AF473831

XU XIAOWEI : SPACING MEMORIES

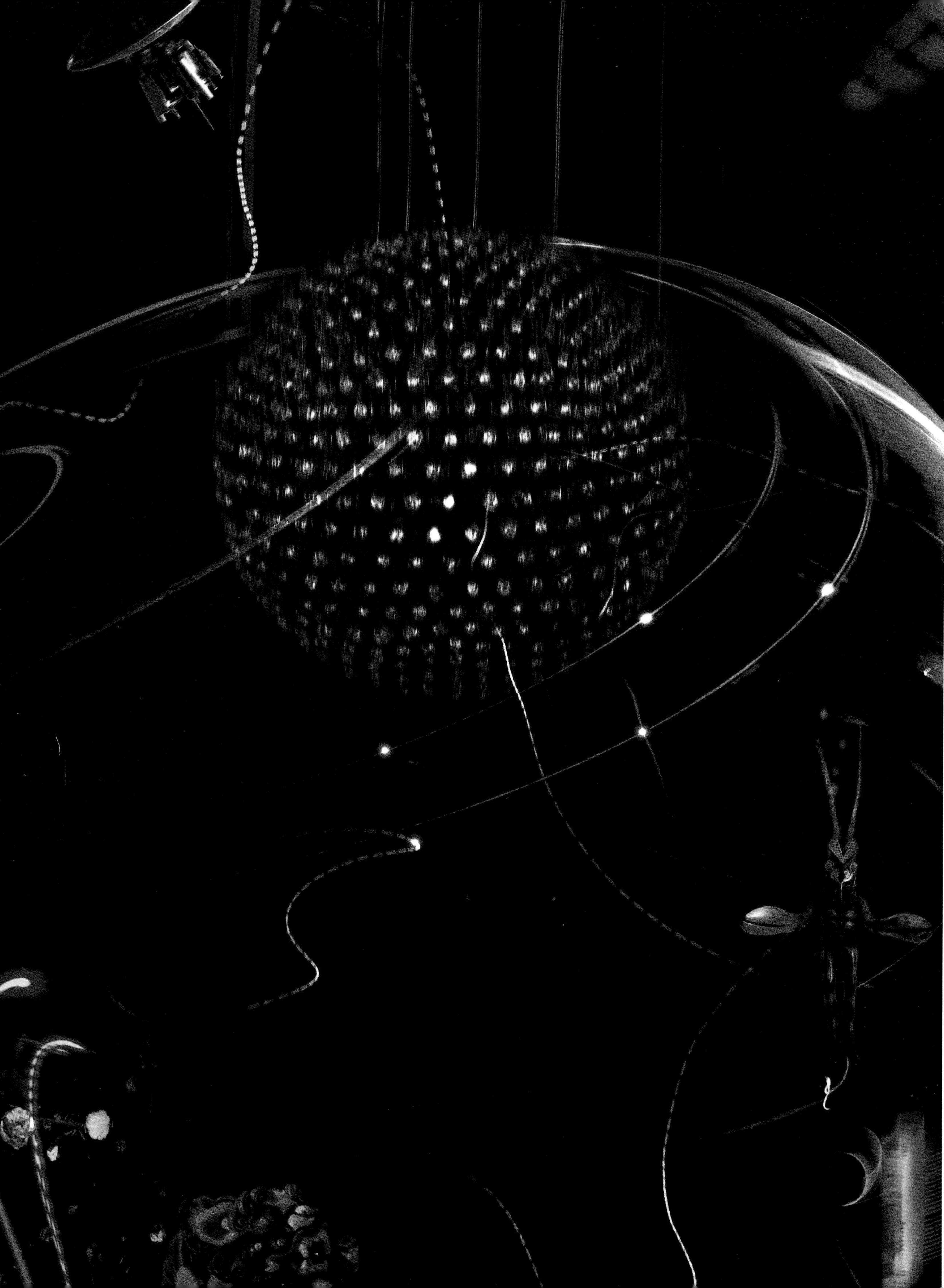

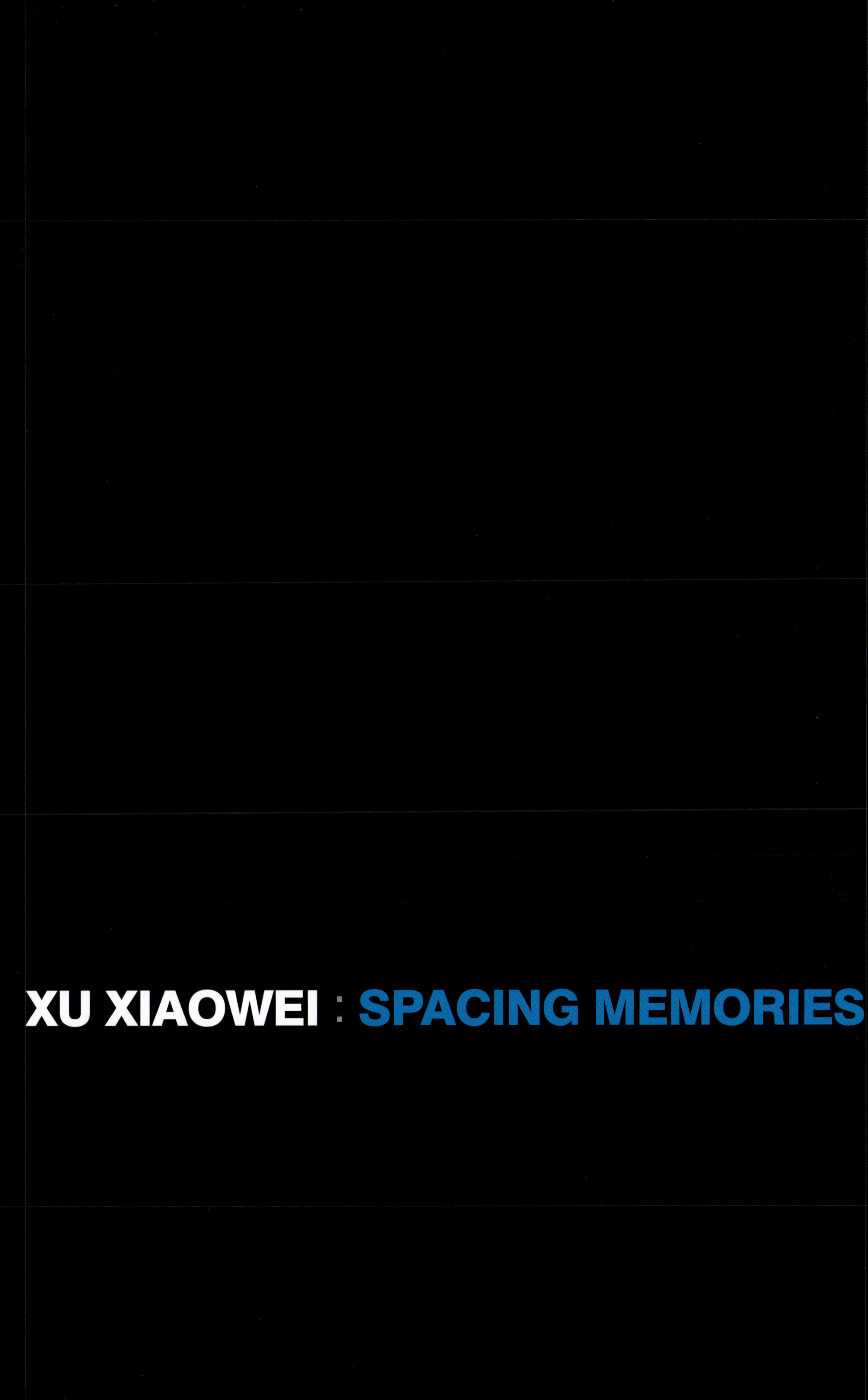
XU XIAOWEI : SPACING MEMORIES

Published in 2025 by Unicorn, an imprint of Unicorn Publishing Group
Charleston Studio
Meadow Business Centre
Lewes
BN8 5RW
www.unicornpublishing.org

ISBN 978-1-916846-39-5

10 9 8 7 6 5 4 3 2 1

Designed by Matthew Wilson

Printed by Gomer Press Ltd, Wales

Previous page:

I Have Always Believed that Humans are Pets of Aliens, 2023 *(see p. 35)*

CONTENTS

FOREWORD

Roger Ballen

As I traverse the landscapes of memory, I am drawn back to my first encounter of China in 1987. I vividly recall the bicycles that filled the streets, the blue uniforms worn by the populace and the overwhelming stillness of a time when cars were a rarity. My days were marked by wandering through the limited aisles of state-controlled supermarkets, where choices were few, and the air was filled with the scent of simple pork and rice dishes served from bustling food stalls. When I returned in 2016 for my 'Theatre of the Absurd' exhibition at the Beijing Academy of Arts, it felt as though I had landed on another planet. The transformation in society, art and photography astounded me – China had shifted from a world of conformity and traditionalism to an industrialised global superpower, a leader in technological and creative innovation.

It is this very intersection of the old and new that forms the crux of Xu Xiaowei's photographs. The artist's work masterfully combines 'anachronistic' black-and-white photography with digital techniques, creating a tapestry that is rich with history yet strikingly contemporary. While there is a lineage of similar subject matter in Chinese photography, Xiaowei's body of work transcends the documentary style that characterised the Reform and Opening-Up era (1970s to 1990s). Photographers like Lu Nan, Liu Heung Shing and Zhang Hai'er captured the rapid changes – urbanisation, industrialisation, poverty, inequality and state control – documenting the lives of marginalised individuals.

Similarly, in Xiaowei's work, we find references to idyllic agrarian life – the 'rural romance' juxtaposed with stark representations of modernity. His photographs create impressions that weave together collective memories and sights of the outside world – landscapes, architecture and cultural insignia. With a surrealist undertone, these seemingly incongruous elements come together as montages, tapestries or a bric-a-brac of experiences. Folkloric symbols and Chinese proverbs evoke a sense of cultural heritage and wisdom, yet they stand in contrast to contemporary themes of fast fashion, consumerism and state surveillance. This 'compression' reveals how visual experiences, perception and memories can layer within the mind: these photographs are projections of a kind of psychic 'flash' or 'multifaceted dramas', as the artist titles one of his chapters.

Like my own work, I see them as mental inscapes where perceptions exist in shallow, flat spaces, allowing the viewer to peer into the depths of their own psyche. Perhaps this is what the artist is referring to in the title of this book, *Spacing Memories*. The concept of 'spacing', suggested by the title of Xiaowei's collection, explores the psychological distance between fragmented memories (or 'ruins', as the artist might call them) and also suggests a deep relationship between the act of remembering and the medium of photography. Photographs become vessels for memory, capturing fleeting moments and emotions that resonate across time and space, akin to 'ruins', as highlighted in Section Two.

But what else renders these photographs as 'psychological'? It is their ability to transcend straightforward depictions of reality. They evoke inner qualities of the mind and personal experience, as abstract elements blur the boundaries between external and internal experiences. For instance, in *Prisoner Dance* (《囚舞》)(2020) on p. 36, the dark, abstract figure against a cracked and textured backdrop evokes feelings of entrapment and disintegration rather than merely mimicking natural phenomena. The figure, resembling a butterfly with parts missing, symbolises transformation or the struggle for freedom. Similarly, in *The Outcast's Competition* (《受排挤的竞争》)(2019–23) on p. 26, dynamic light trails against a shadowy background intensifying feelings of confusion and estrangement.

As a photographer and artist for over fifty years, my raison d'être has always been to reveal hidden, repressed and elusive parts of the psyche, and I resonate with

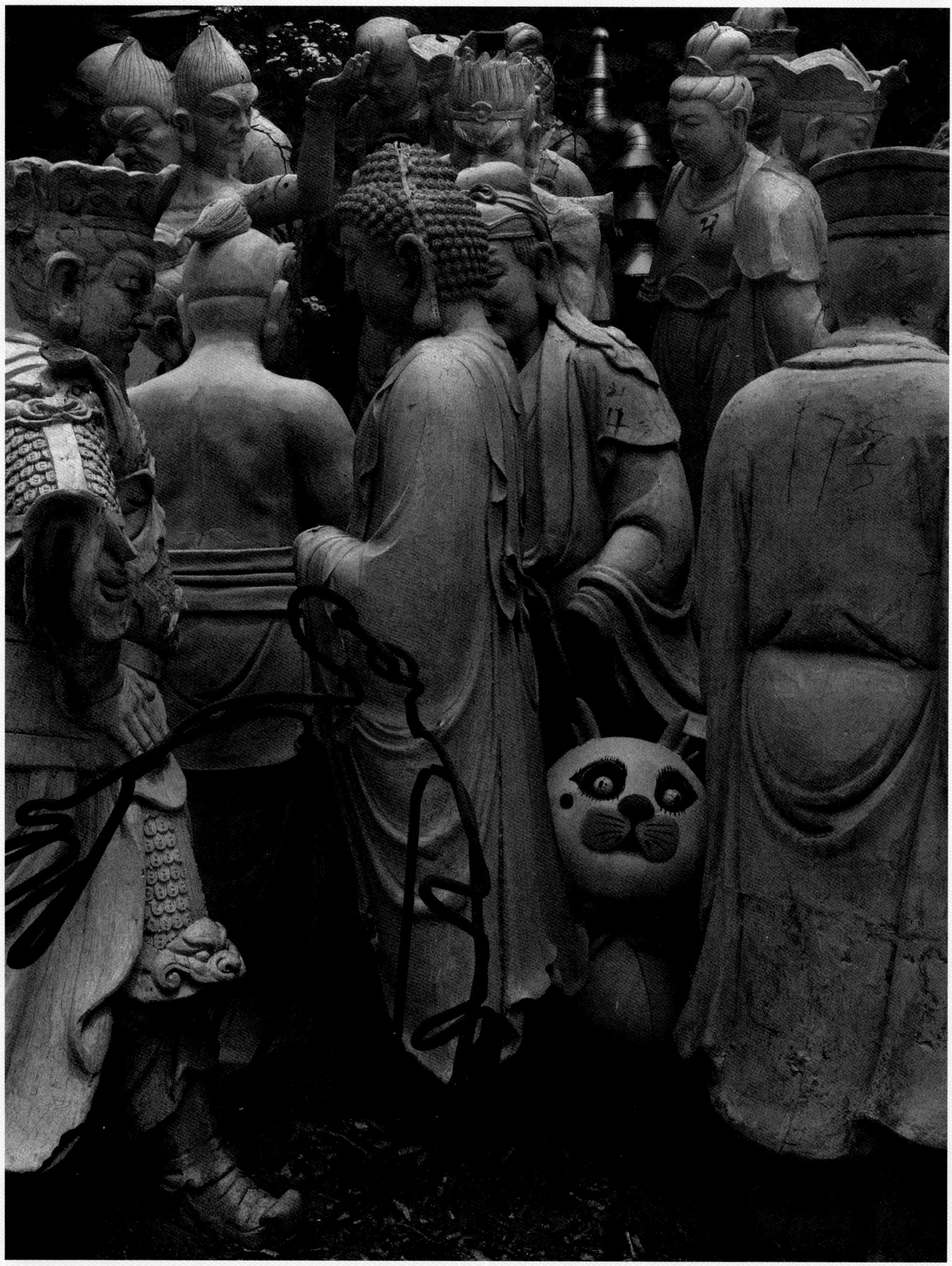

The Feast of the Gods, 2020 *(see p. 75)*

Xiaowei's capacity to surface such unsettling truths – hidden desires or fears. The artist's childhood terror of fireflies, evident in *Get Rid of Those Shiny Bugs* (《赶走那些闪光的虫子》) (see p. 22), for instance, symbolises associations with death and the unknown, serving as metaphors for deeper psychological states within a fast-paced, technologically driven society. In one haunting scene, a doorman sits at a stark white table with three clocks, symbols of unfulfilled life and expectations. Another portrays a face overlooked by dispersed goldfish, who, in an existential entrapment, are 'always looking for something'. The eerie or uncanny sense of imprisonment, of being 'watched', is evoked in the sight of a woman who bears puppeteer handles and, in the background, a man being tube-fed like a pet, as well as a solitary figure who walks through a narrow door set into a tall, curved concrete wall with strong shadows stretching across the lower part of it.

Further, the presence of absurdity in Xiaowei's work is what renders it particularly disturbing, unsettling, and psychologically provocative. The irrational and out-of-place elements create tension and humour, disrupting our sense of order. In *The Feast of the Gods* (《众神之宴》) (see p. 75), for example, traditional statues are interrupted by a cartoonish cat, juxtaposing sacred traditions with modern consumerism. Similarly, *Torture,* on pp. 64–65, depicts figures wearing animal masks, evoking alienation and the struggle for personal identity in the face of societal control. The prevalence of masks in different forms – from clowns to facial paper covers to animal heads – heeds a profound sense of otherness and outsiderness that has always perplexed and captivated me.

Ultimately, Xiaowei's work admirably embodies the complexities of modern Chinese culture, revealing the interplay between tradition and progress, absurdity and reality, within the framework of collective memory. Through this lens, I find not only kinship with the artist but also a mirror reflecting my own artistic journey.

As I continue to explore the depths of memory, I am reminded of the power of photography as a medium that transcends time and space, capturing the ephemeral essence of our experiences and emotions. One needs to travel deep into oneself to take a picture – into the dark and subterranean – and Xiaowei has taken me there. I think of the words of the Tang Dynasty Chinese poet and painter Wang Wei, who wrote: 'In the mountains, there are always things to enjoy; in the valley, there are always things to see.'

Get Rid of Those Shiny Bugs, 2020 *(see p. 22)*

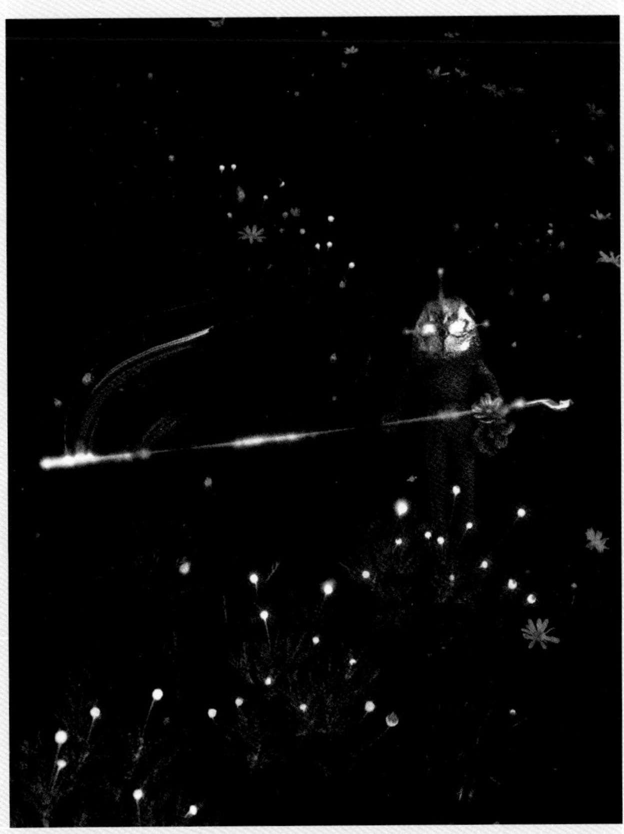

INTRODUCTION

Dr Joshua Gong

Personal memory provides an inexhaustible source of inspiration for Xu Xiaowei's visual art. In an ever-shifting landscape of contemporary visual culture, people continually reenact absurd yet realistic tragicomedies. Through the language of lens and intuitive impulses, Xiaowei creates a distinctive artistic texture. His artworks strive to transcend static black-and-white images, allowing imagery of people and objects to evolve with hidden symbols. In a digital era, replication and distortion of images grant artists significant creative freedom. Xiaowei's memory (a sense of time), after a sudden flash of inspiration, transforms into a new visual order (a spatial entity) through a novel combination of light and shadow.

His visual art deepens the exploration of media art in terms of content, form and life experience, maintaining a unique texture while fostering empathy with his audience.

The Outcast's Competition, 2019–23 *(see p. 26)*

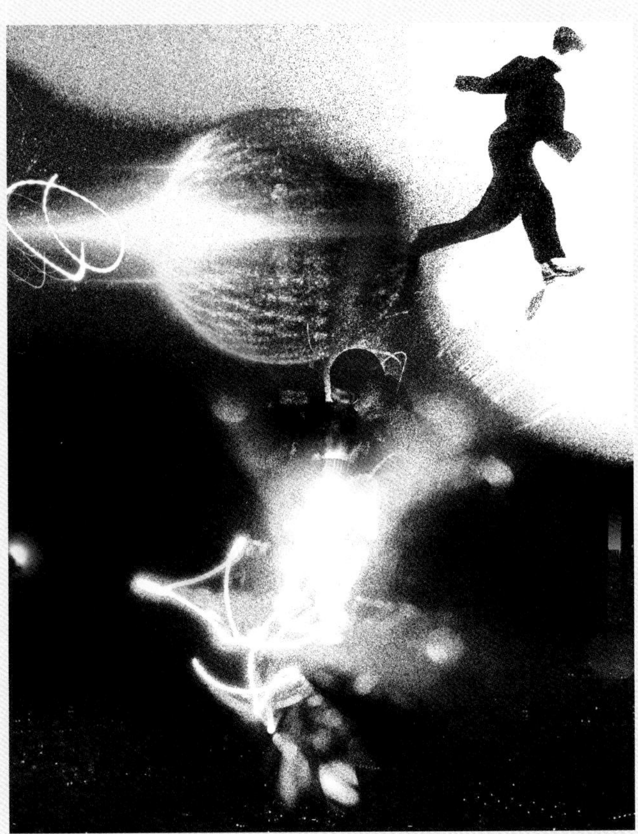

Firstly, in terms of content, Xiaowei's image narratives stem from the rapidly evolving contemporary society. The twenty-first century, an era of information, sees mechanically reproduced and digitally collaged images dominate production and consumption. The current perception of time has a more intricate relationship with image symbols. Images not only create history and reshape memory but also document the future. In *The Outcast's Competition* (《受排挤的竞争》) on p. 26, the artist creates an energy field. Light leaps and gathers into spheres, forming rhythmic images, while human figures blur and scramble. In the centre, three faint human shapes appear on a stage enveloped in mist. Complex lighting, chaotic imagery and anxious emotions converge into a portrayal of the present. A distinct yet indescribable unease is captured and projected through multi-angled lens language. Absurd competition, eerie existence and chaotic energy transformation depict the reality of an ordinary person amidst sweeping changes in production and consumption. After transforming various concrete images, the scenes attain an abstract quality. This abstractness is not mere surrealism, which releases creativity through the subconscious, but a postmodern abstraction of existence. As contemporary sociologist Antonio Negri (1933–2023) pointed out:

> In reality, in this miserable situation, something has happened: our experience and our desire have serenely tested the absolute character of the limit. Here, starting from this ferocious and extraordinary discovery, our soul has taken its distance from the market, and has once again declared – epically, starting from the nothingness of existence, in the flood of abstraction – the value of utopia, of the ethical gesture, of the rational mythology – the irreducibility of dystopia.[1]

1 Antonio Negri, *Art and Multitude*, transl. by Ed Emery, Cambridge: Polity Press, 2011, pp. 17–18.

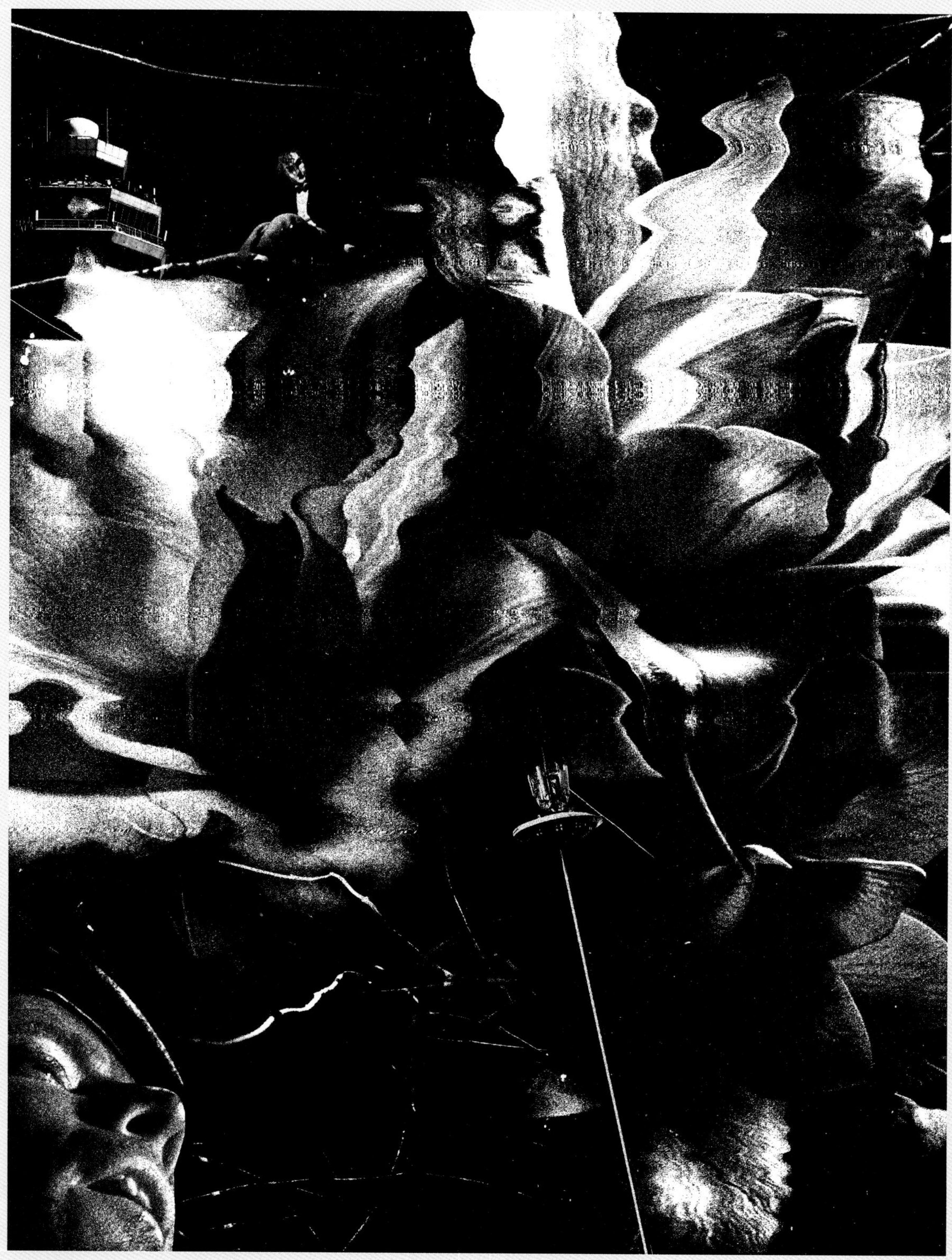

All Kinds of Imagination in Life are Just Some Simple Thoughts, 2017–23 *(see p. 33)*

The environment in which Xiaowei grew up and created art underwent dramatic changes in just a few years. He was born in a seaside town in Haiyang, Shandong, China. Due to his parents' work in freight transportation, he was largely left to his own devices, He spent time with his aunt by the sea. His childhood memories are intertwined with pastoral and maritime scenes. The mountains, woods and beaches – those primordial landscapes – provided the backdrop for Xiaowei's visual art.

Xiaowei gradually began to perceive the profound impact of industrialisation, urbanisation and globalisation on his worldview. In recent years, a floating rocket launch pad has been built off the coast of Haiyang; the first launch in 2019 was a marvel. The rocket launch pad, mobile phone signal towers, skyscrapers of reinforced concrete, colour televisions from abroad, Japanese anime and American Hollywood blockbusters all collided in a fantastical blend of globalisation. More absurdly, the old rural landscapes, temples and farms were not completely replaced but were reused over time among the ruins, thus forming new symbols and functions. The modernisation and contemporisation of China occurred simultaneously.[2]

As a result, people in this region have experienced multiple transitions – from agrarian civilisation to industrial civilisation and then to the post-industrial era. These rapid changes render surrounding images increasingly illogical. While life 'progresses', many new issues also arise. Physiological and psychological responses intertwine in the subconscious.

Regardless of how cultural architects might rationally depict a beautiful new world and epic heroic scenes, the classical core of tragedy is deconstructed and reshaped in Xu Xiaowei's imagery. The linear axis of time is dispersed, allowing the viewer's perspective to be transformed beyond the image by the energy field presented by the picture. Through careful observation of the images, the complexity and helplessness of human nature are revealed layer by layer. Xu Xiaowei's works, for example, *All Kinds of Imagination in Life are Just Some Simple Thoughts* (《生活中的各种想象就是想想》) on p. 33, *The Escaping Soul* (《外逃的灵魂》) on p. 54, and *Coming to Save You* (《来救你了》) on pp. 118–19, use the language of light and shadow to compose a silent poetry of postmodern existence.

This aligns with photography art critic Charlotte Cotton's belief that image art can uphold Duchamp's concept – that is, it possesses the artistic charm of questioning the essence of objects:

> Both contemporary sculpture … and photography can activate the same conceptual dynamic; they both create puzzles and confound our expectation of, say, the weight or scale of objects, or the permanency of an artwork.[3]

In terms of form, Xu Xiaowei consistently seeks a distinctive visual texture, highlighting the potential of deconstructing and reorganising time and space through the language of light and shadow. Xiaowei's uncle was the only photographer in their small town who took family portraits. After the photo session, the developing of the prints was the part Xiaowei anticipated most eagerly. As a child, he could spend an entire day in a small darkroom, perhaps sowing the seeds of his future in photographic art.

In Chinese families, family portrait photography holds a special ritual significance, rooted in ancestor worship and the importance of the extended family. Contemporary artist Zhang Xiaogang's *Bloodline – Big Family* series uses family portrait imagery as a creative template, exploring collective and individual visual memory through painting. Zhang's paintings reappropriate the concept of photography, blurring the boundaries between the 'human' and 'object' nature of images. This allows viewers to adopt a critical viewing perspective,

2 Joshua Gong, *Chinese Art Today: From 20th-Century Tradition to Contemporary Practice*, Lewes: Unicorn Publishing Group, 2023, p. 149.

3 Charlotte Cotton, *The Photograph as Contemporary Art*, Kindle Edition, New York: Thames & Hudson, 2020, p. 160.

making the framework of image-meaning more open.[4] In Xiaowei's era, the solemnity of black-and-white family portraits was swiftly replaced by the vividness of colour images. Colour television images quickly supplanted black-and-white photos, and it became the new medium through which Xiaowei experienced visual perception in his childhood. The light from cathode ray tube screens fuelled the artist's anticipation of big cities and the future. As an undergraduate, Xiaowei majored in painting. By then, the internet had become widespread. Online games, web literature and e-commerce were thriving in China, no longer strictly following the commercial logic of Western-developed capitalist regions. China's rapid economic development captured global attention, and luxury brands from all over the world prepared to enter the Chinese market.

Since graduating from university, Xiaowei has achieved remarkable success in fashion and commercial photography. He regularly shoots fashion spreads for *Vogue*, *ELLE*, *Cosmopolitan* and *Le Figaro*, among other domestic and international media, and works for luxury brands. Fashion and commercial photography in China have undergone dramatic changes in just a few years, transitioning from traditional analogue film shooting to video-streaming production and short video live-streaming. The digital photography process, from pre-production to post-production and dissemination, can now be completed in minutes using smartphones and artificial intelligence.

The meaning of images has been further fragmented and TikTok-ified. The significance of photography has undergone a major transformation. Before the rise of mobile imagery, critic Susan Sontag (1933–2004) stated that 'Photography has become almost as widely practiced an amusement as sex and dancing – which means that, like every mass art form, photography is not practiced by most people as an art. It is mainly a social rite, a defense against anxiety, and a tool of power.'[5]

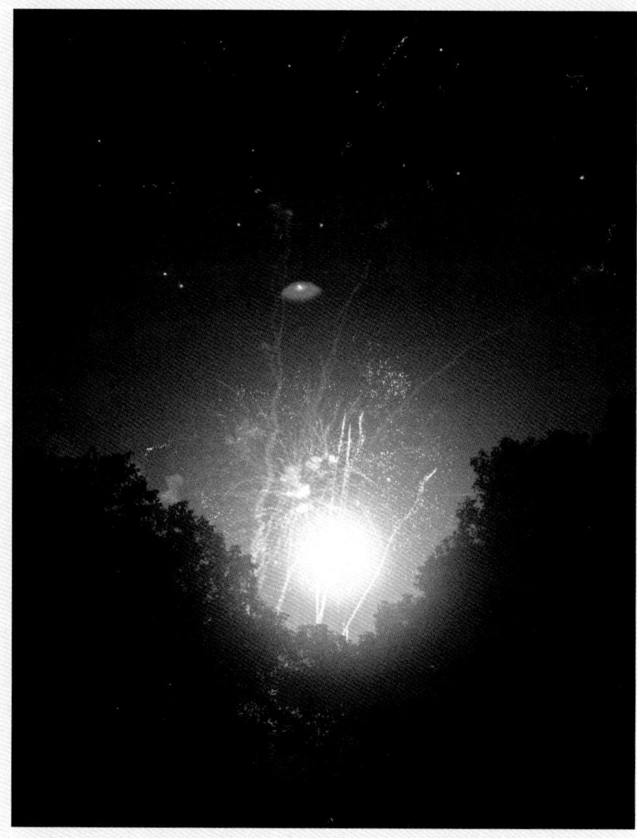

Burst Silently, 2024 *(see p. 124)*

Unfortunately, Sontag passed away before the advent of computational photography. In the new era, photography has become not a method to combat anxiety but a form of acknowledging the diversity of human nature. In *Burst Silently* (《爆裂无声》) on p. 125, *Father and Son* (《父与子》) on pp. 128–29, and *Waiting for Feedback* (《等待反馈》) on pp. 84–85, Xiaowei's works question the immediacy of photographic documentation, revealing the multiplicity of real space, the distortions of memory and the ritual nature of recollection. The combination of illuminated framing and the integration of images and painting expresses the postmodern characteristics of image appropriation and the contradictory attitudes of visual language towards interpretation. In *Burst Silently* (《爆裂无声》), light is perceived before sound by the photographer. Simultaneously, the explosive sound is

4 易丹：《物/像：观看的意义之旅》，中信出版集团2023年，第35页。
[Yi Dan, *Things & Images: The Significances of Seeing*, Beijing: Citic Publishing, 2023, p. 35.]

5 Susan Sontag, *On Photography*, Kindle Edition, London: Penguin Group, 1979, p. 7.

integrated into the image system through the initial image. Within the artist's designed viewing path (inside the frame), observers can engage in diverse viewing behaviours not entirely dictated by the photographer's preset intentions (outside the frame).

Photography's evolution from maturity to global dissemination took just a few years, and it spread visual culture more widely than painting, sculpture or architecture. Now, through smartphones and social media platforms, the trend is for the digital world to encroach on the physical. The nature of images becomes more malleable with the increased convenience and speed of digital replication and dissemination.

Xu Xiaowei, through comparative media analysis, seeks to explore the unique texture of digital imagery. Beyond the general concept of digital fission, he makes viewers aware that digital replication, like mechanical reproduction, has differences in field and aura.[6]

Today's screen technology has attained new heights. The precision of resolution and colour thresholds have, to some extent, exceeded the limits of the human eye. Many subtle changes in nature are detected and received through mechanical lenses, silicon chip calculations, digital signal processing and LCD screens. Nowadays, people can see and realise images which earlier technologies were incapable of producing.

Historically, Antonie Philips van Leeuwenhoek (1632–1723) introduced the micro perspective to human society, but it was Johannes Vermeer (1632–75) who truly added artistic value to new optics. Xiaowei combines the characteristics of physical and digital images, exploring a new dimension of dramatic light-and-shadow art. He particularly emphasises the atmosphere in his works, adding visual uniqueness and individuality to digital images through differentiated analogue film grain. The grain in Xiaowei's works is not simply from the digital simulation filters developed by traditional film manufacturers such as Kodak and Fujifilm; he crafts them himself, based on his experience and the specific needs of his works. This graininess transforms the texture of digital images and allows the audience to perceive the essence of film. This is the unique visual language of an image artist. The distinctive texture of lens and digital collage images reflects the postmodern disorder arising from the current imbalance in consumer supply.

Finally, in contemplating humanism, Xiaowei captures a sense of eternity in fleeting moments, presenting it across the entire image. The wave of globalisation in the post-consumer era and China's reform and opening-up provided a unique soil for the artist's memory and growth. A free and slow-paced childhood allowed Xiaowei's visual memory to retain the last traces of his hometown while inevitably aligning with the post-consumer era. From idyllic rural scenes with curling smoke to bustling city traffic, the intense changes, collisions and combinations were later reinterpreted by Xiaowei through mixed media in his images. For example, in *Get Rid of Those Shiny Bugs* (《赶走那些闪光的虫子》) on p. 22, an eerie, monster-like figure holds a long, glowing instrument and seemingly drives away fireflies. The black-and-white images make ambiguous symbols that were previously clear. The scattered dots and the monster's gaze seem to share the same light source and energy. The transformation and arrangement of potential energy between light and shadow reflect an abstract symbolic concept. This surreal artistic treatment further blurs the traditional documentary function of photography.

It seems Xiaowei was propelled to the forefront of society by the tide of history. His first job after graduation was working with stars he had only seen in films as a child or with supermodels he knew from the covers of top magazines. These environmental changes felt inexplicable to him, yet they were undeniably real. At times, this made him question whether the changes in his life were tied to his talent and whether his creativity was truly as impressive as it seemed.

6 Walter Benjamin proposed that mechanical reproduction, depending on the context of its display, possesses a unique 'aura' distinct from the original.

China's economic miracle mirrors the experiences of the Four Asian Tigers, leveraging the population dividend and focusing on labour-intensive development. However, this alone cannot explain how China successfully avoided the financial crises of 1997 and 2008. The mobile internet boom in 2014 indicated that the new population dividend was not just cheap labour but also the efficient financial transformation of big data. Silicon Valley, through social media giants such as Facebook and Instagram, introduced unprecedented ways of sharing images. However, the rise of TikTok marked a new paradigm of image production and mindset, originating as it did from a non-Western model. Xu Xiaowei's visual art reflects the collective subconscious during this unique developmental period: a delayed adaptation and acceptance of a reality without historical precedent.

For example, Xiaowei's *Longing* (《思念》) on p. 93 taps into the collective subconscious, where people in everyday China can unconsciously encounter the shadow of international superstar Michael Jackson, representing the once-certain American Dream: the assurance of happiness through hard work. In the early days of China's reform and opening-up, almost every Chinese person harboured a Chinese version of the American Dream. American pop songs, TV shows, movies and fast food are indelible collective memories and realities for Chinese youth. Works such as *The Doorman's Dream Came True* (《门卫大叔的梦想实现了》) on p. 101 and *The Dream of Getting Rich was Ruined by a Big Pot Lid* (《发财的梦却被一个大锅盖给毁了》) on p. 60 critique the illusion of the Wall Street wolf through reflections on identity symbols. Contemporary Chinese people oscillate between

The Doorman's Dream Came True, 2018 *(see p. 101)*

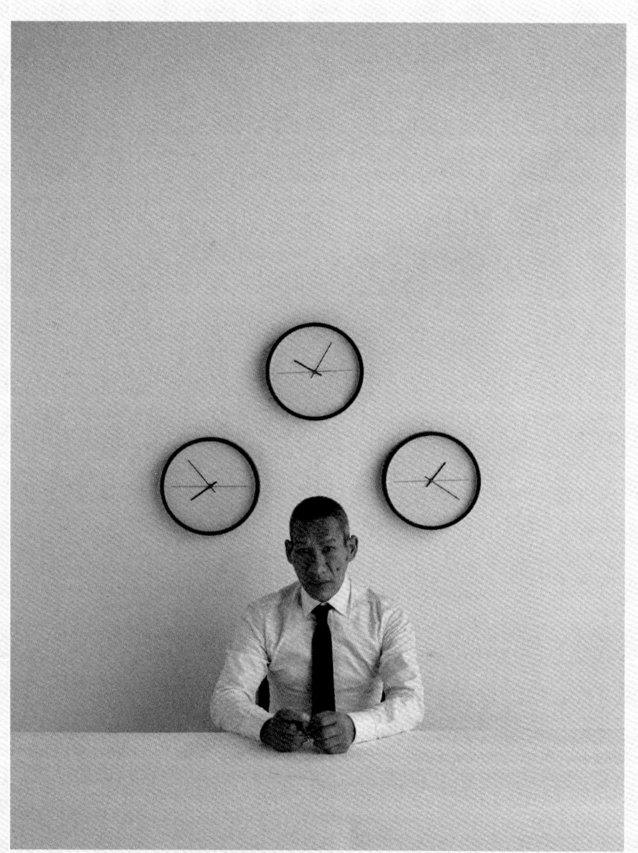

Longing, 2012 *(see p. 93)*

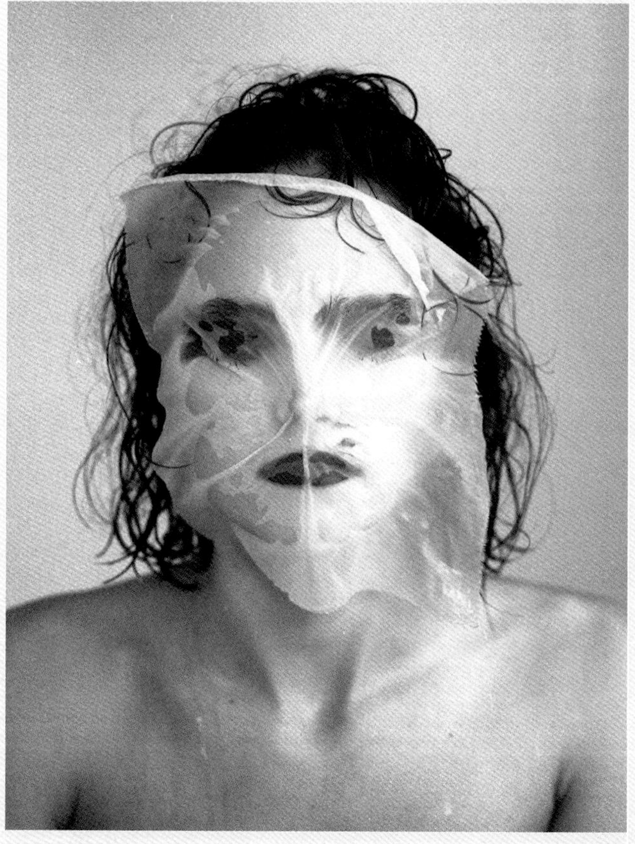

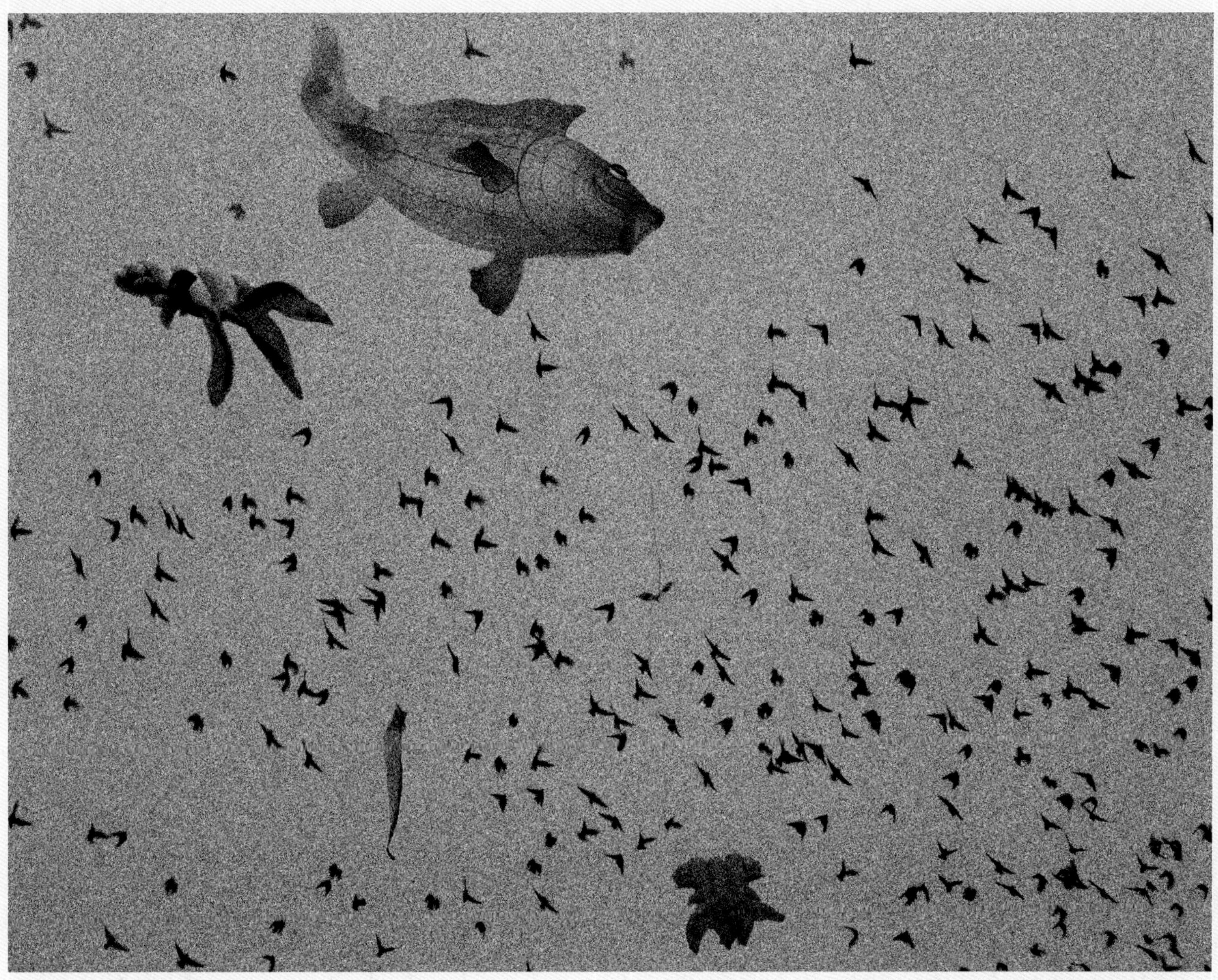

Peaceful, 2020–21 *(see pp. 136–37)*

order and wild growth, as the myth of the American Dream gradually fades. 'Time is money, efficiency is life', reflects the aspirations, frustrations and realities of Third World countries striving for rapid development.

However, it must be emphasised that humanistic care is a universal consciousness, regardless of country or region. Xiaowei's work presents more than just images unique to China. Postmodernism is complex and dazzling, but this does not hinder his focus on ritual, empathy for ordinary people, nostalgia for pastoral life, and ambivalence towards opulence. In a gilded age, a touch of green light[7] signifies the individual's yearning for a brave new world.[8] *The Escaping Soul* (《外逃的灵魂》) on p. 54 captures people's thrill and longing for ritual and mysticism. The more complex the world, the more people yearn for simplicity. Ritual and mysticism provide substantial emotional value for these human desires. The pursuit of spirituality cannot be fully achieved through rational analysis. Xiaowei's compositions reveal the sensuous acceptance and expression of the world. The empathy, sense of ritual and desire for happiness required by humanism have not changed with the advent of new ways of composing images. Instead, they have been enriched, gaining depth in expression through diverse forms. Works such as *Astigmatic Eyes Need a Mirror* (《散光的眼睛需要一面镜子》) on p. 120, *Peaceful* (《游心》) on pp. 136–37, and *Act Within Your Capabilities* (《量力而行》) on pp. 134–35 convey a warmth towards

7 The concept of the green light comes from F. Scott Fitzgerald's *The Great Gatsby*, which critiques opulent American society.

8 The idea originates from *Brave New World,* a dystopian novel by Aldous Huxley.

humanity. Conservatism is a distrust of rational radicalism. The utopia of the virtual world reminds people to honour their inner selves and treat themselves and others kindly. Xiaowei's seemingly chaotic interplay of light and shadow respects indescribable, universal human emotions.

Ultimately, the universe consists of two main coordinates: time and space. Since its invention, photography has been considered a magical tool that surpasses painting in recording the past. It is also regarded as an immortal treasure that transcends death. Over the past 180 years, countless art enthusiasts have tried to replace painting with photography as the best solution for recording time. Conversely, countless painters have sought to prove that photography – relying as it does on mechanical light reproduction – is not the best method for expressing visual creativity. Thus, painting and photography compete with and complement each other. In the digital era, and even in the era of computational photography, the documentary and immediate qualities of photography are as questionable as those of realist paintings of the past. At the same time, the value and standards of photographic art become increasingly perplexing. Yet, this undoubtedly opens up new possibilities for the language of photography. It can both document the past and create new realities, thus allowing the space of memory to grow within reality.

Xu Xiaowei's works, blending painting and photography, showcase the reality, visuality and emotionality of humanity's quest for existence and uncertainty. He weaves spectacles and stories, existing in a space of self-doubt and certainty, and empathises with his audience. As Jean-Paul Sartre said, 'Man is always outside of himself, and it is in projecting and losing himself beyond himself that man is realised; and, on the other hand, it is in pursuing transcendent goals that he is able to exist.'[9]

9 Jean-Paul Sartre, 2007, *Existentialism is a Humanism*, transl. by Carol Macomber, London: Yale University Press, p. 52.

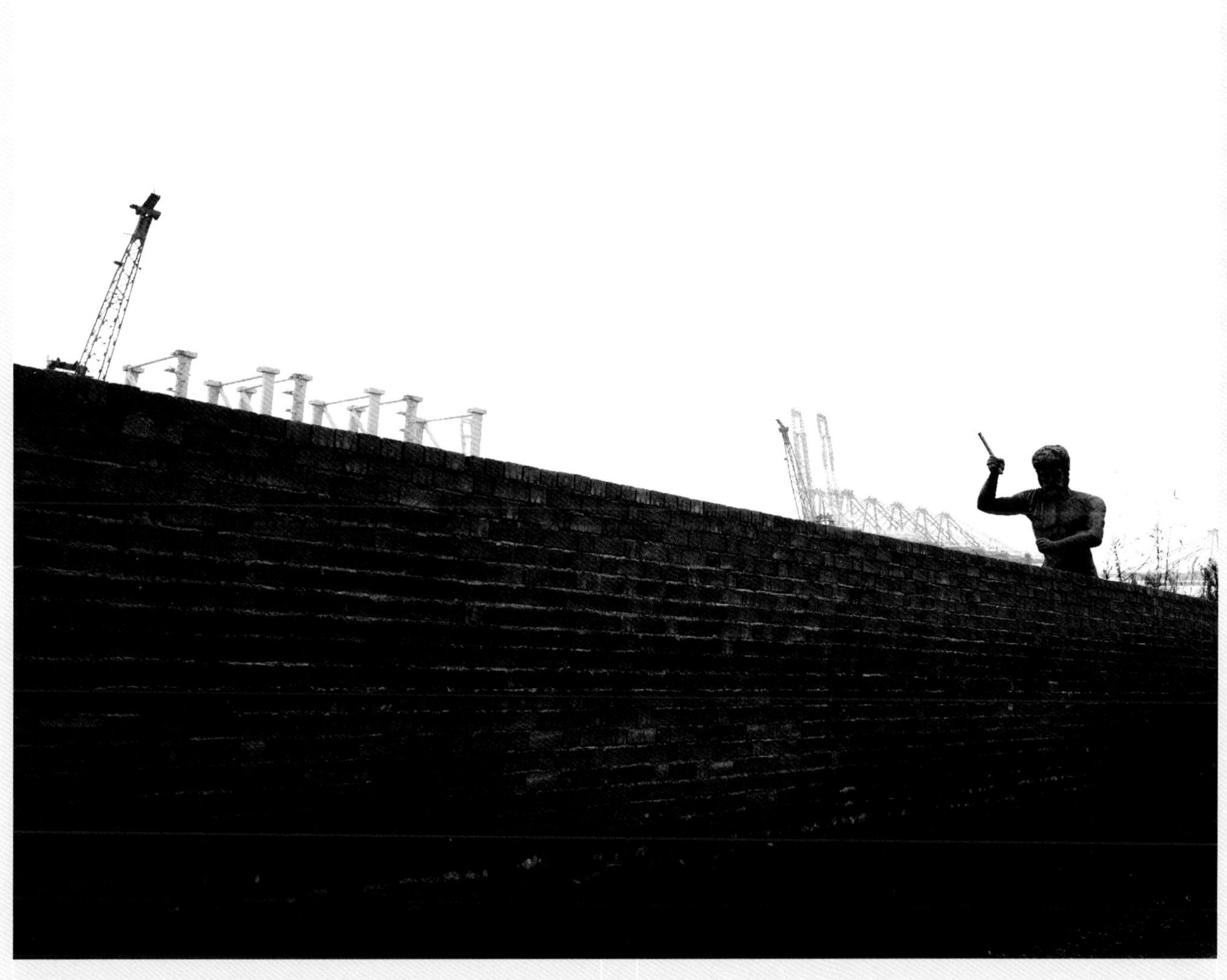

Act Within Your Capabilities, 2023 *(see pp.134–35)*

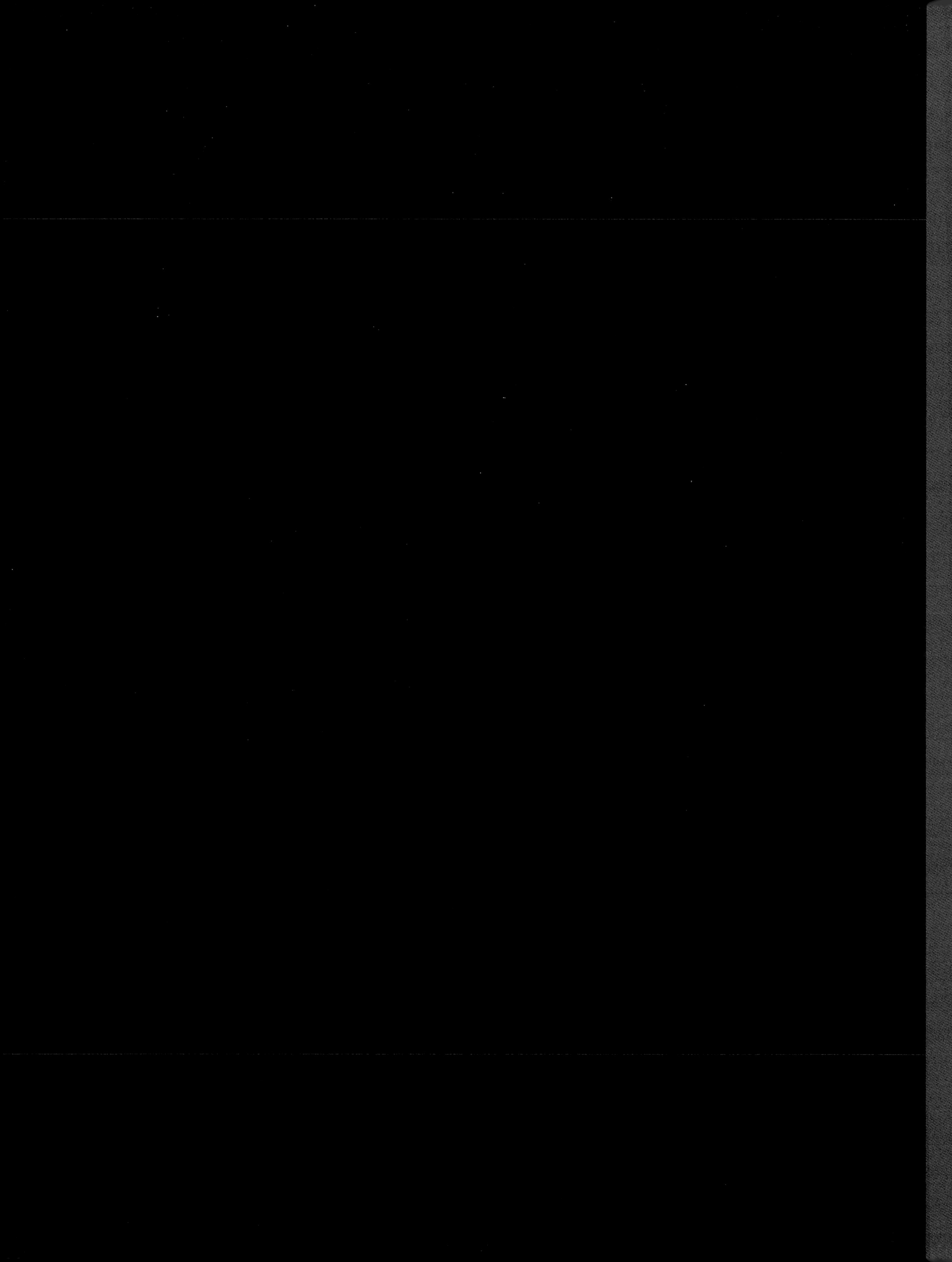

SECTION ONE

The Beating Soul

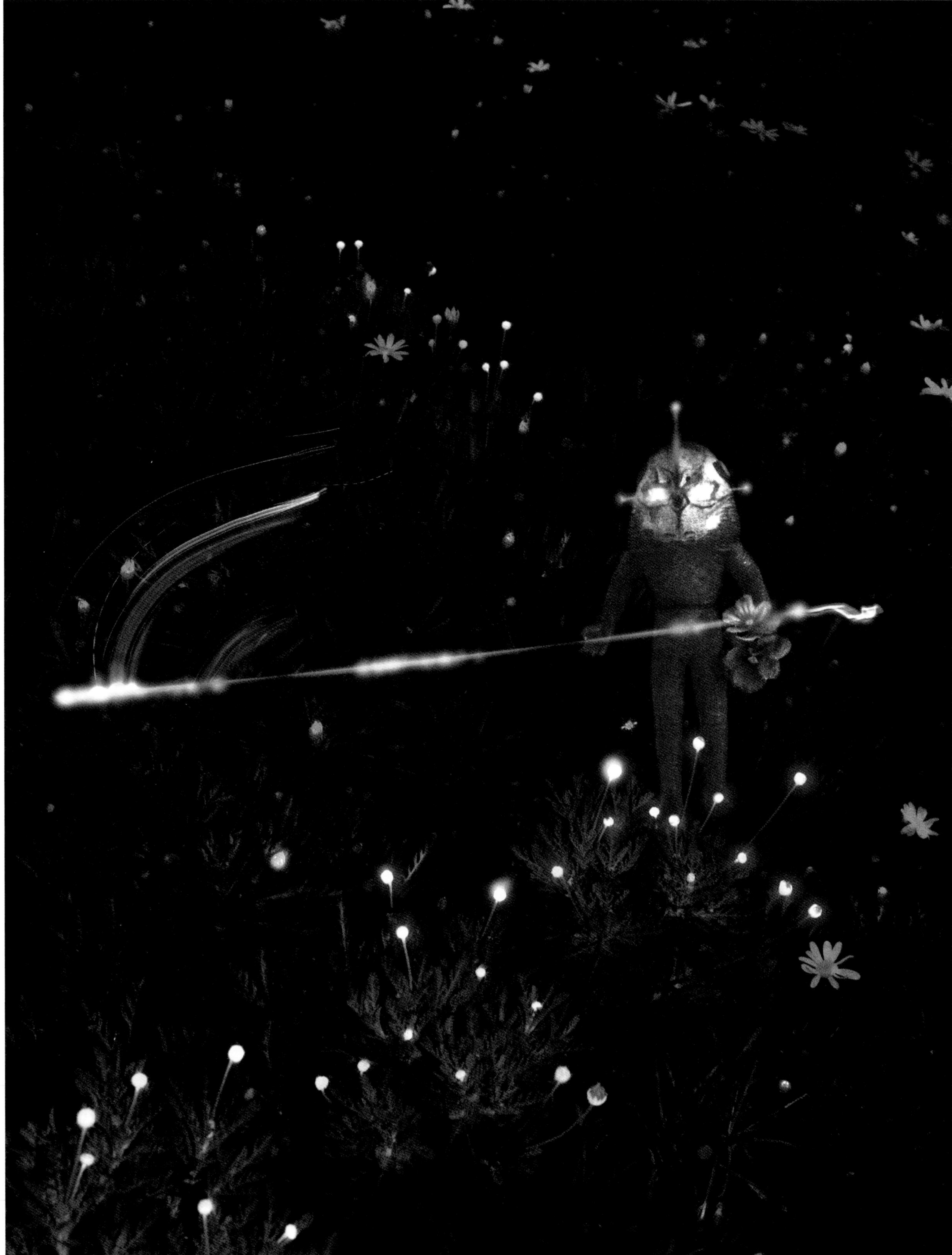

赶走那些闪光的虫子
Get Rid of Those Shiny Bugs, 2020
600 × 800mm

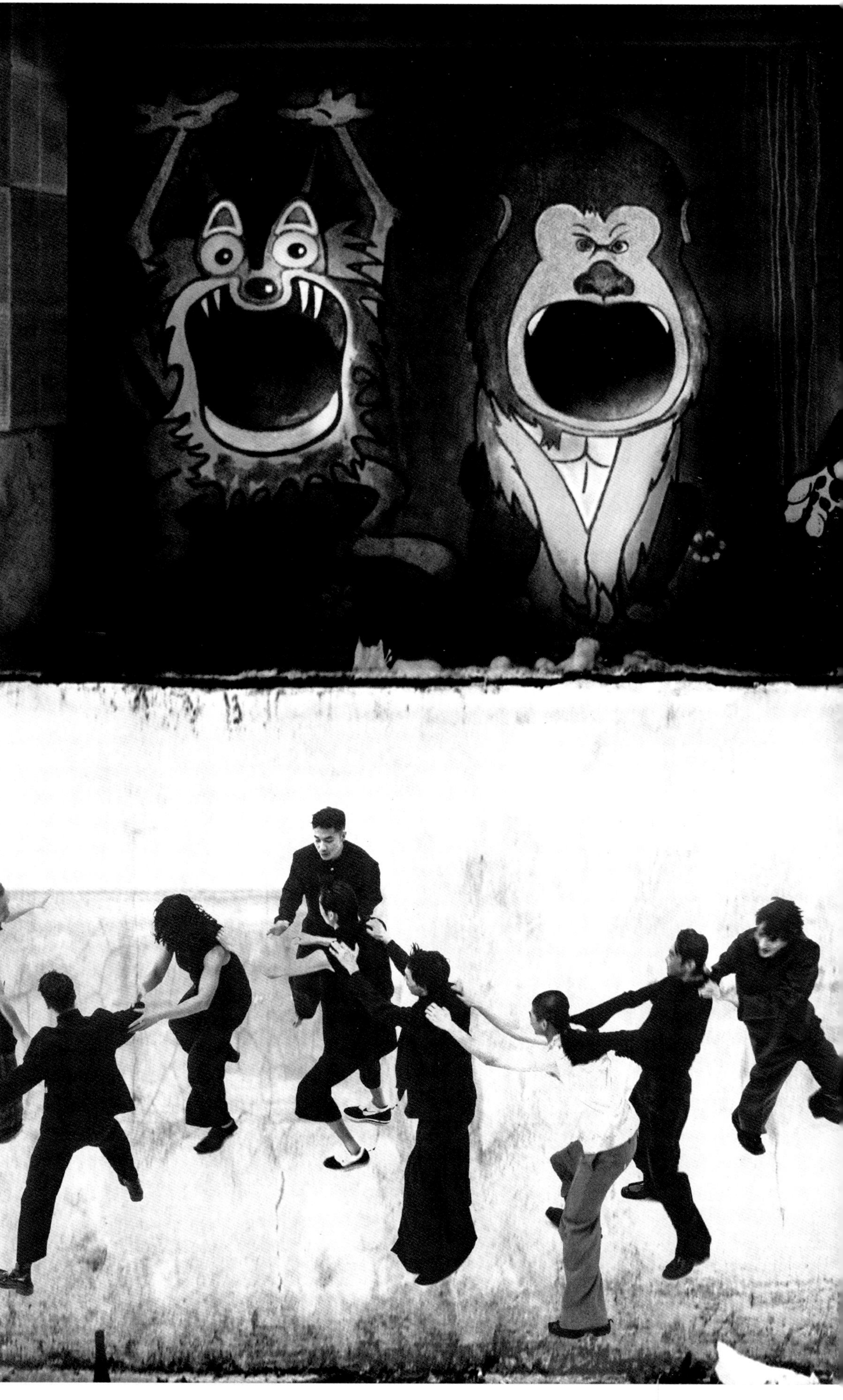

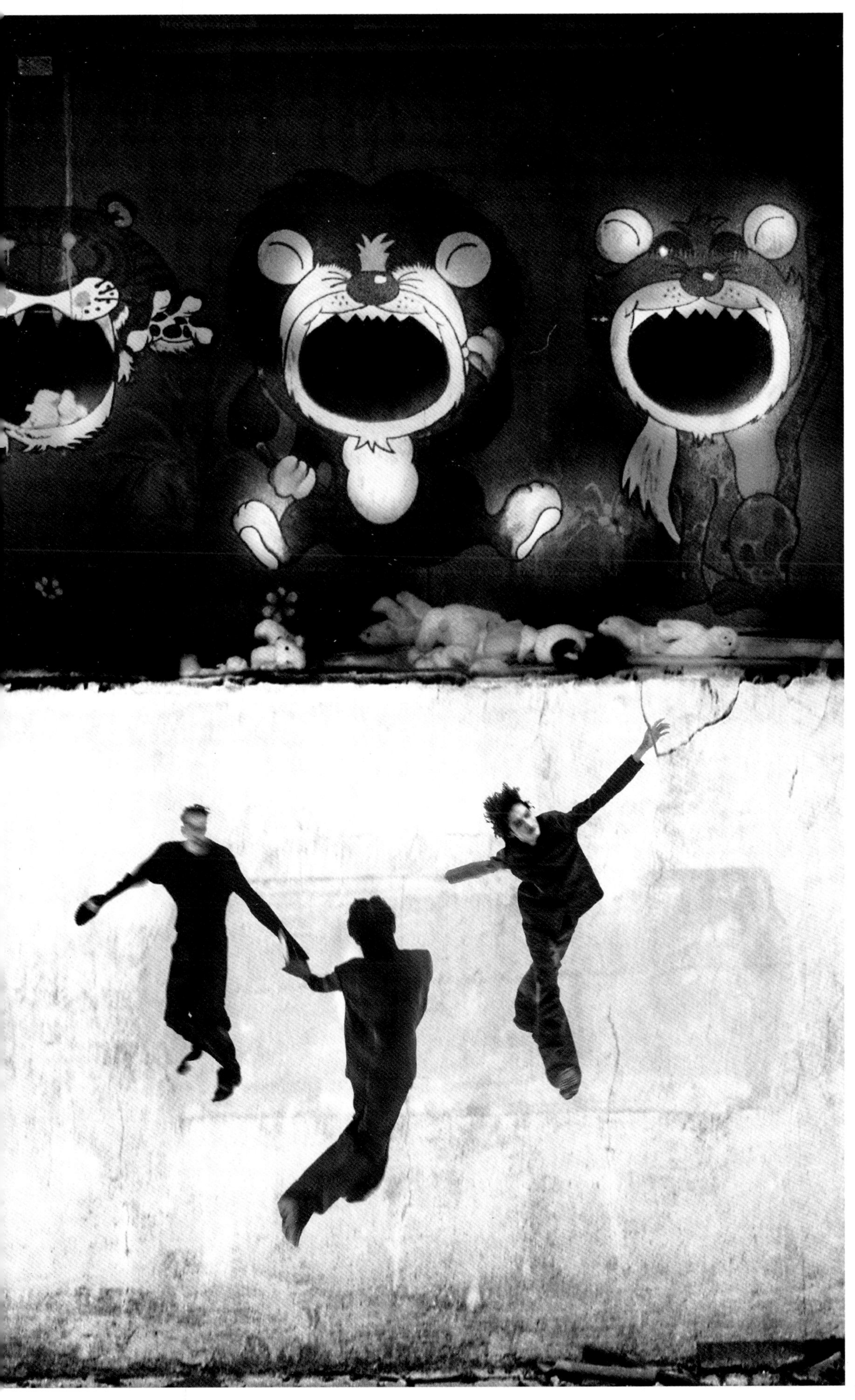

人类知道我们是怎么想的
Humans Know What We Think, 2018–21
1000 × 800mm

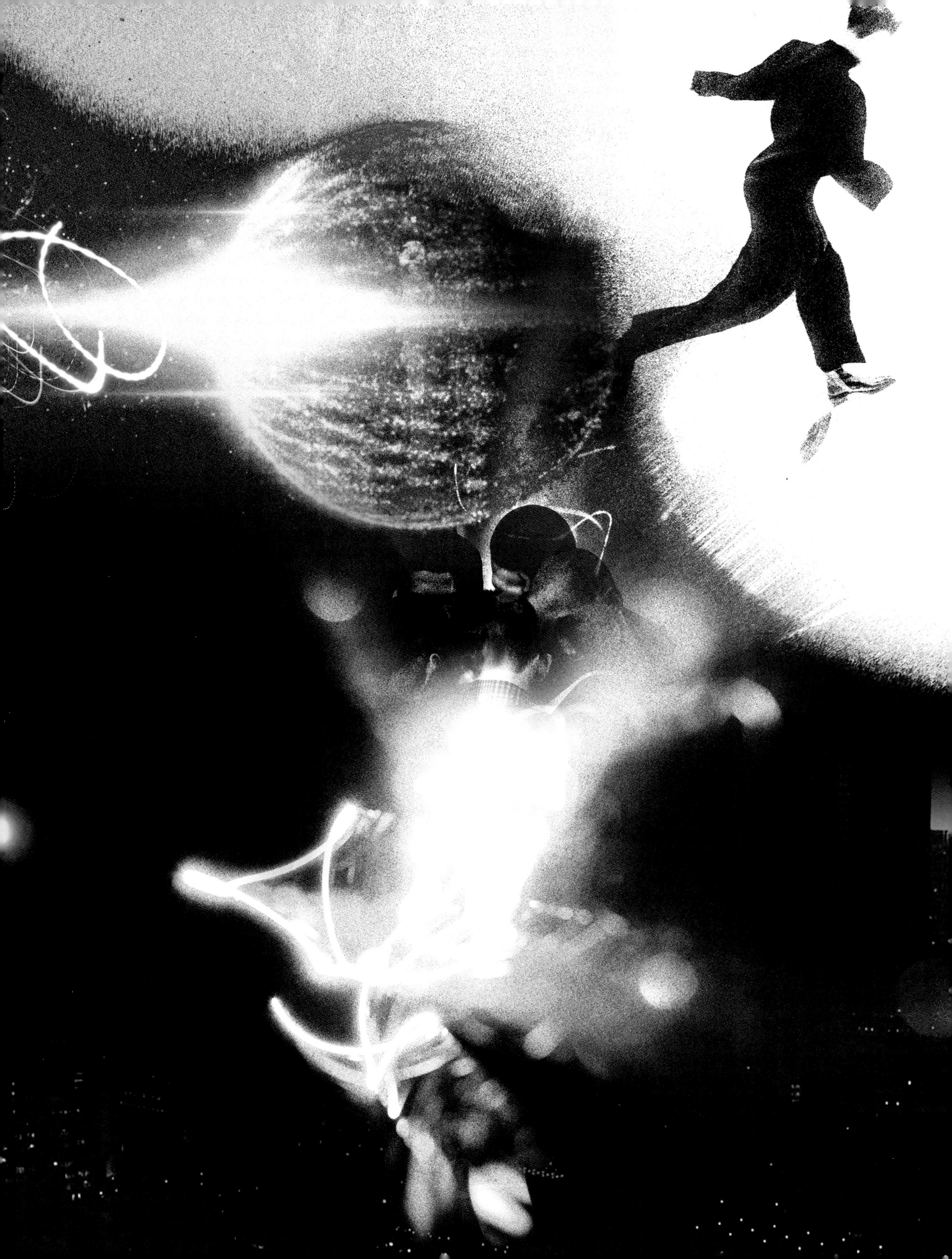

受排挤的竞争
The Outcast's Competition, 2019–23
600 × 800mm

大王叫我来巡山
The King of Bandits Asked Me to Patrol the Mountain, 2024
600 × 800mm

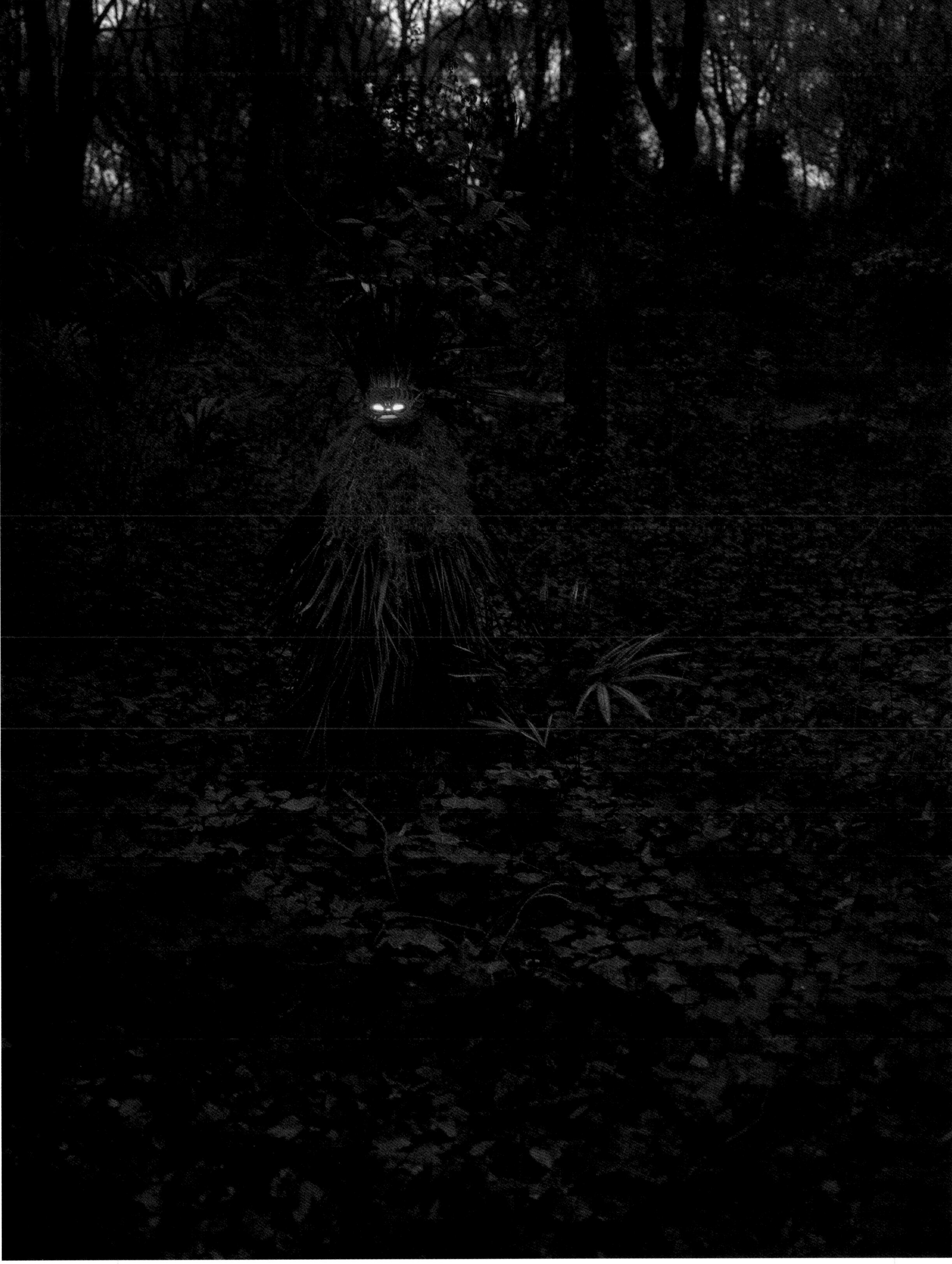

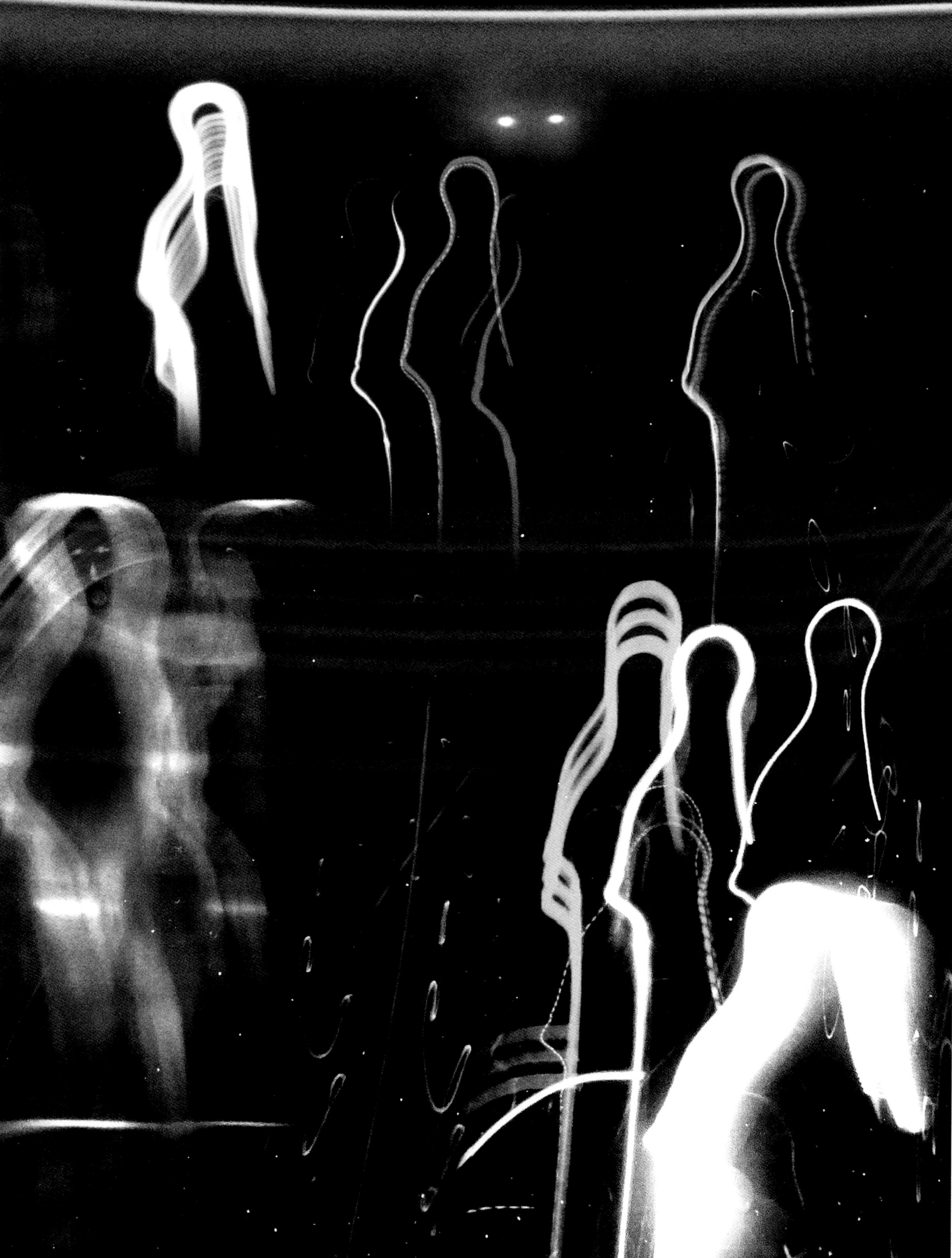

快乐的灵魂
Happy Souls, 2024
600 × 800mm

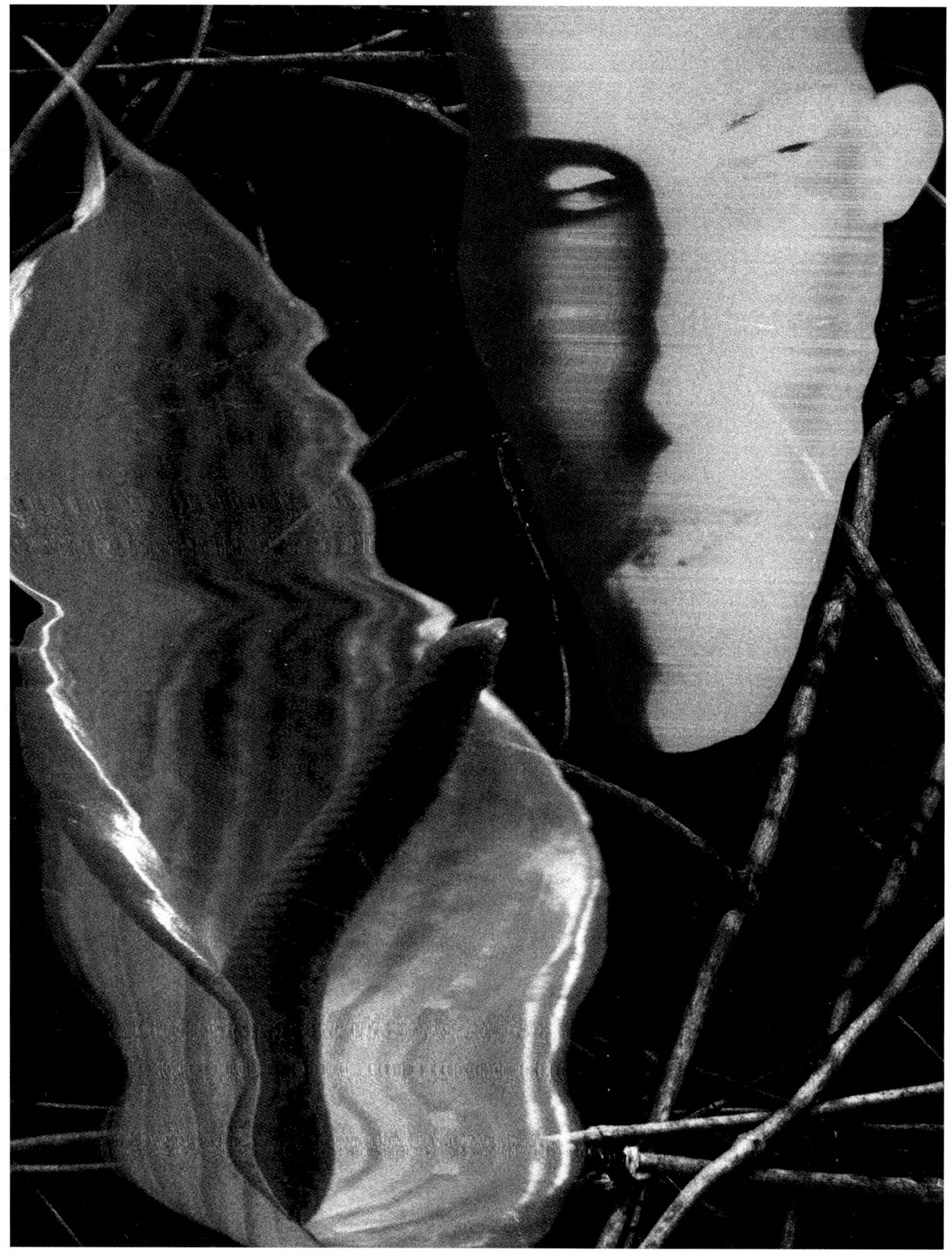

水中的美人
Beauty in Water, 2022
600 × 800mm

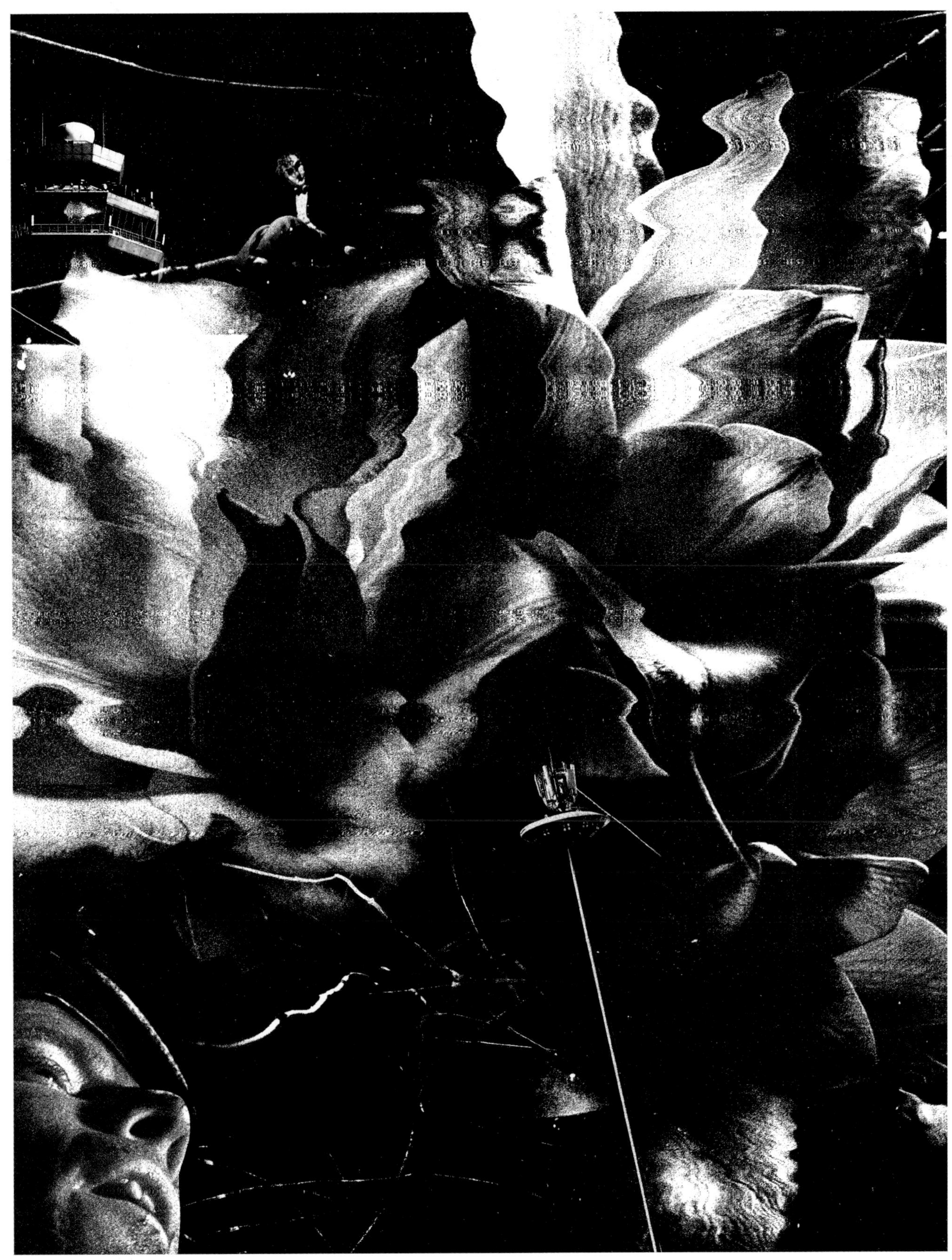

生活中的各种想象就是想想
All Kinds of Imagination in Life are Just Some Simple Thoughts, 2017–23
600 × 800mm

自始自终的认为人是外星人的宠物
I Have Always Believed that Humans are Pets of Aliens, 2023
600 × 800mm

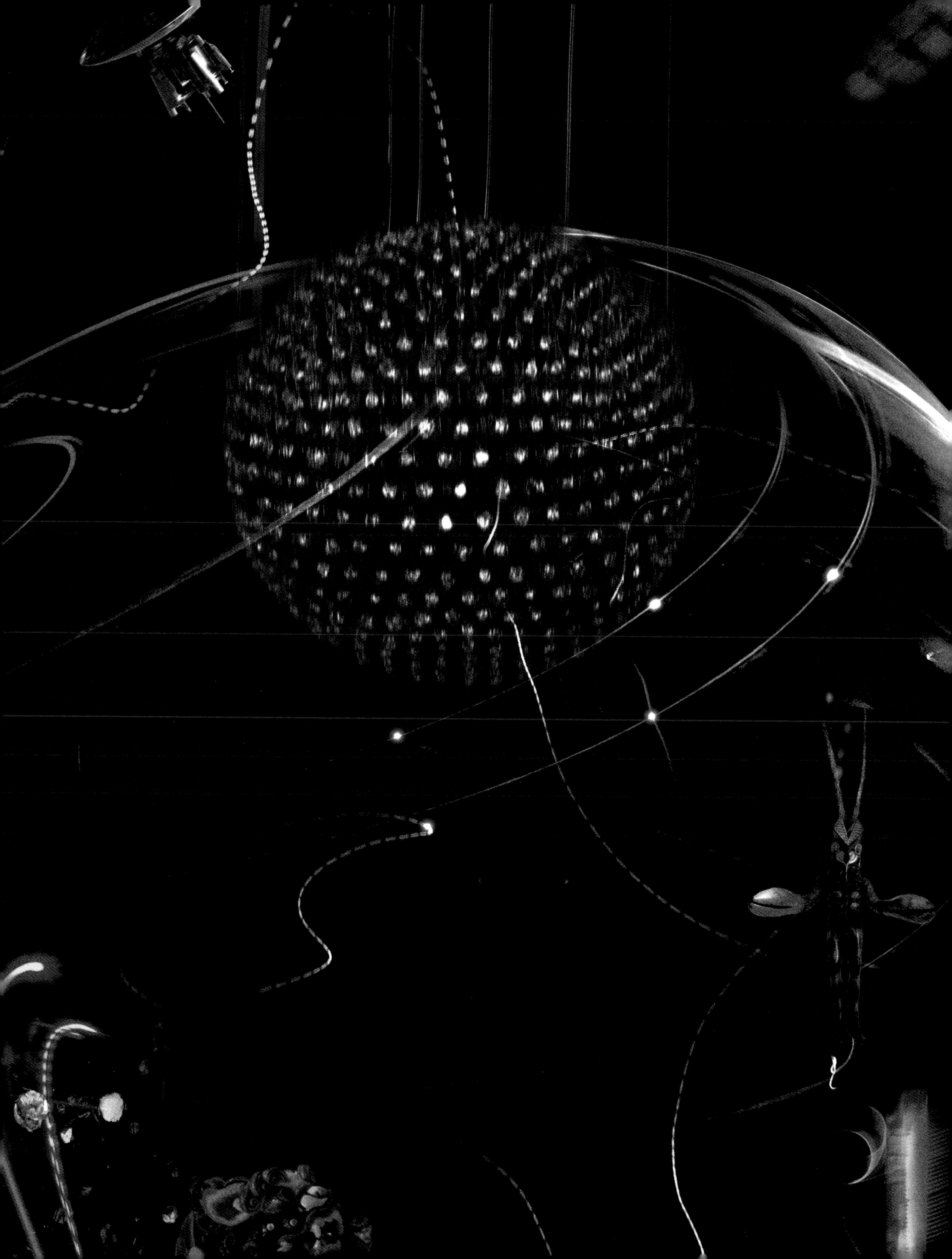

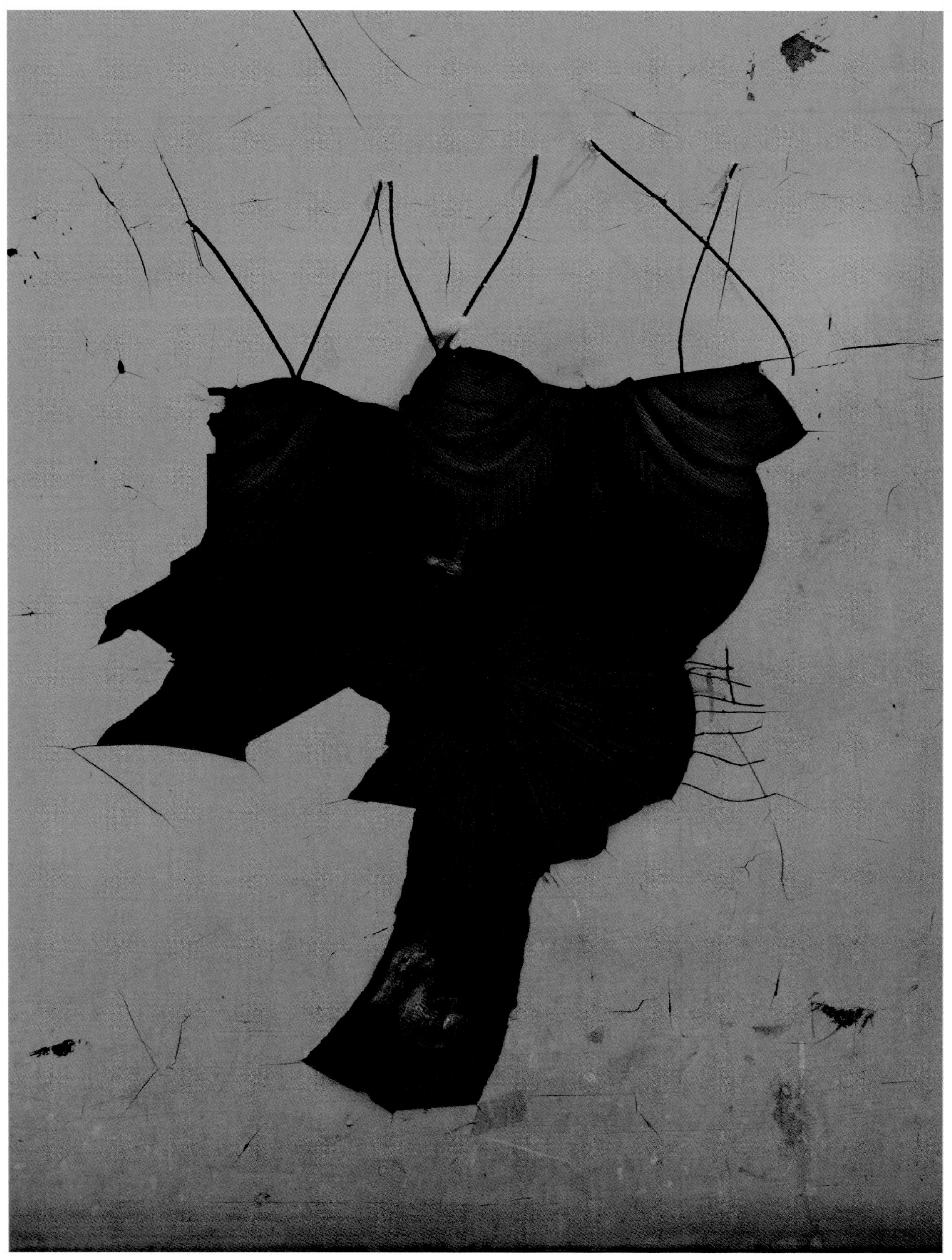

囚舞
Prisoner Dance, 2020
600 × 800mm

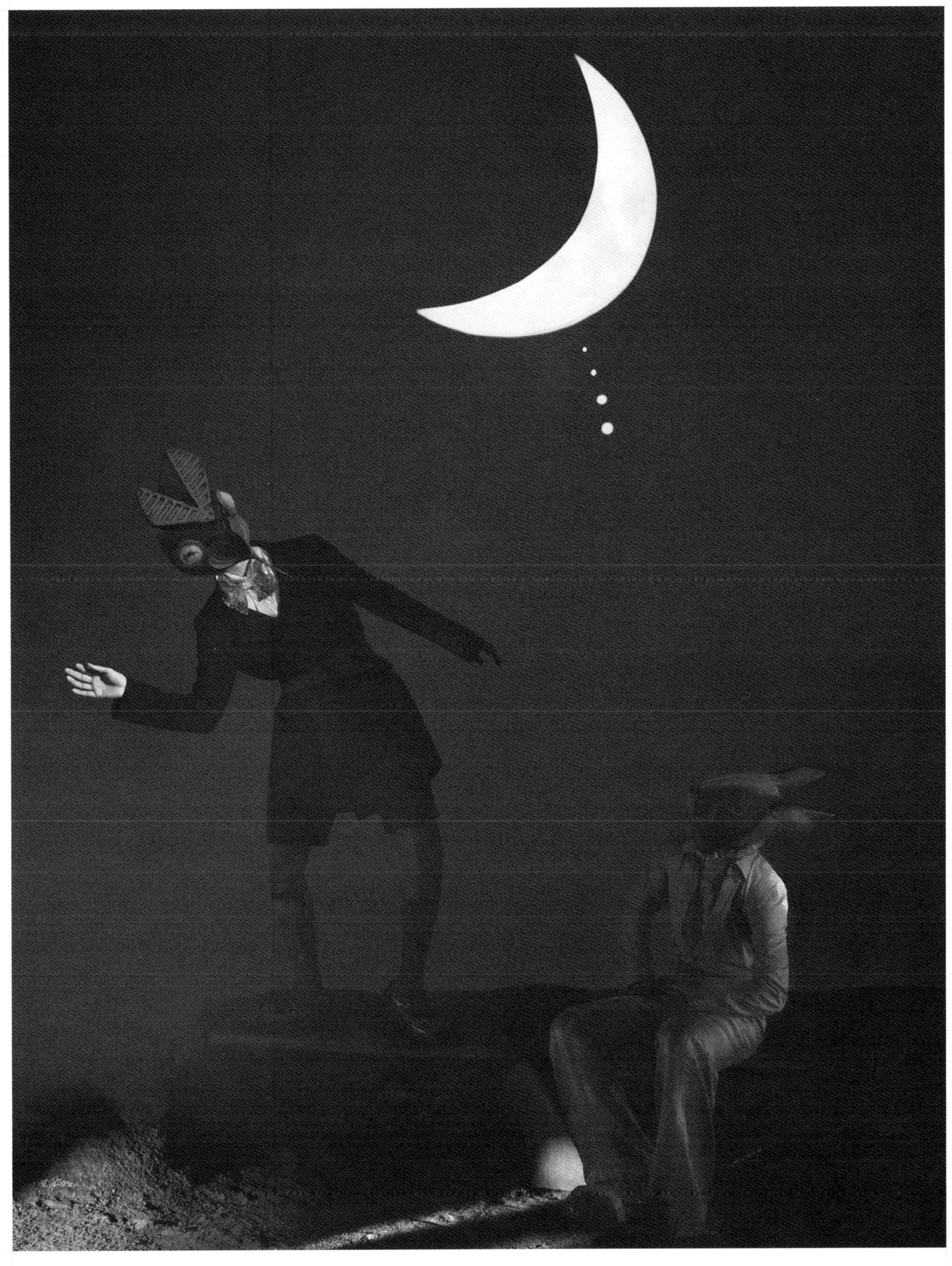

就这样静静地看着你
Just Looking at You Quietly, 2019
600 × 800mm

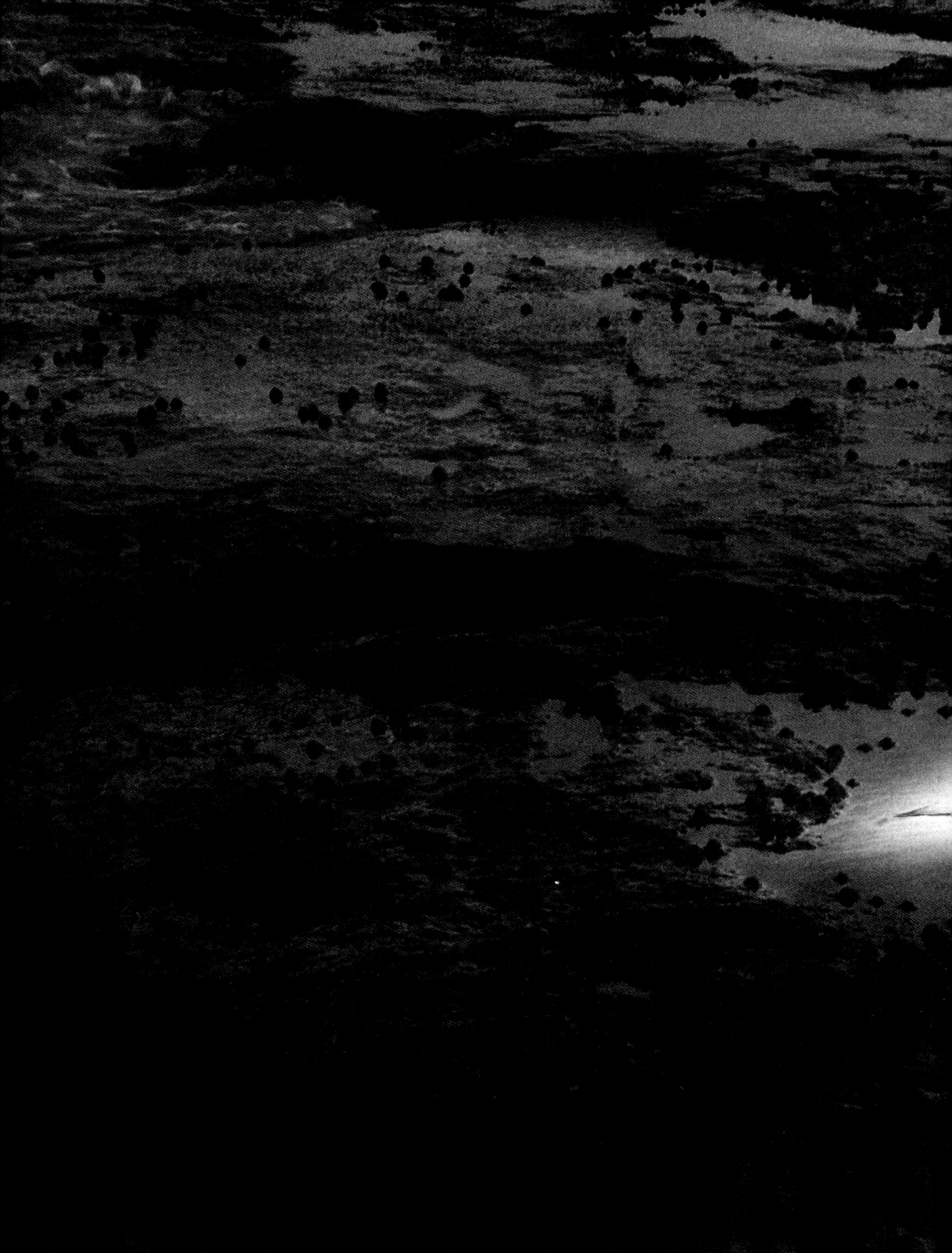

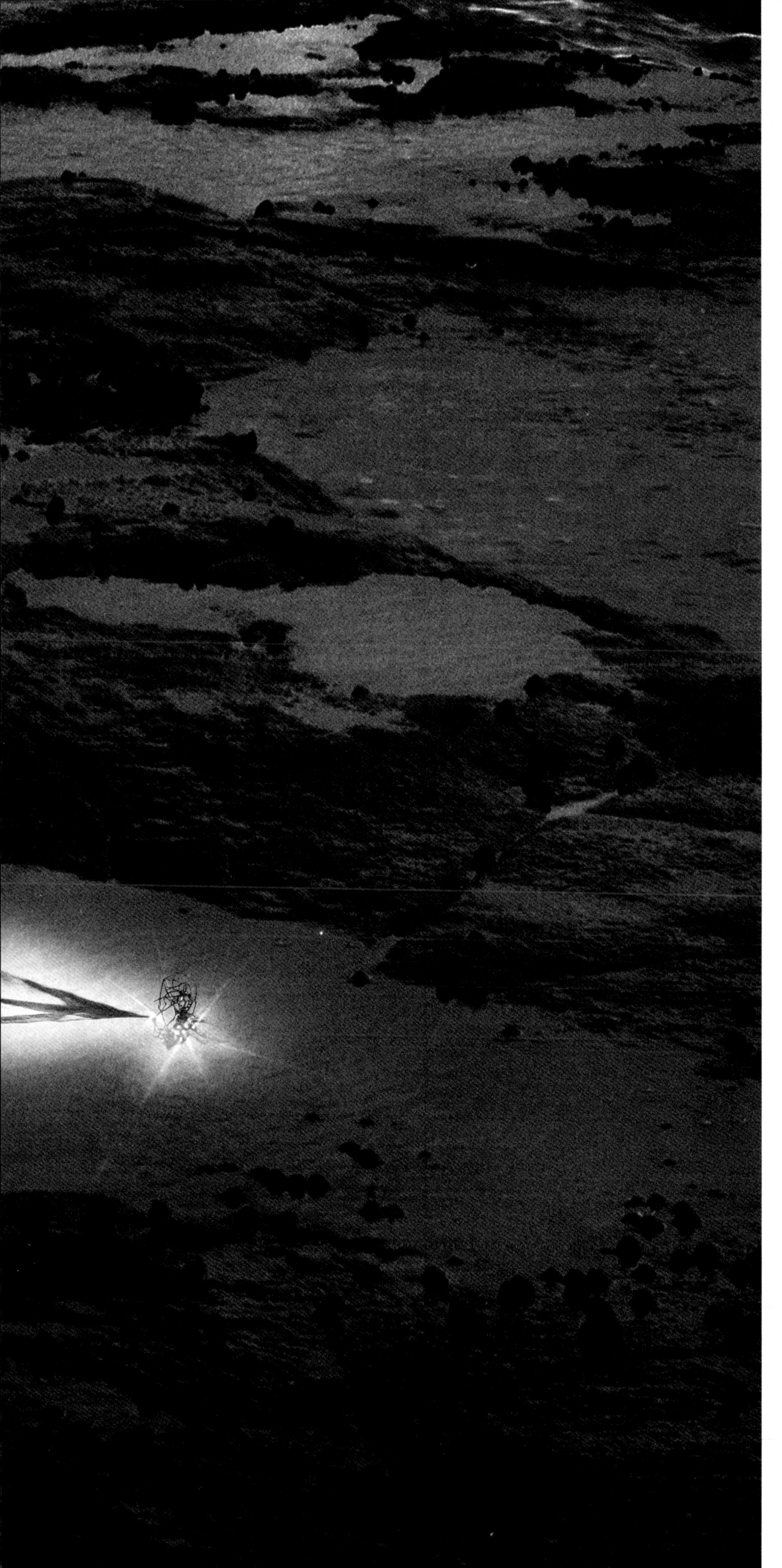

隐秘在角落

Hidden in the Corner, 2020

1000 × 800mm

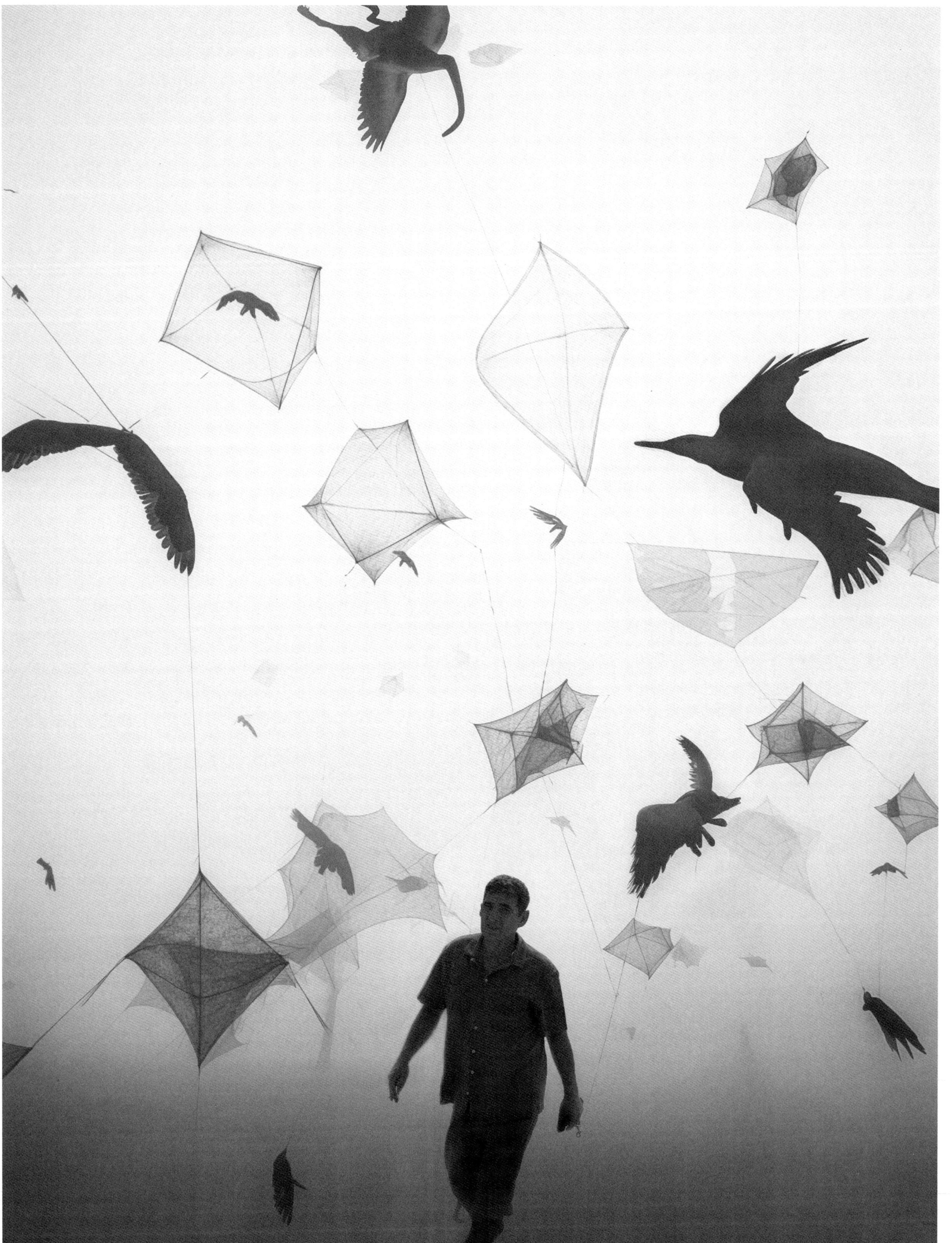

礼物
The Gift, 2022–24
600 × 800mm

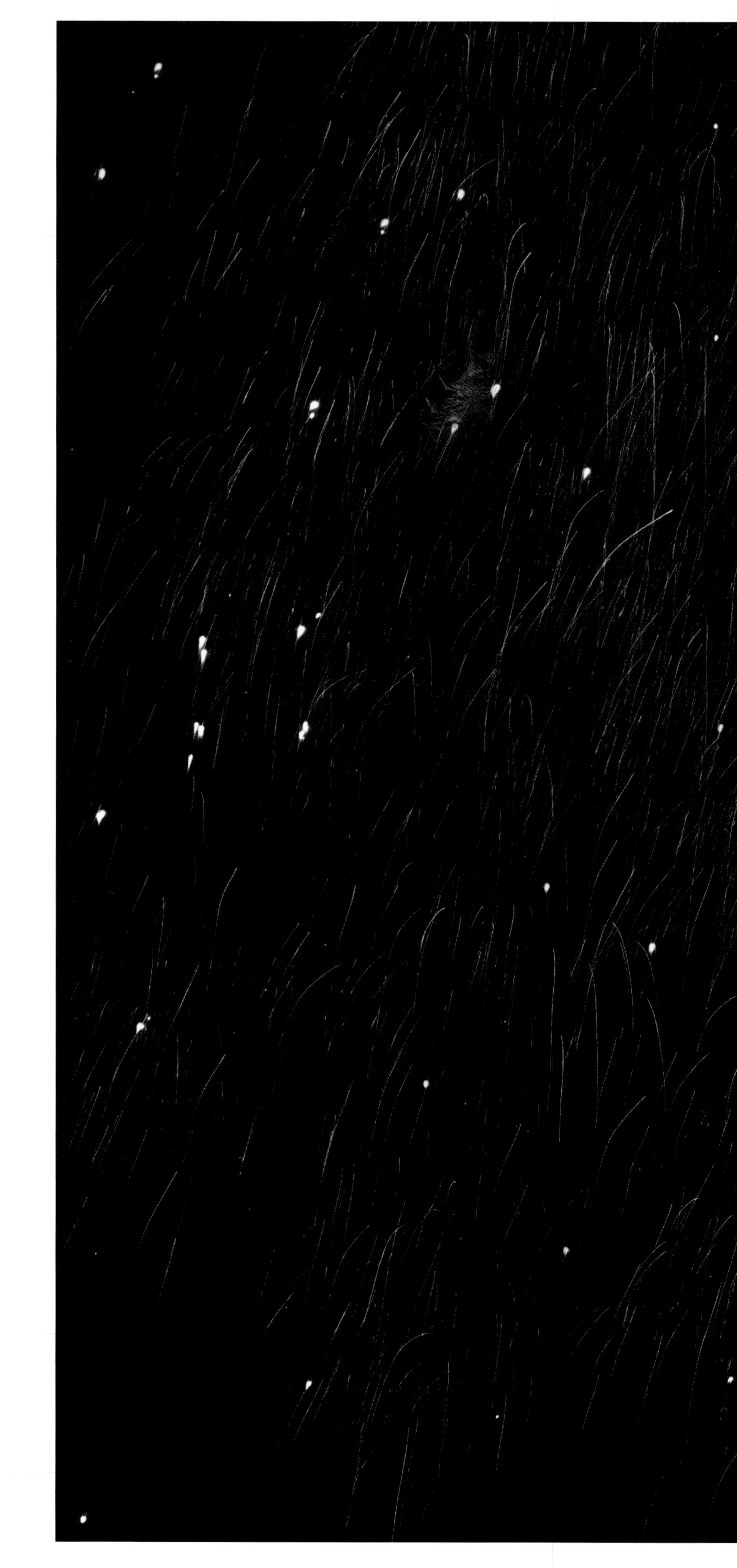

休憩
Recuperation, 2021
1000 × 800mm

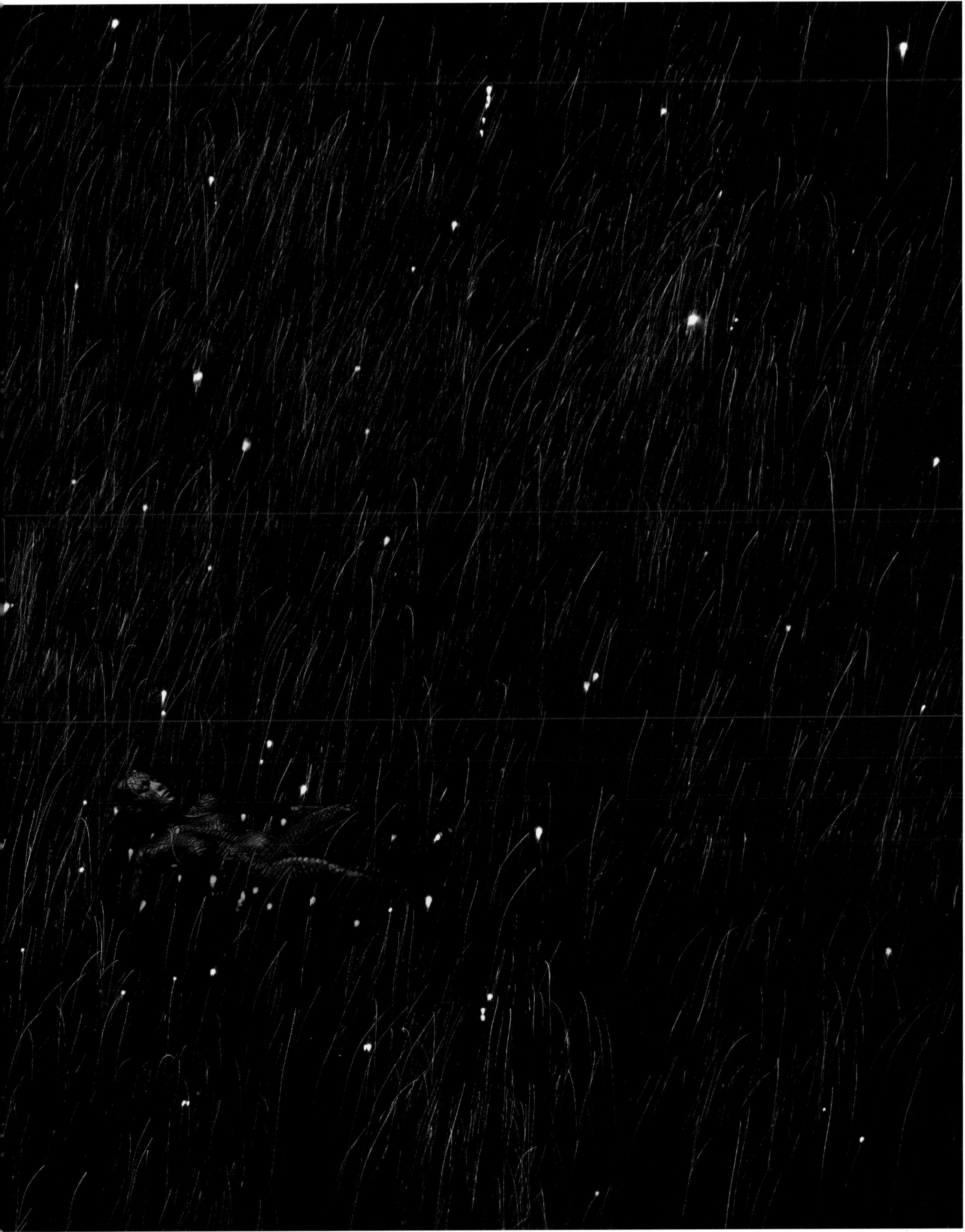

SECTION TWO

Ruins and Civilisations

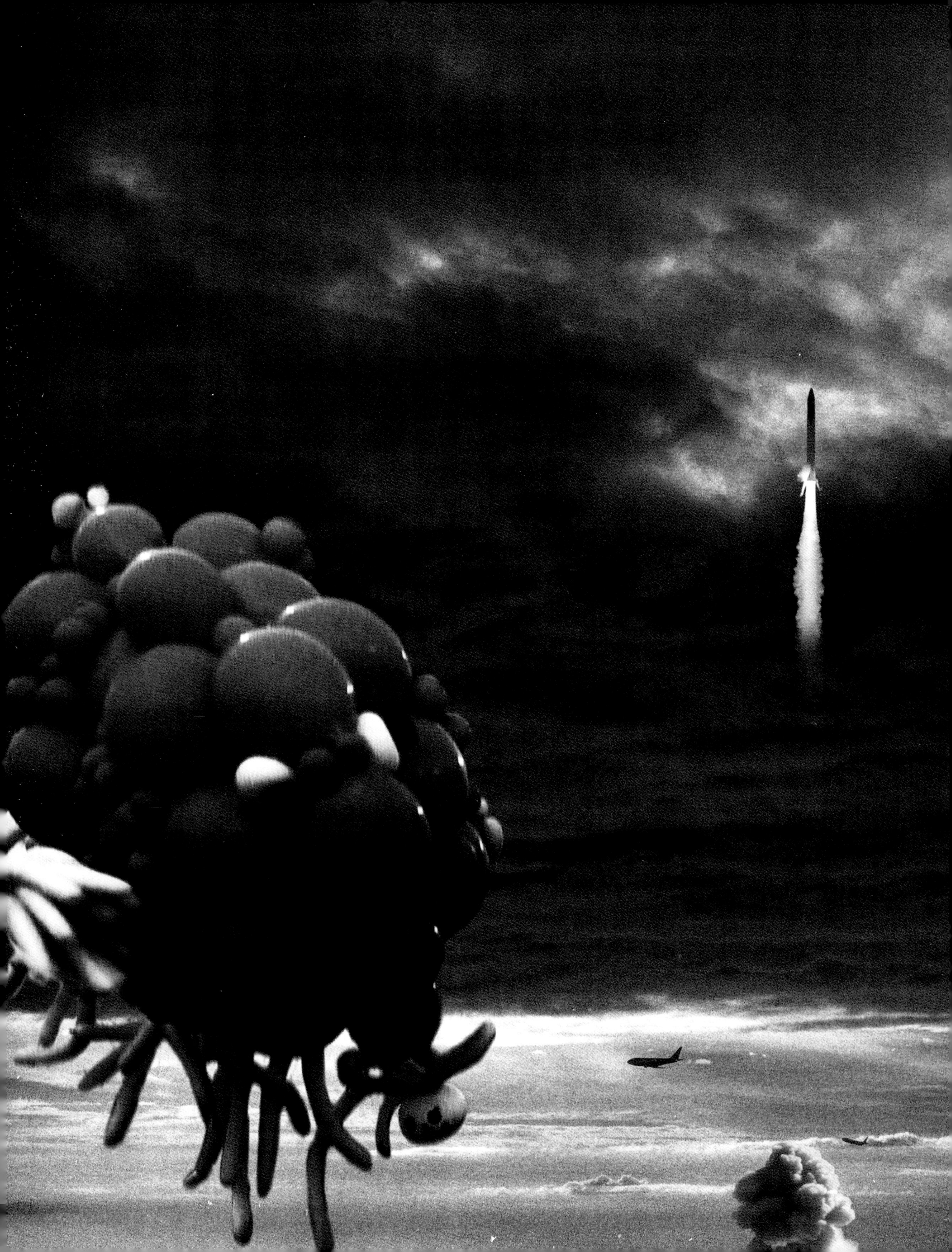

徒有其表
Have a Good Appearance Only, 2022–23
1000 × 800mm

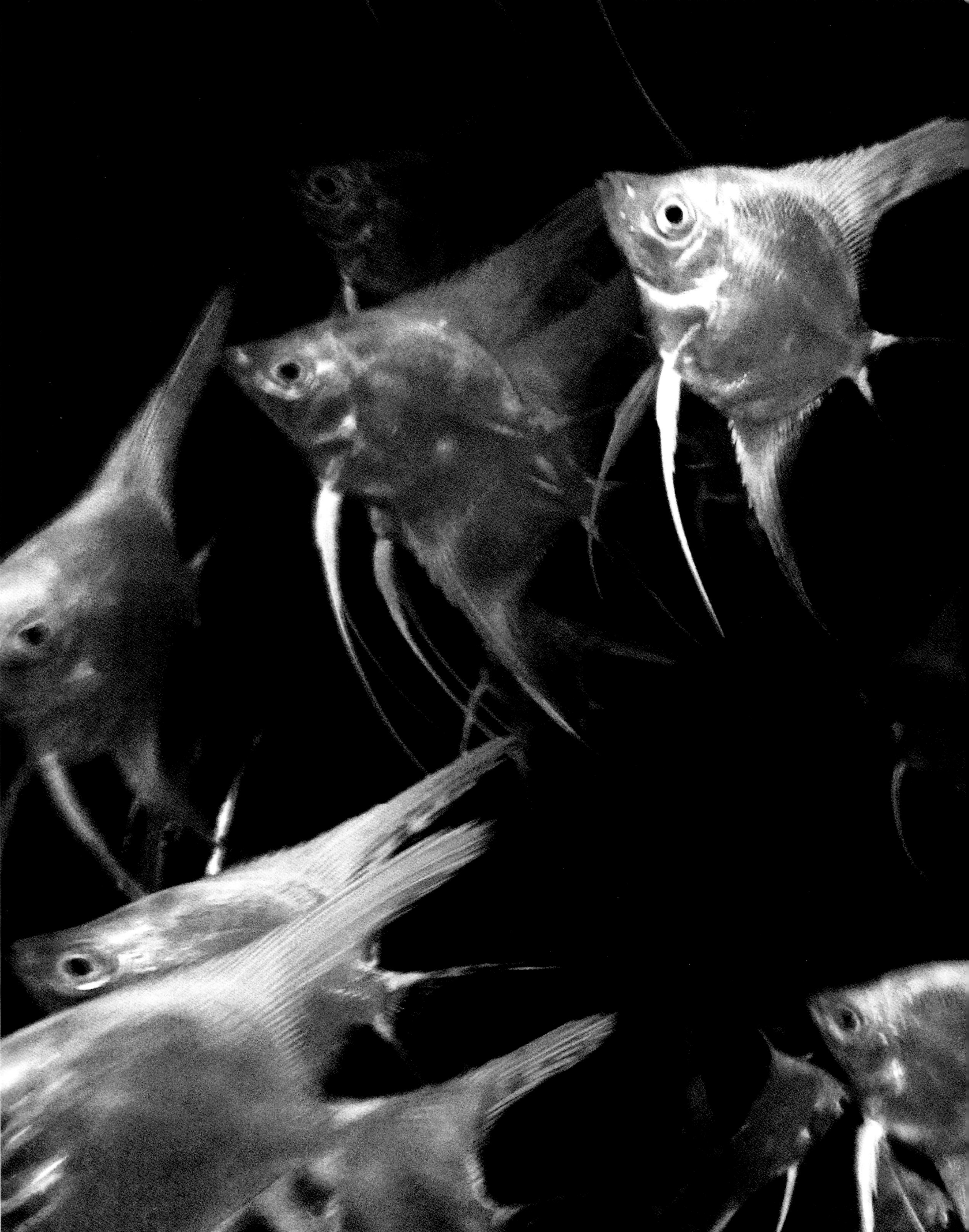

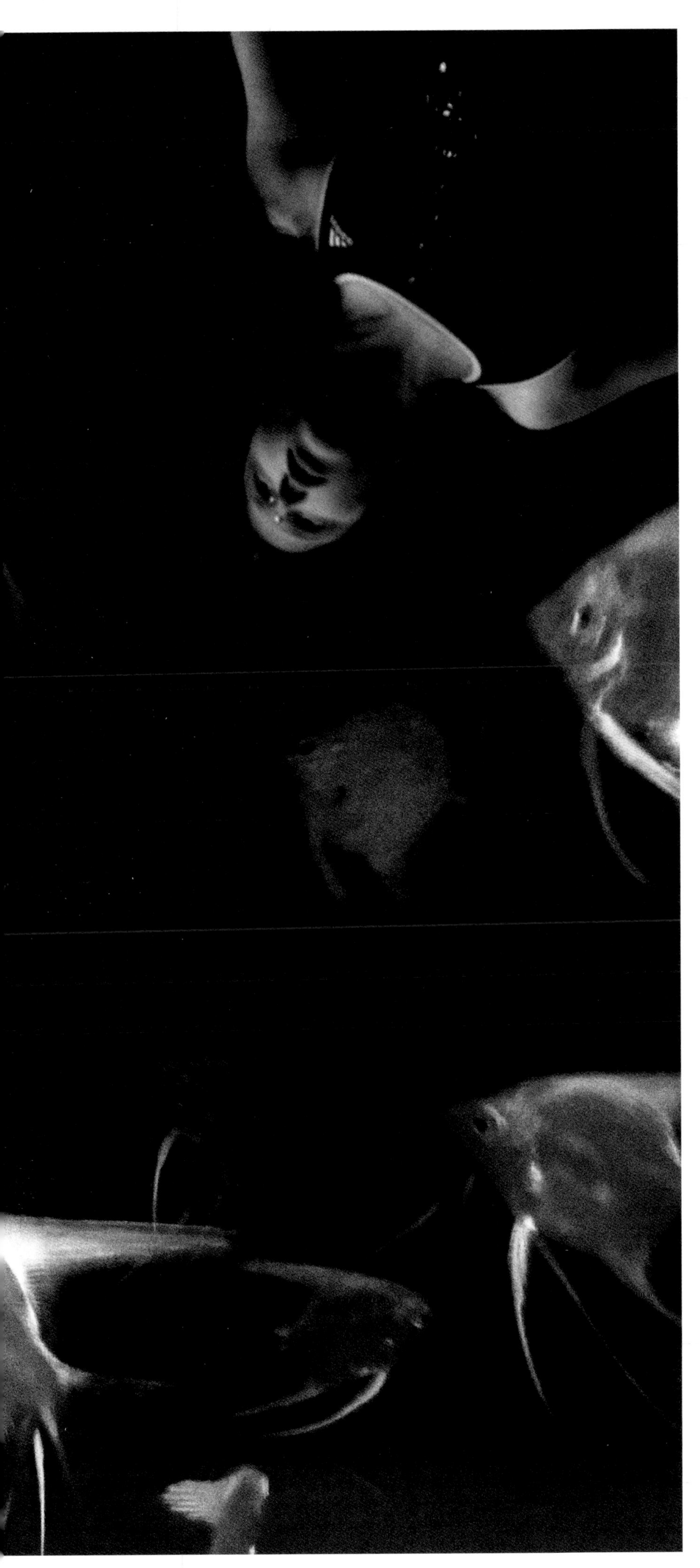

一直在找
Always Looking for Something, 2024
1000 × 800mm

主宰的猪
The Pig is the Overlord,
2017–22

1000 × 800mm

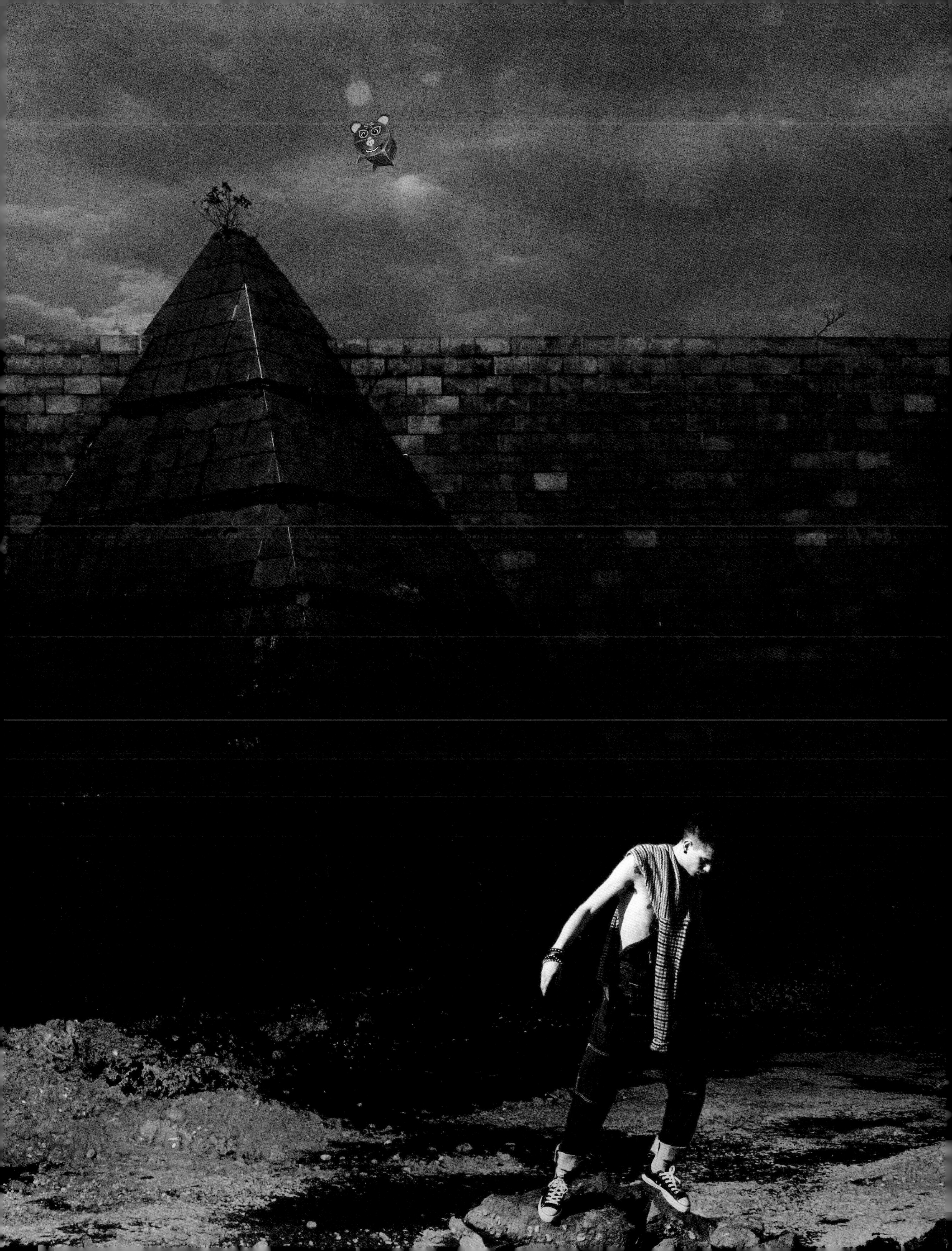

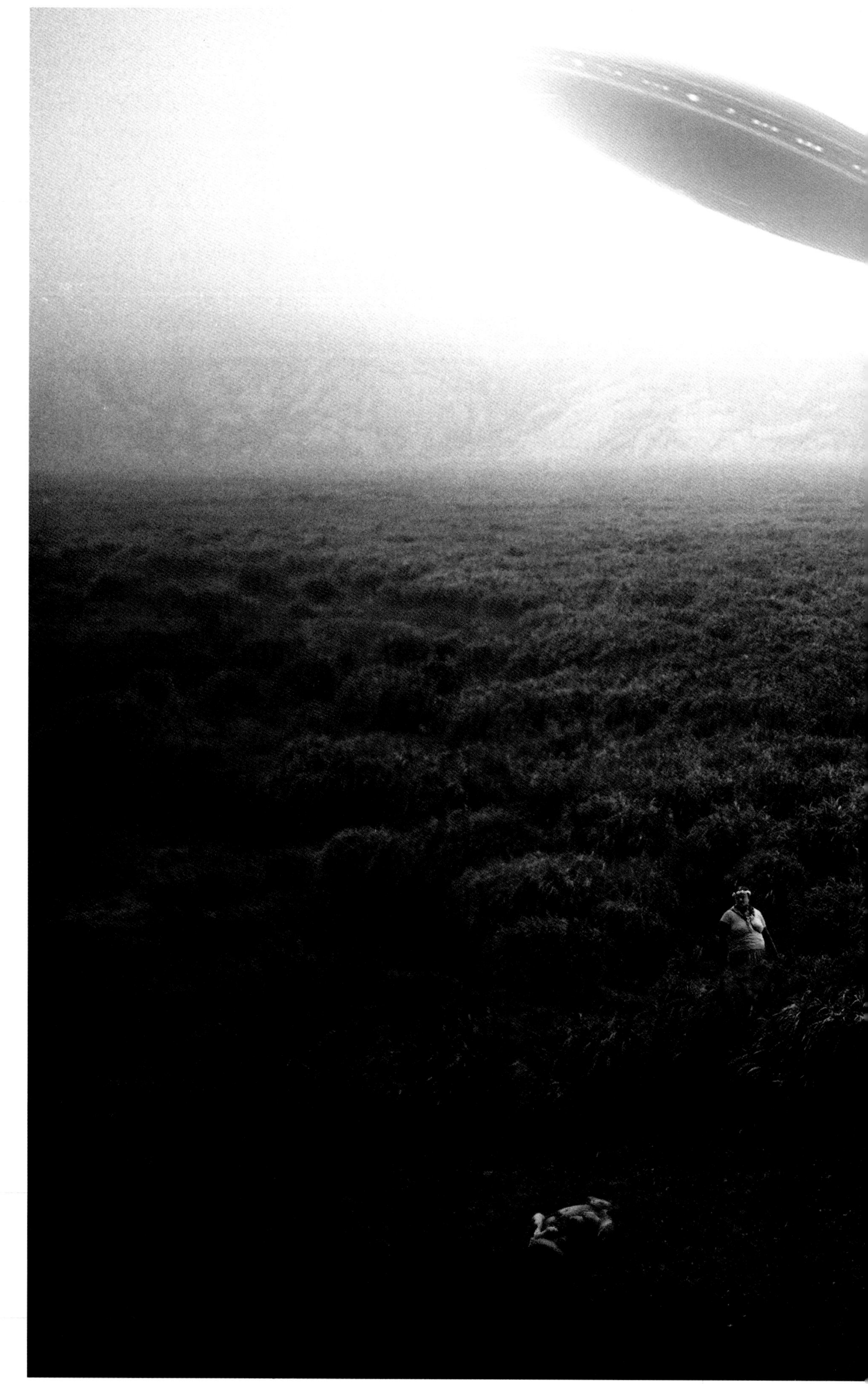

谁是曾经的征服者
Who Conquered this Place Before?, 2017–19
1000 × 800mm

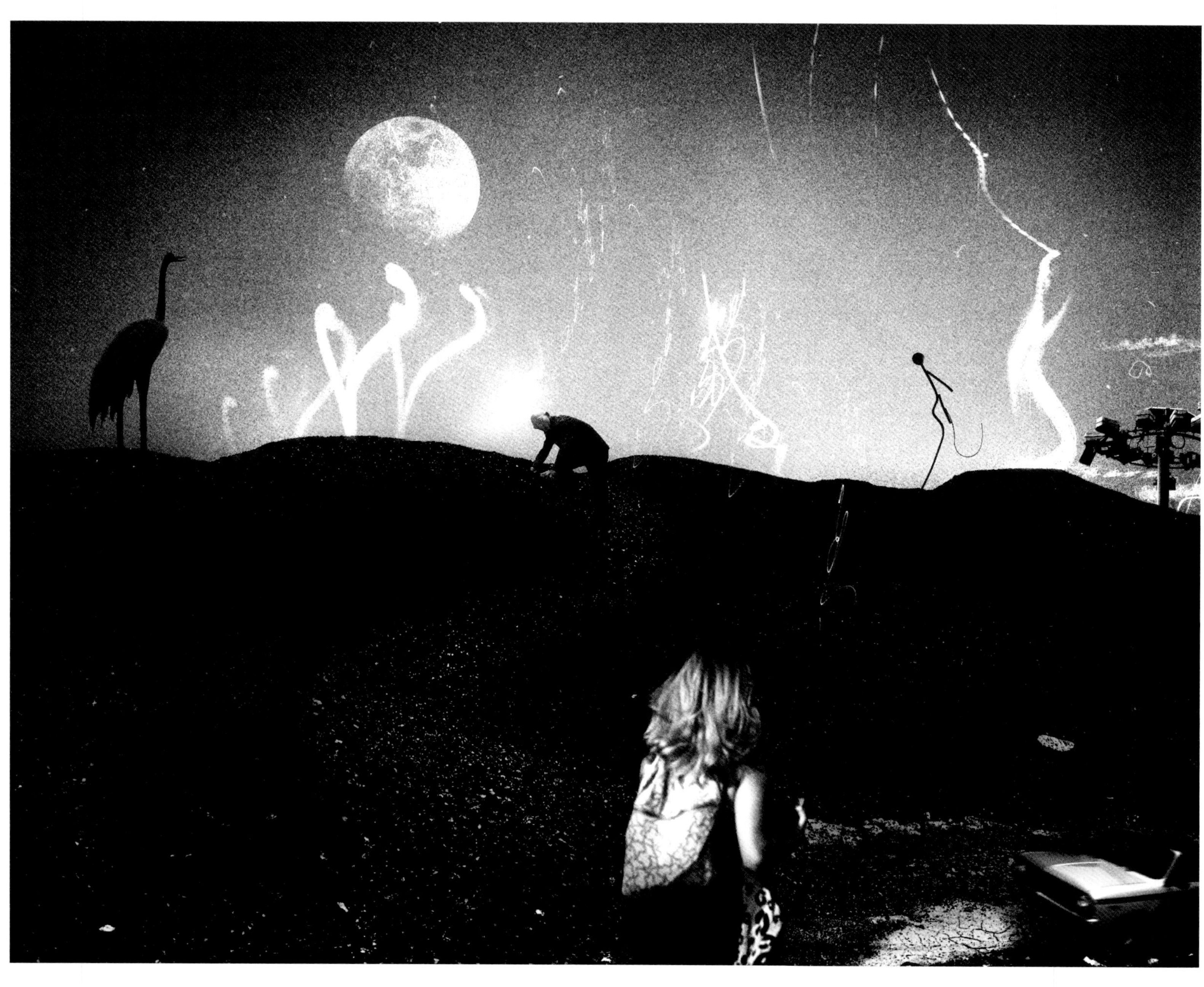

外逃的灵魂
The Escaping Soul, 2014–22
1000 × 800mm

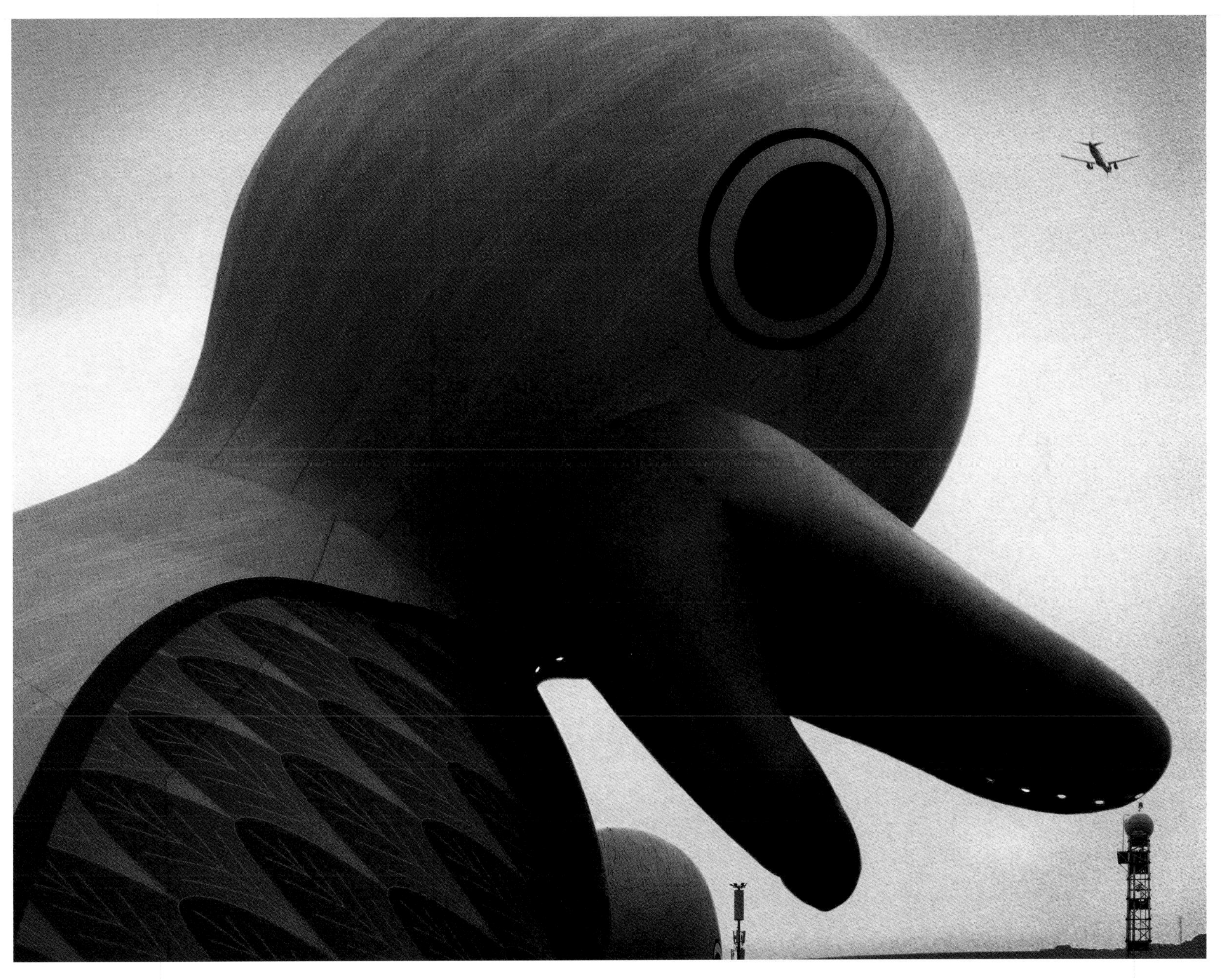

变强了他们就会怕
They Will Be Afraid When You Become Stronger, 2009–21
1000 × 800mm

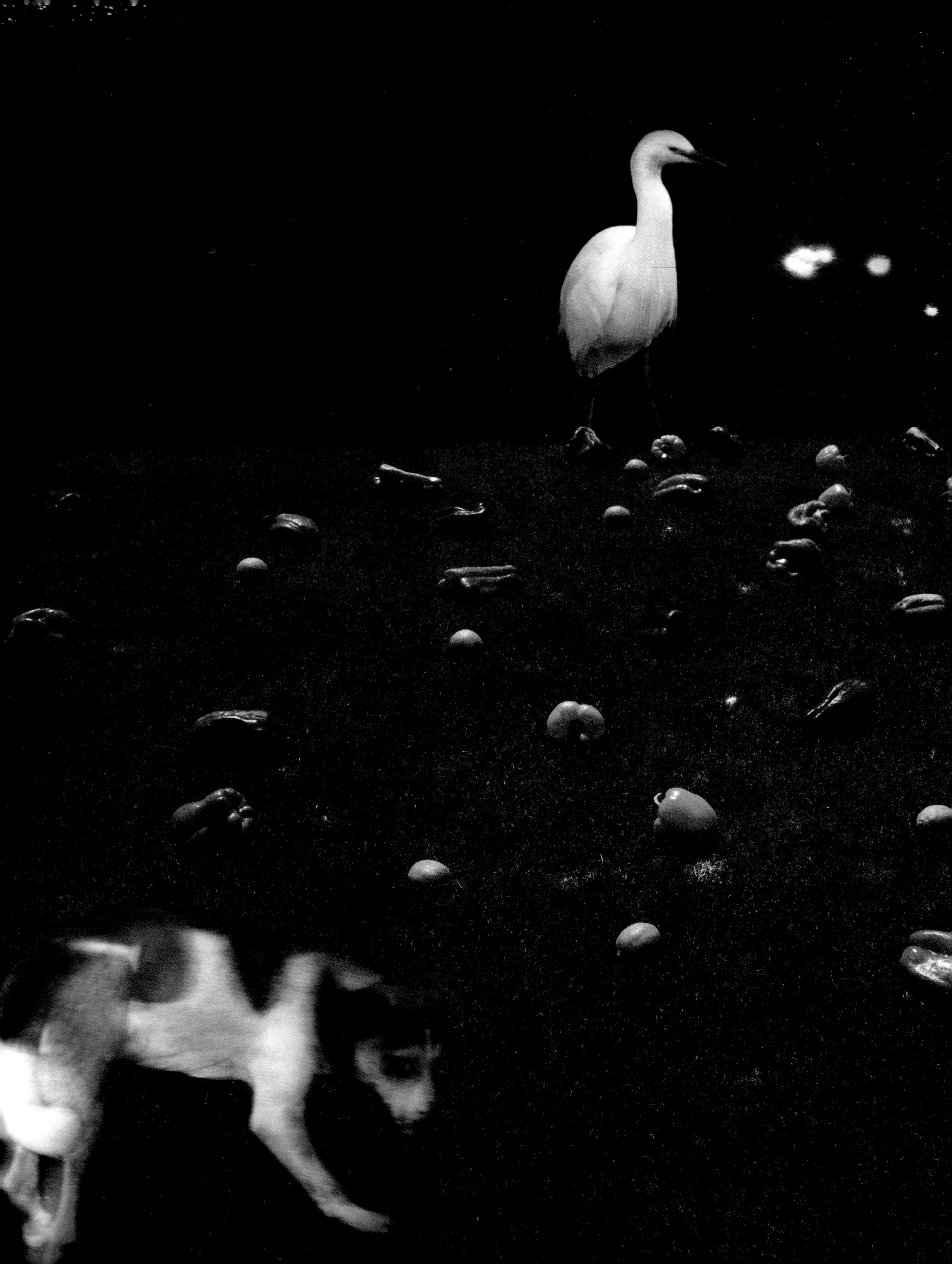

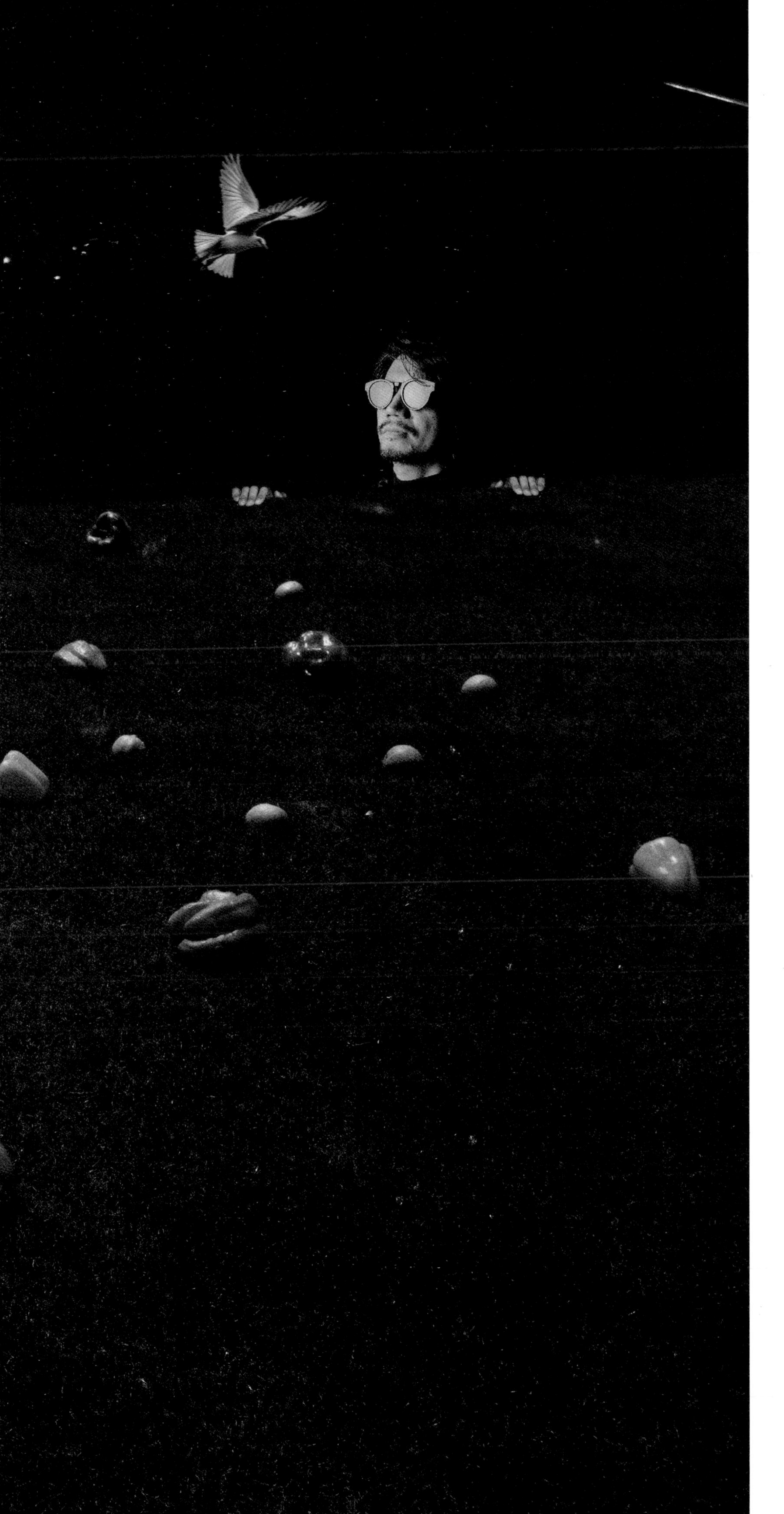

后院
The Backyard, 2020–24
1000 × 800mm

墙
Wall, 2023
600 × 800mm

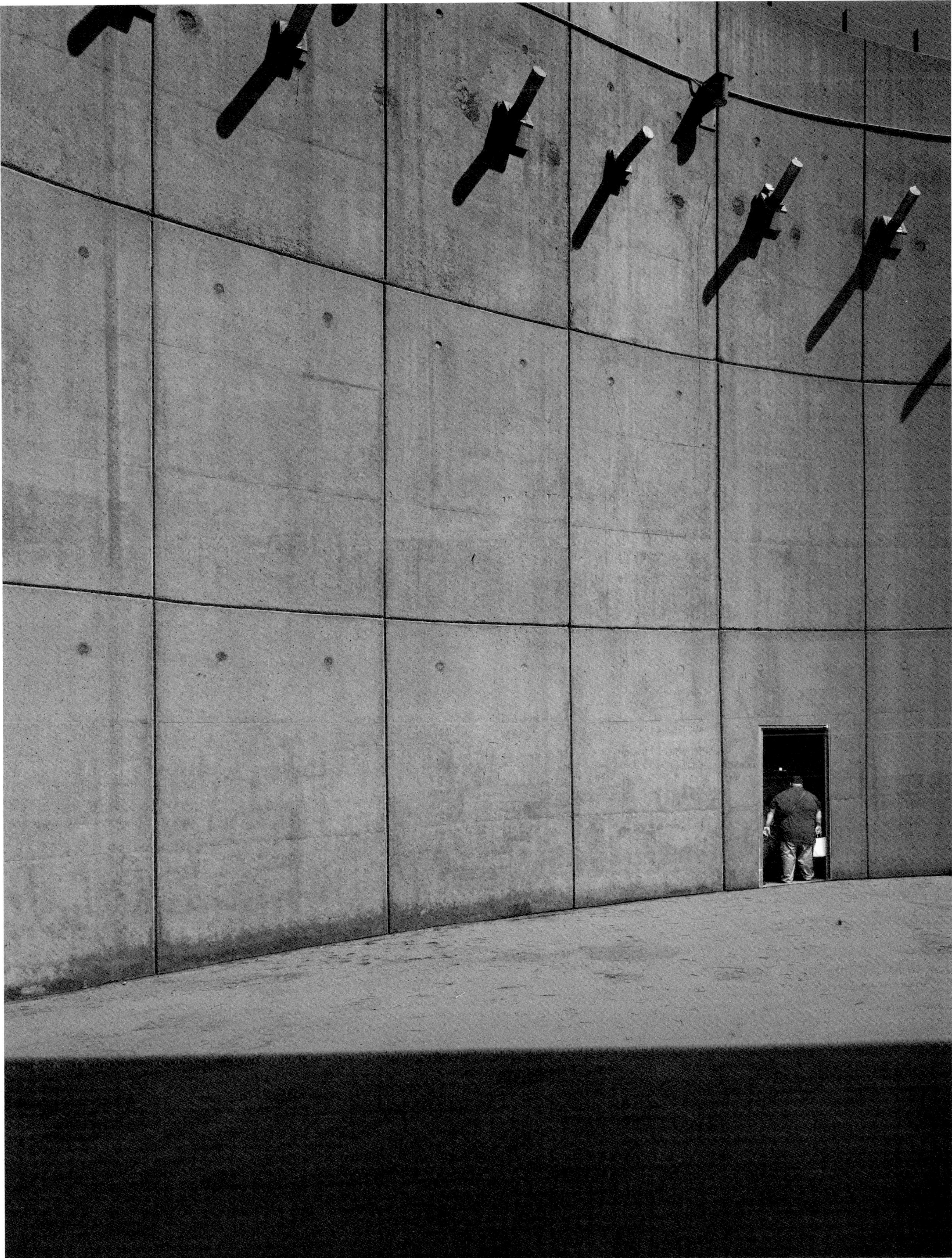

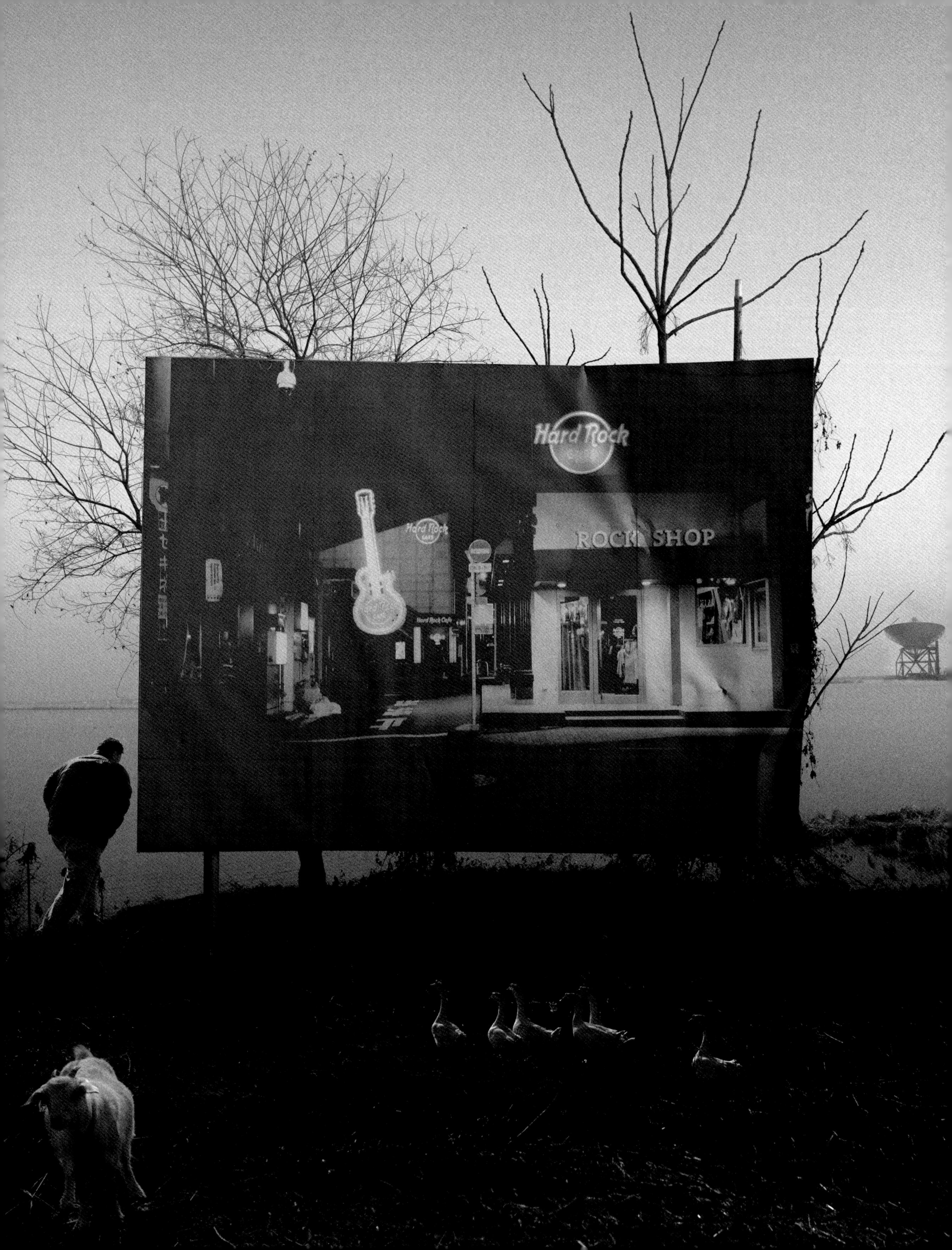
Hard Rock
ROCK SHOP

发财的梦却被一
个大锅盖给毁了
The Dream of Getting Rich was Ruined by a Big Pot Lid, 2010–20
600 × 800mm

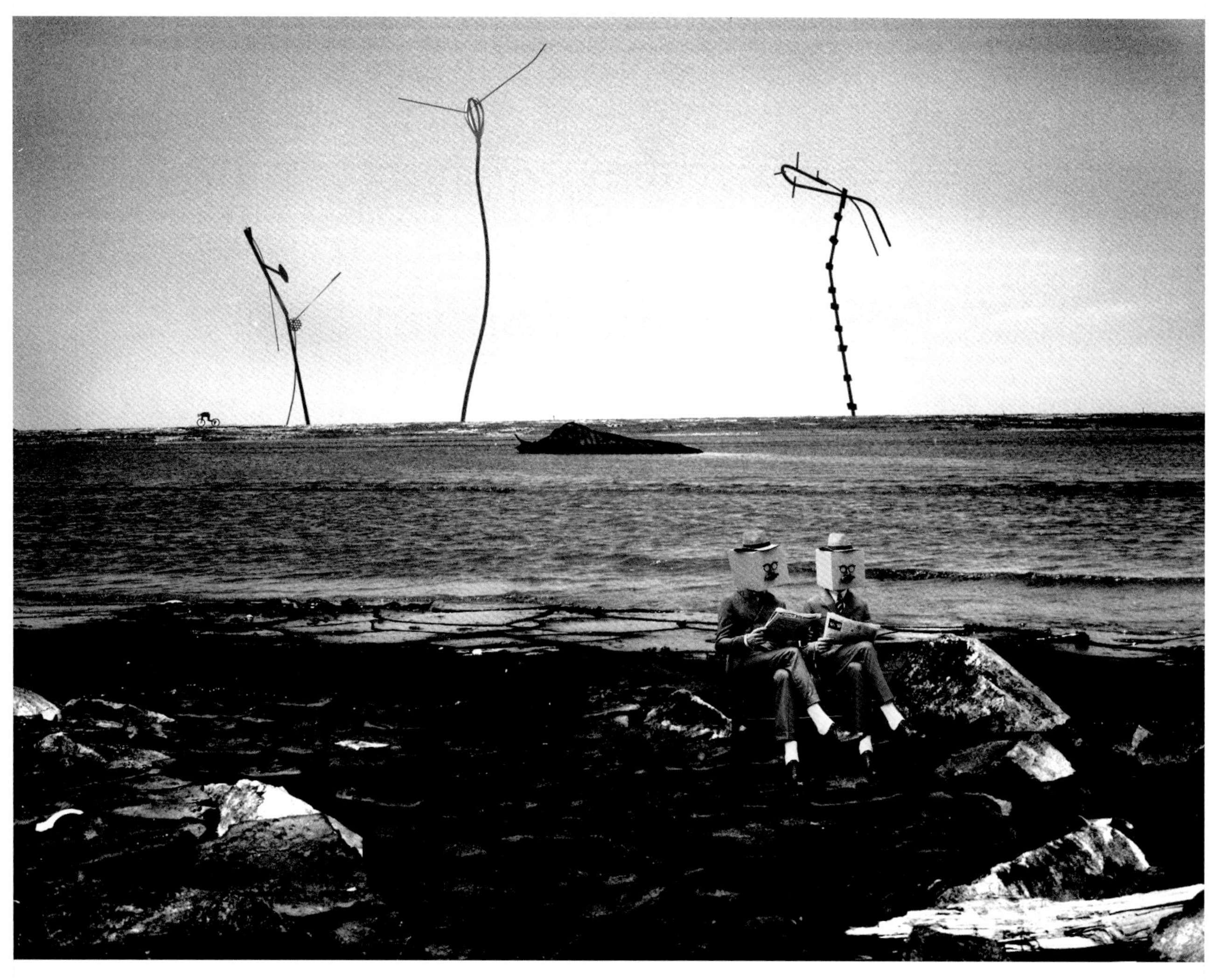

远离伪装者
Stay Away From Pretenders, 2012–23
1000 × 800mm

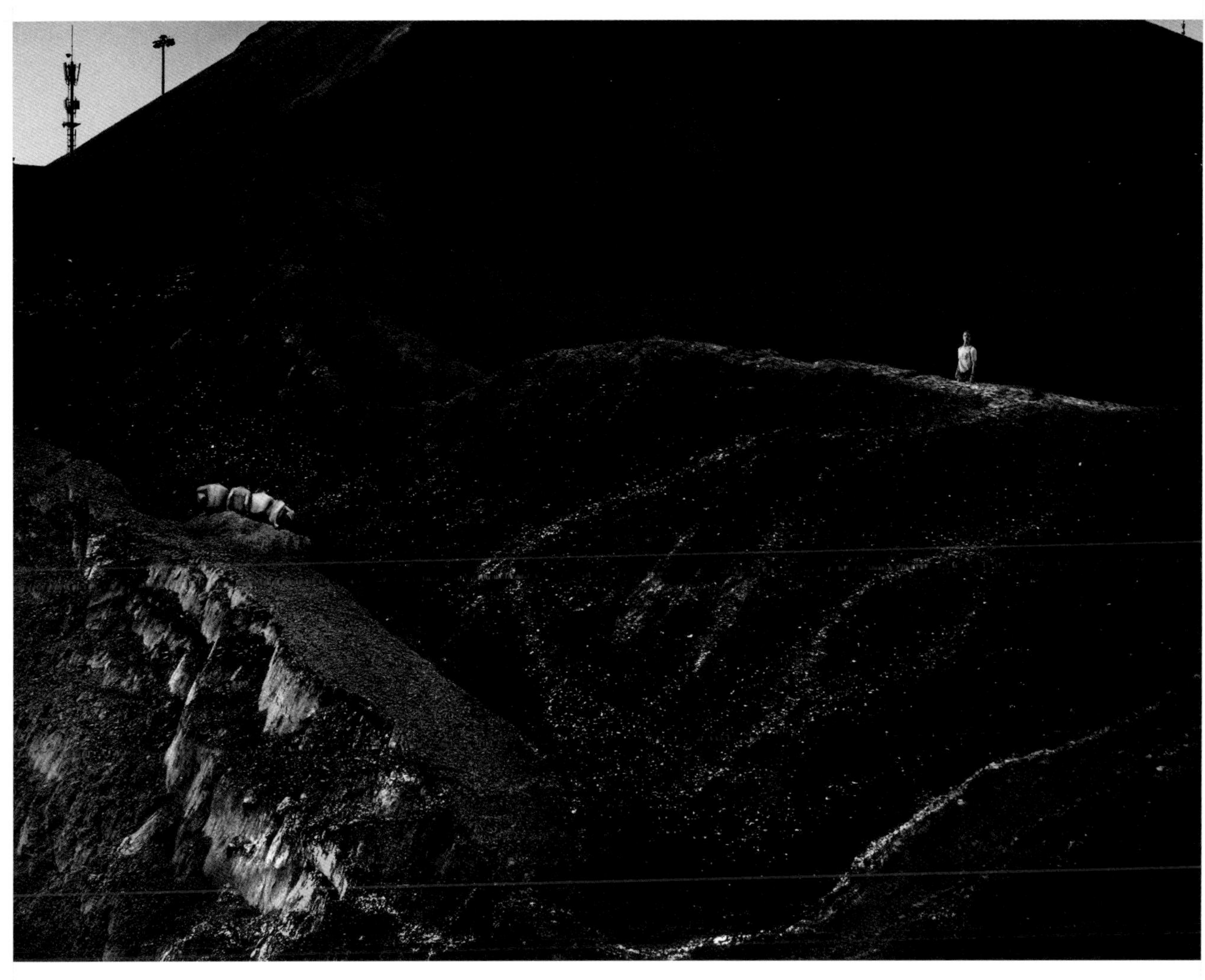

曾经的兄弟
Former Brothers, 2016–23
1000 × 800mm

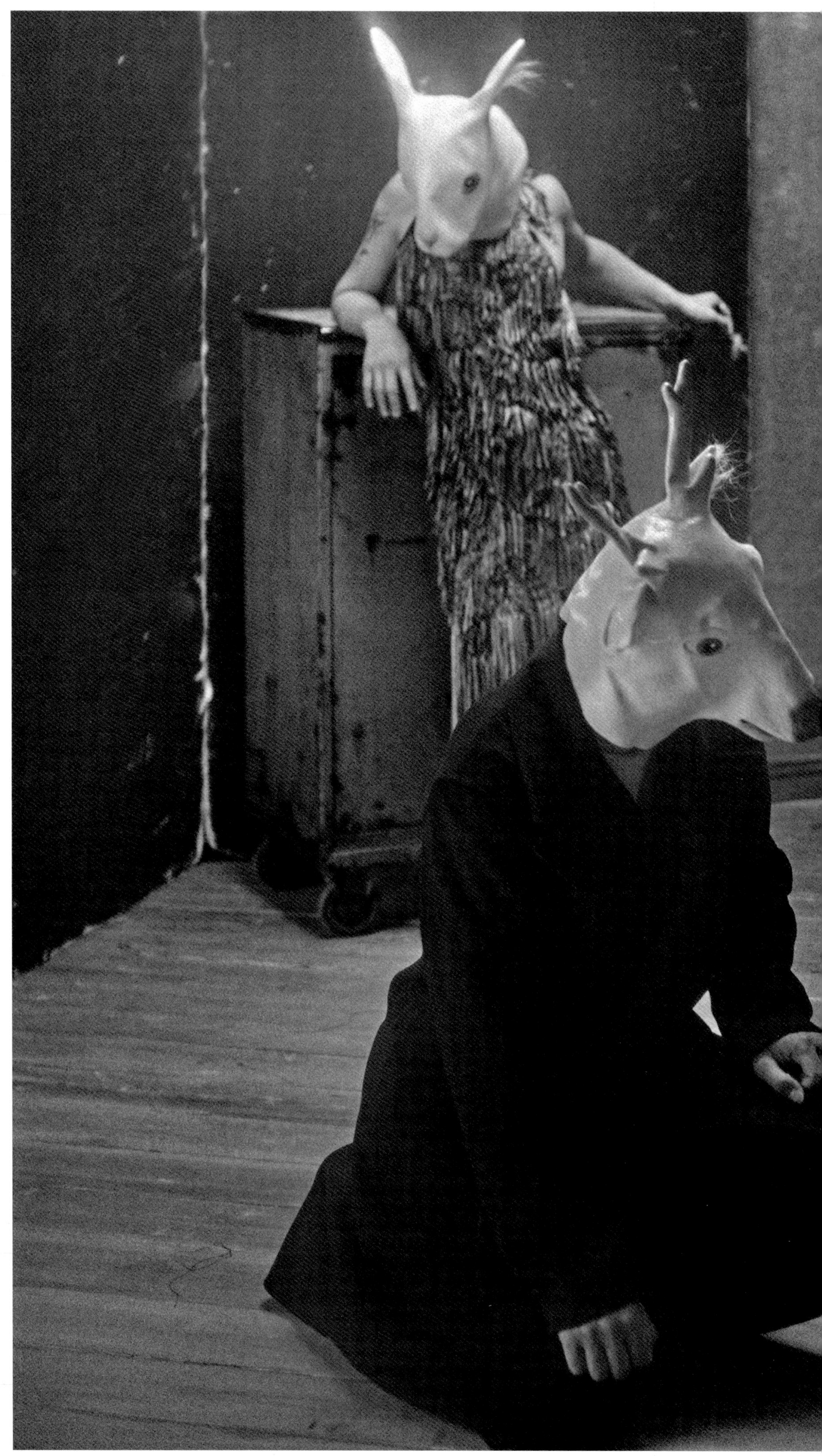

拷问
Torture, 2018
1000 × 800mm

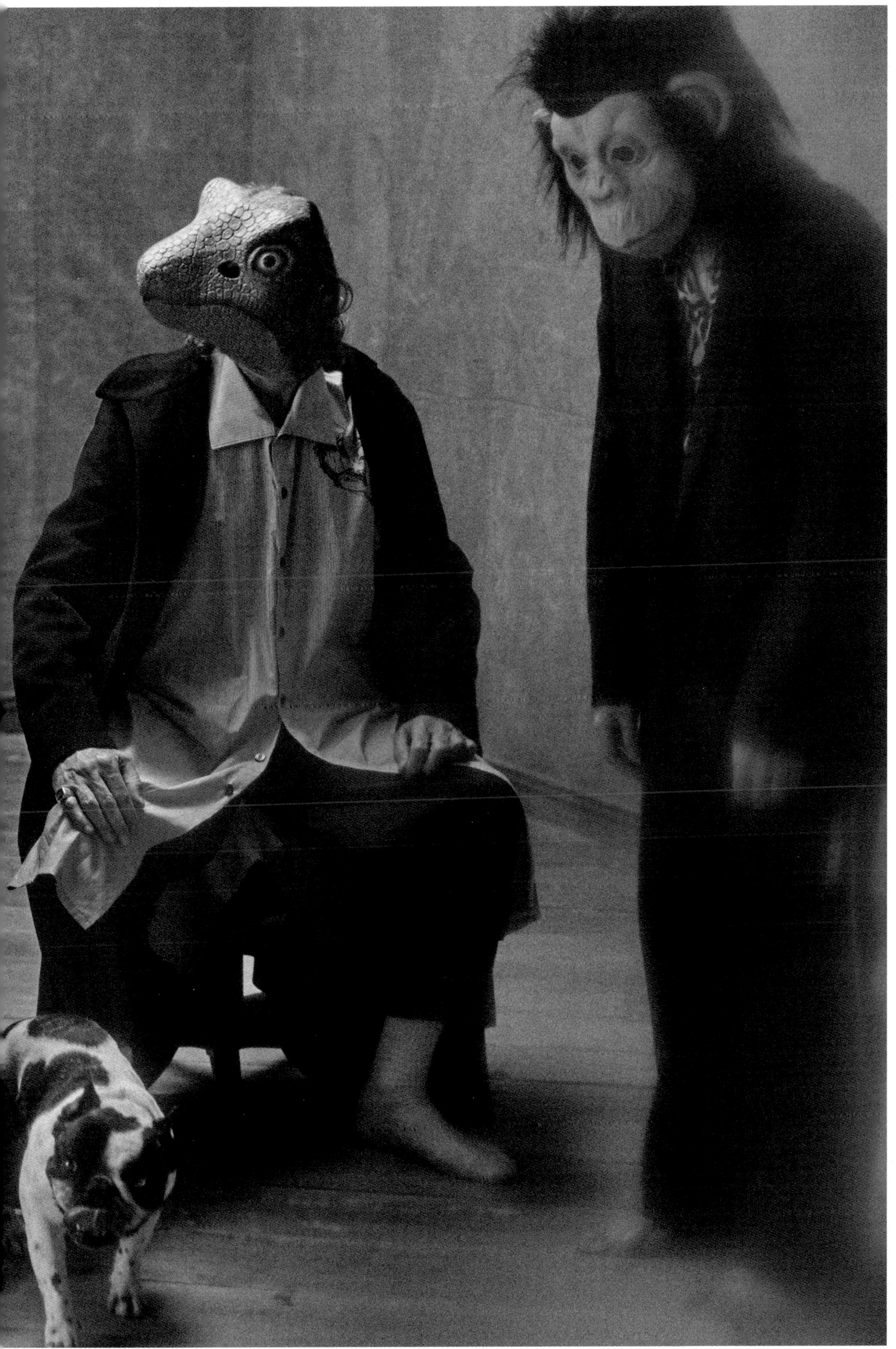

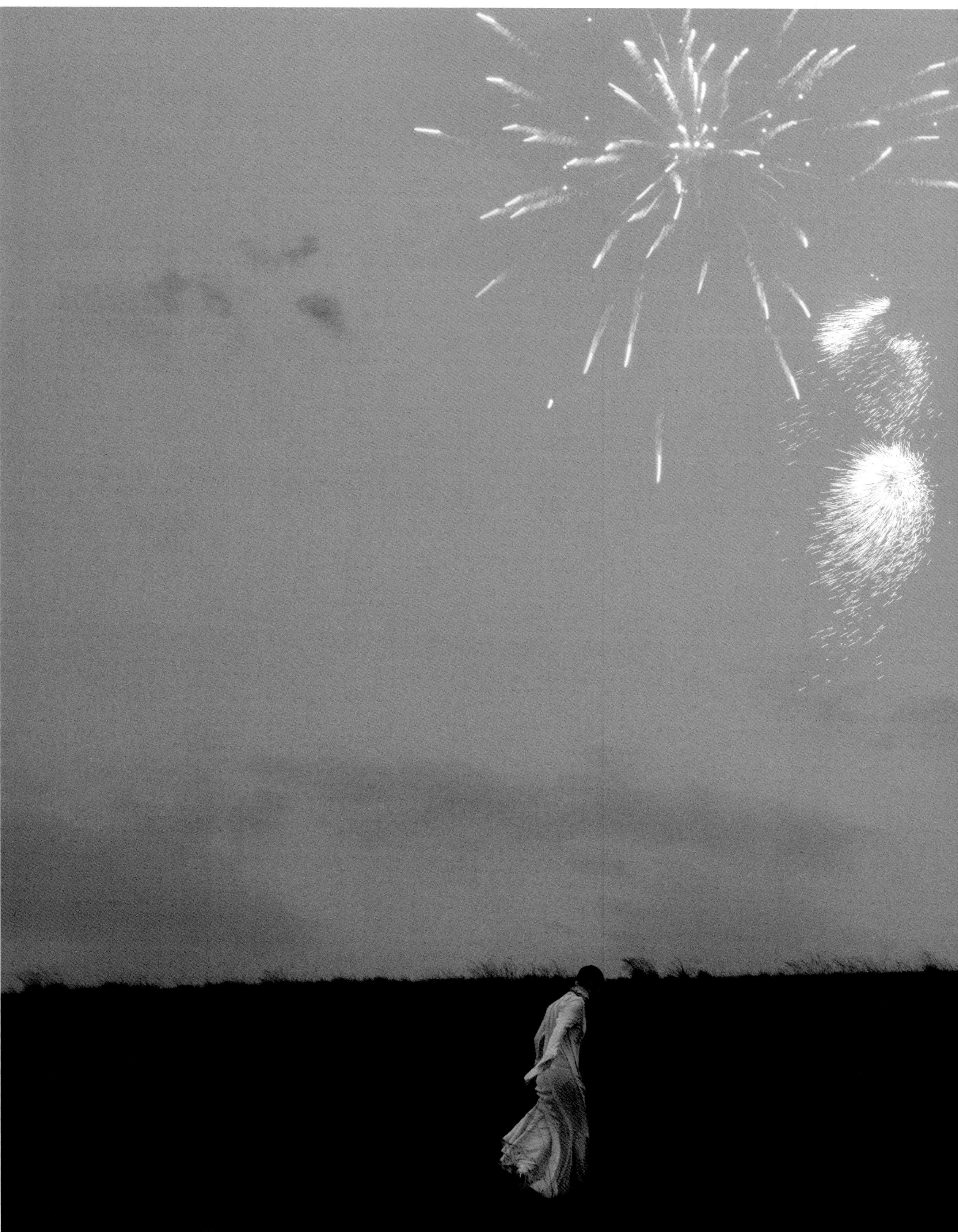

白日焰火
Fire During the Day,
2017–18
1000 × 800mm

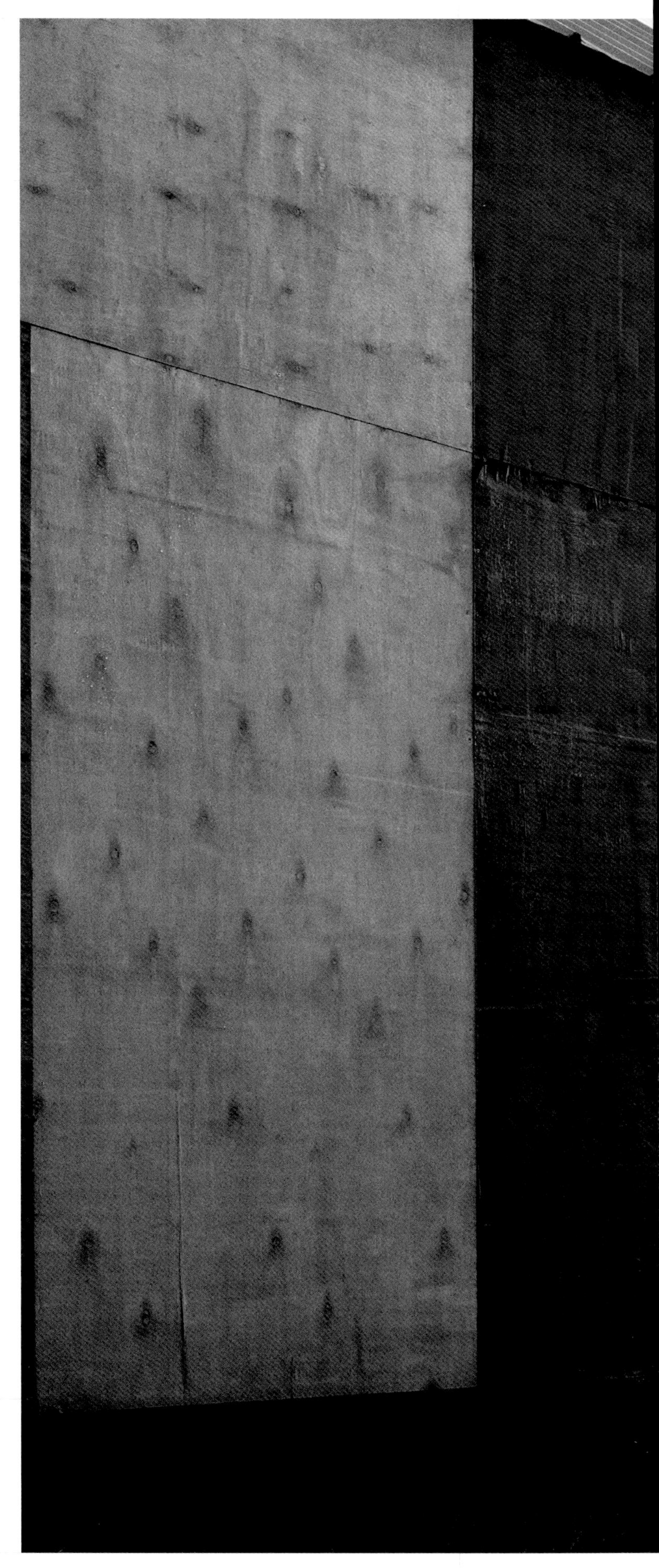

通缉
List as Wanted, 2022–23
1000 × 800mm

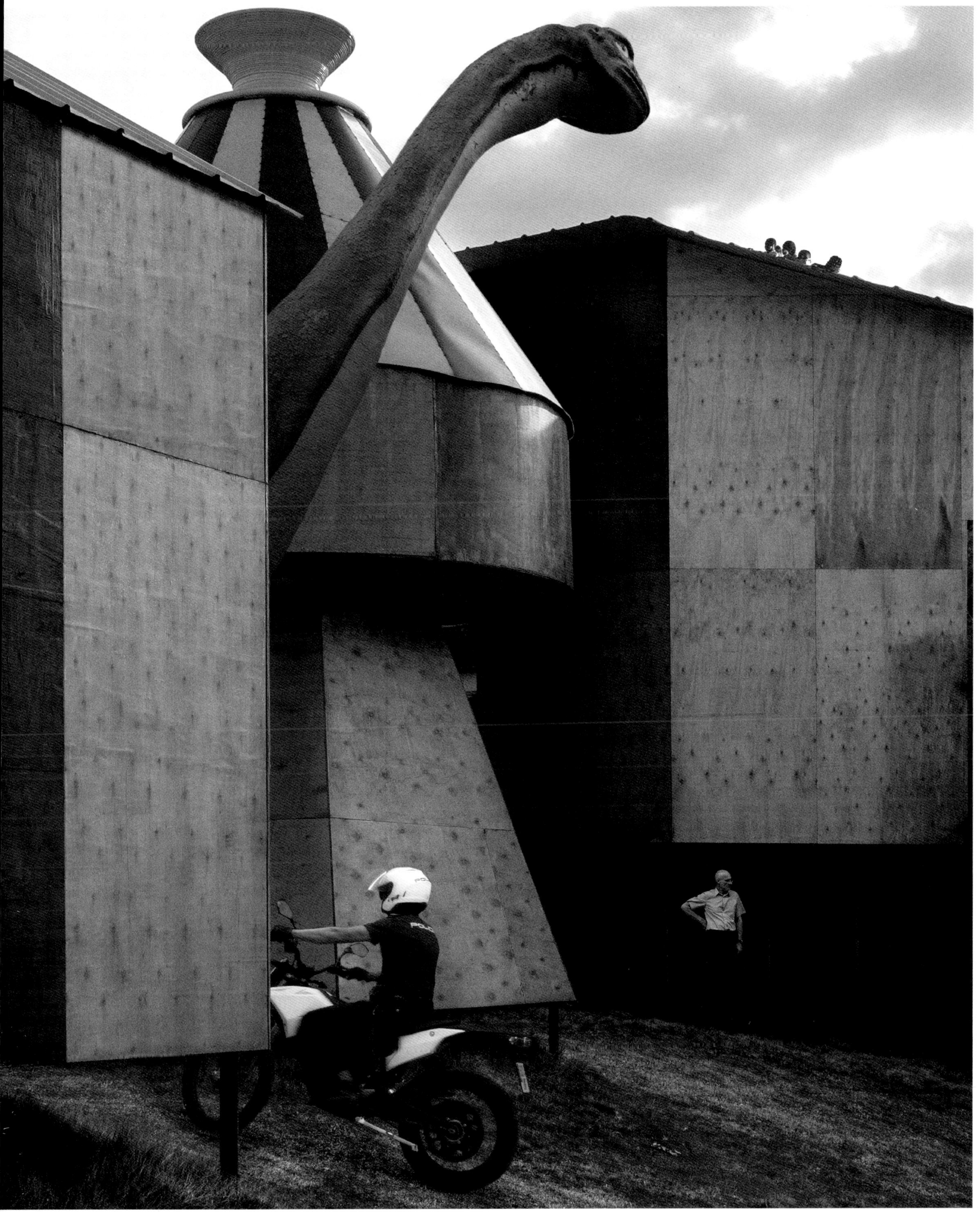

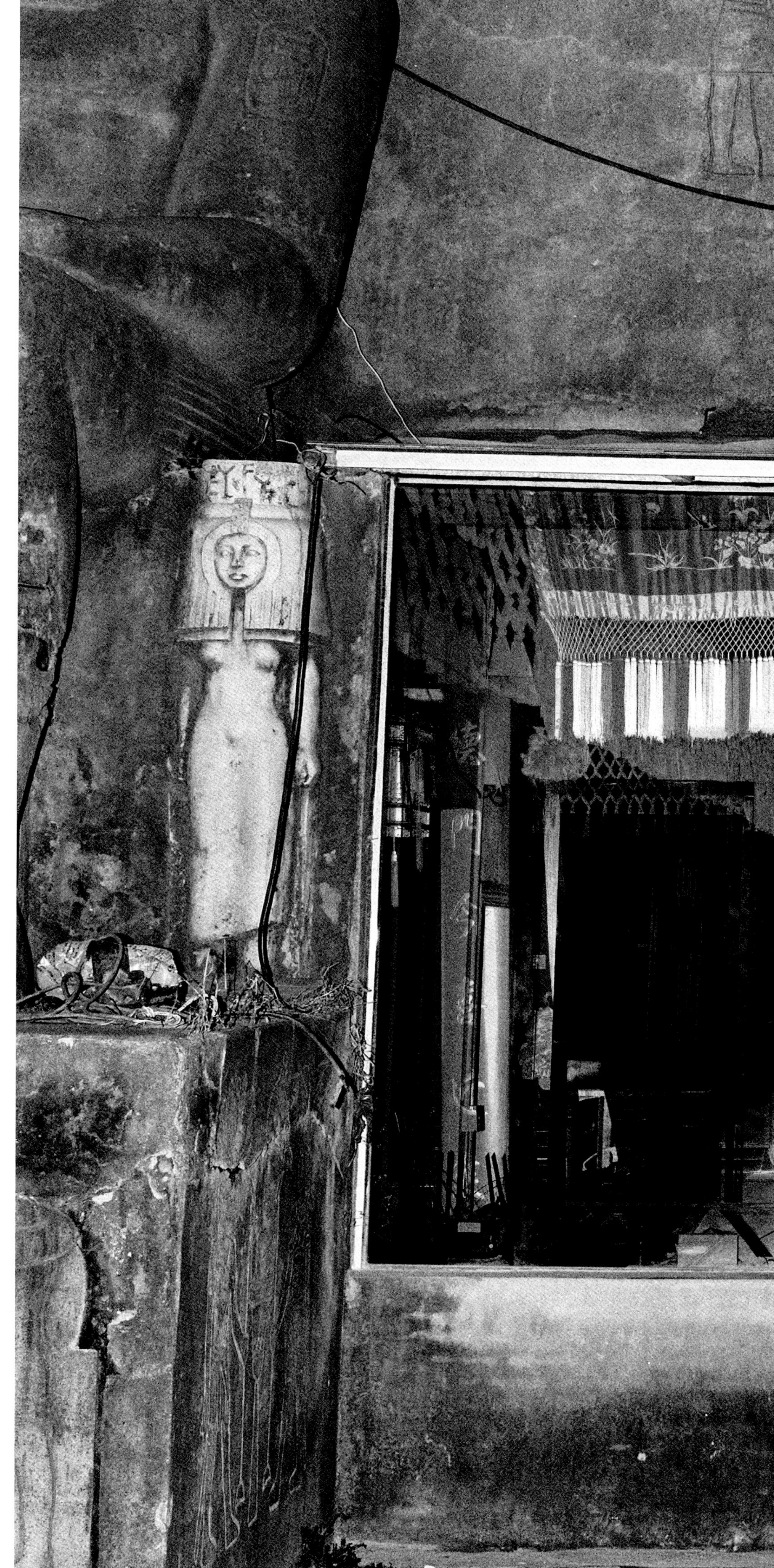

那天的婚礼
The Wedding on that Day, 2016–23
1000 × 800mm

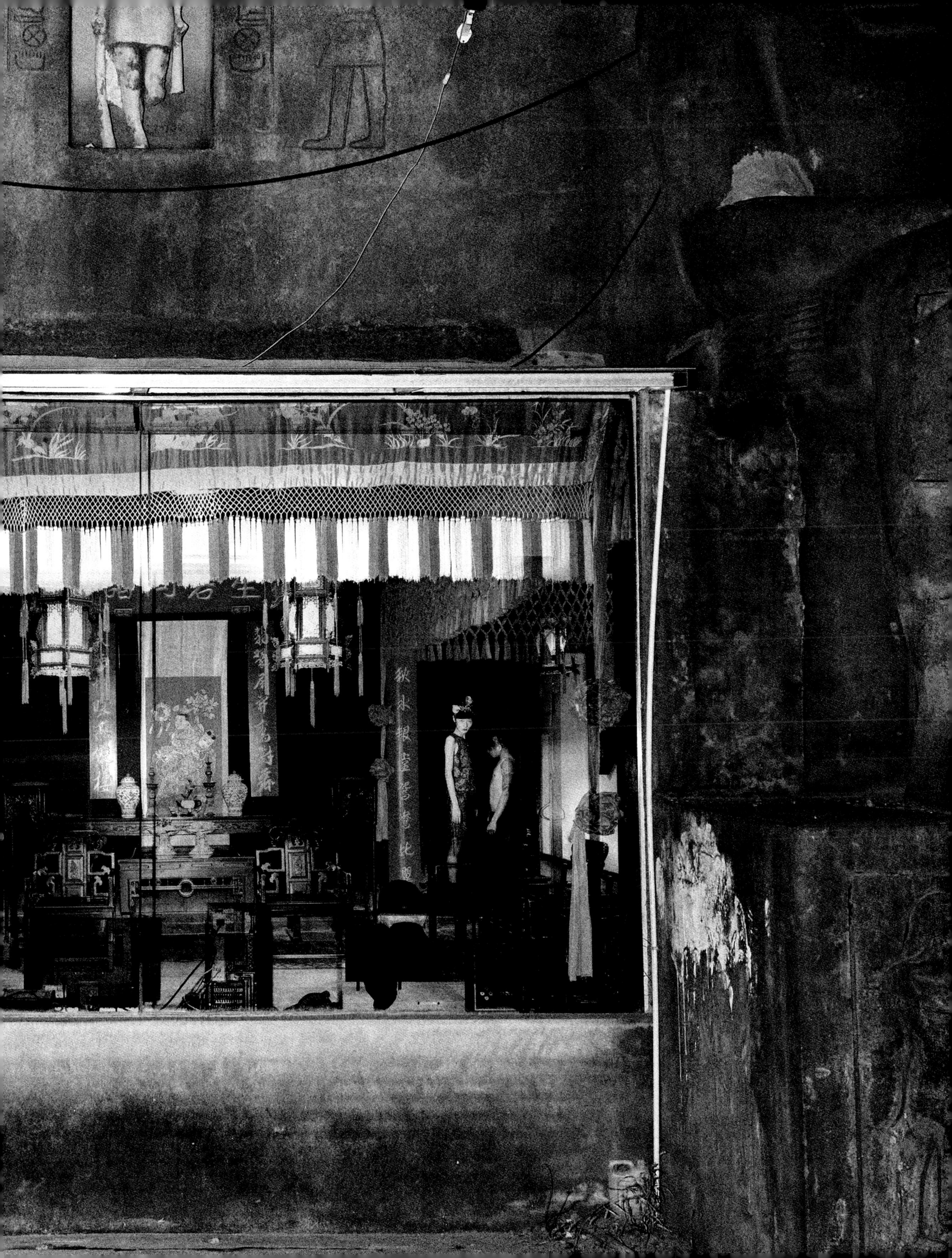

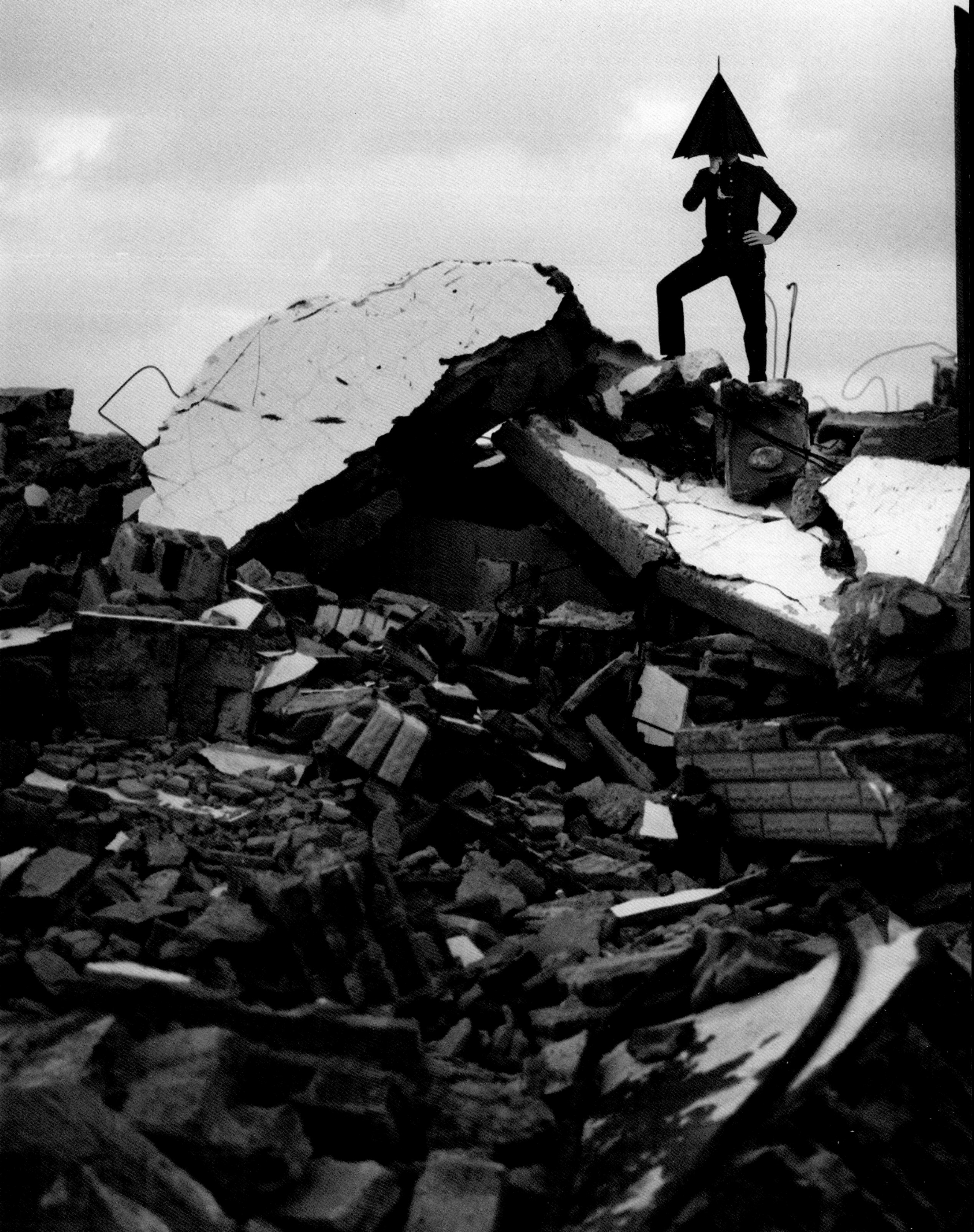

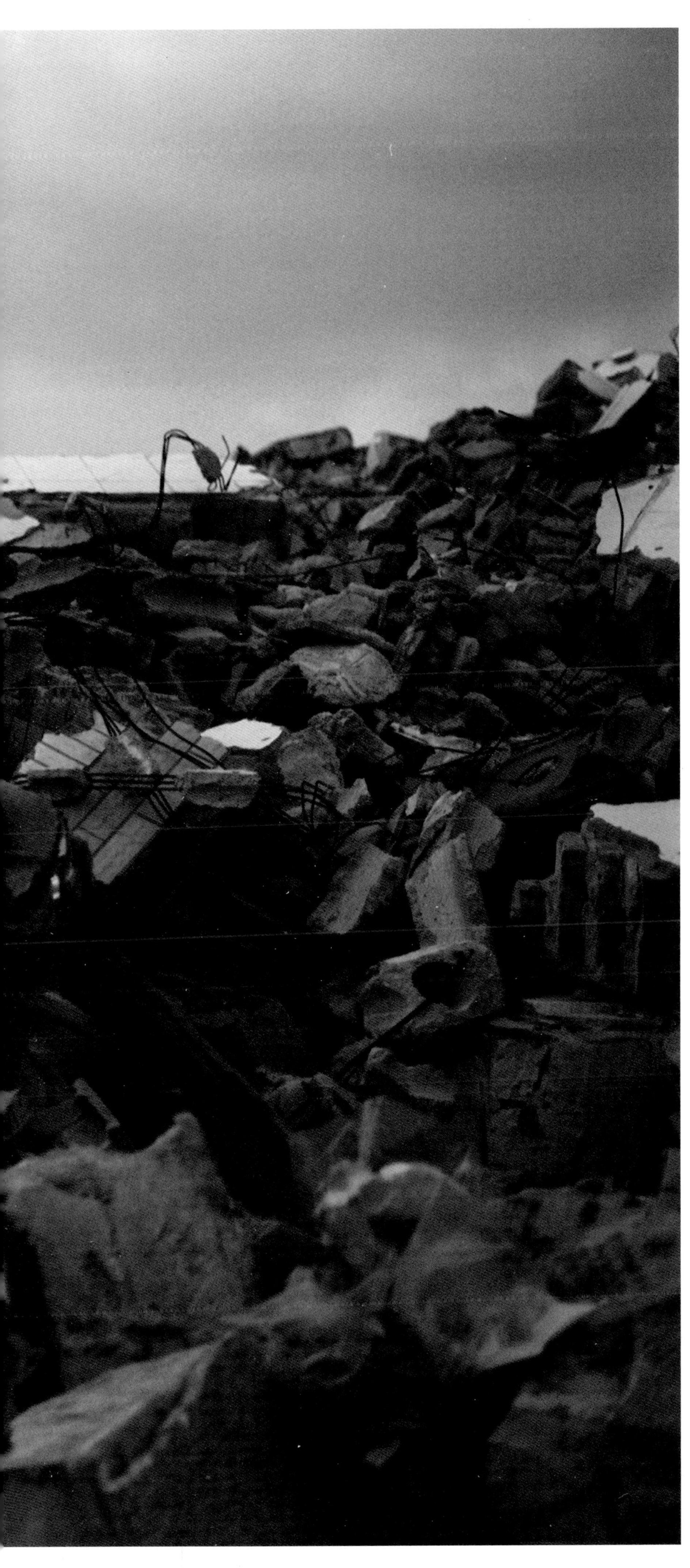

面对难题
Facing Problems, 2012–15
1000 × 800mm

众神之宴
The Feast of the Gods, 2020
600 × 800mm

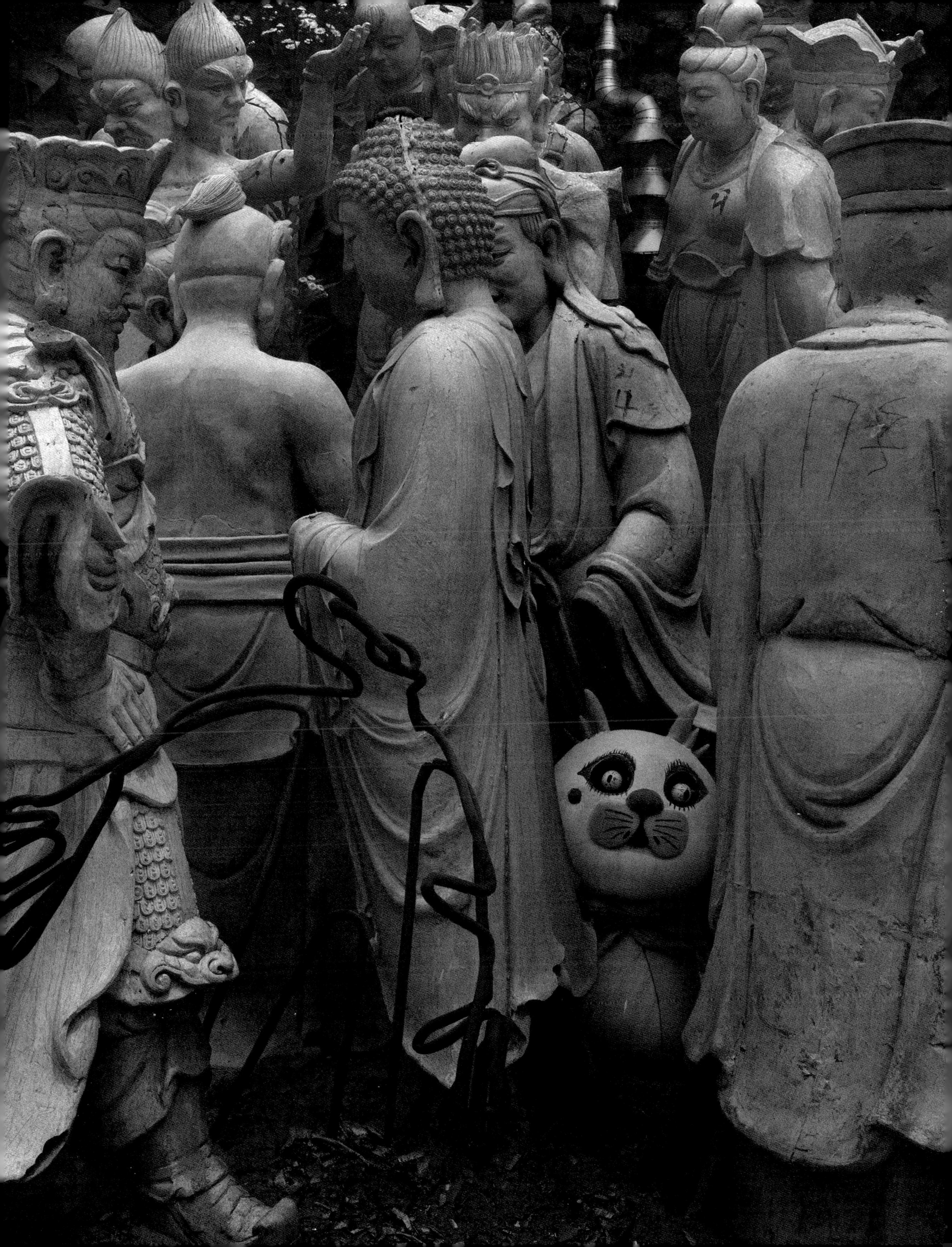

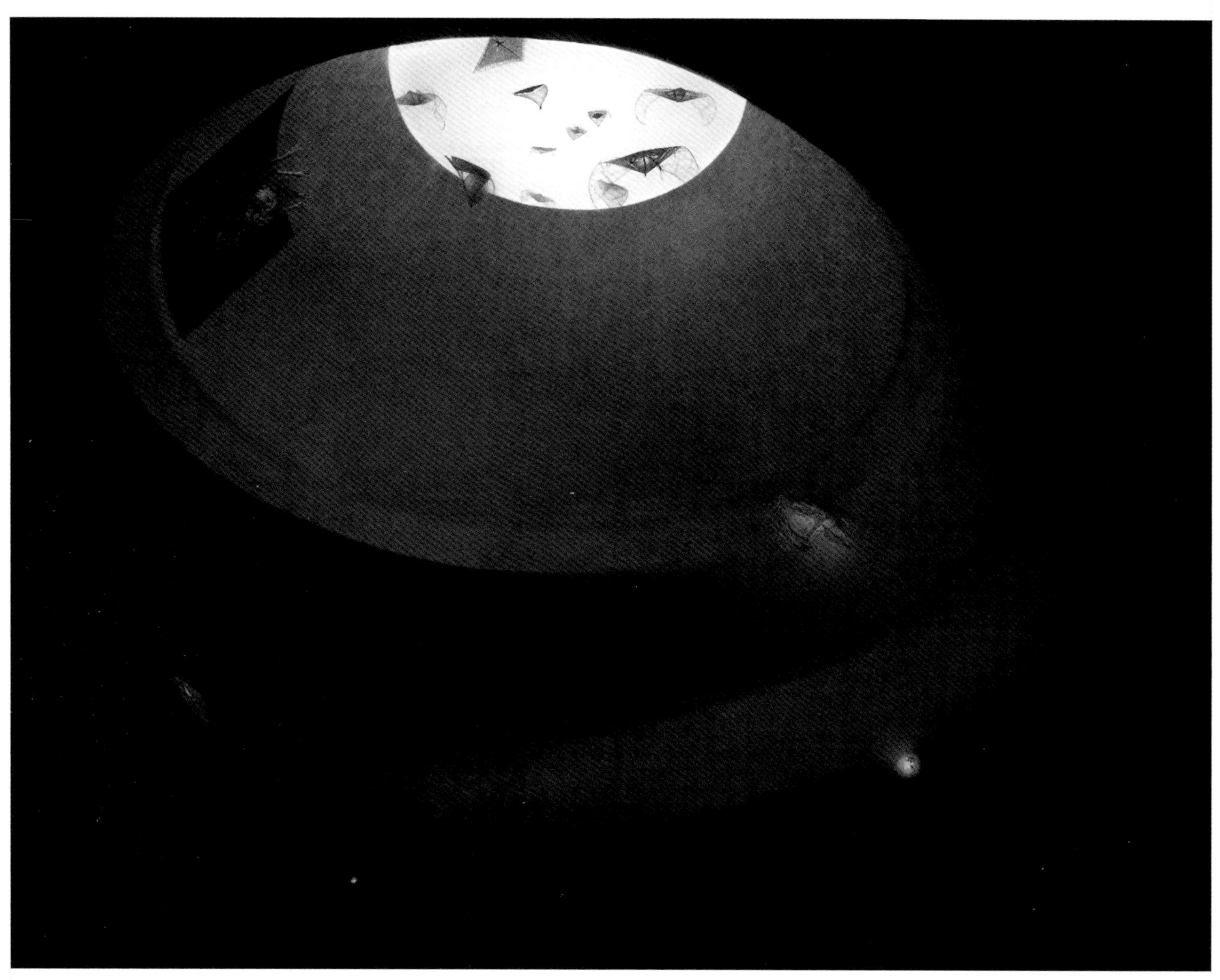

天外天
Beyond Heaven,
2020–23
1000 × 800mm

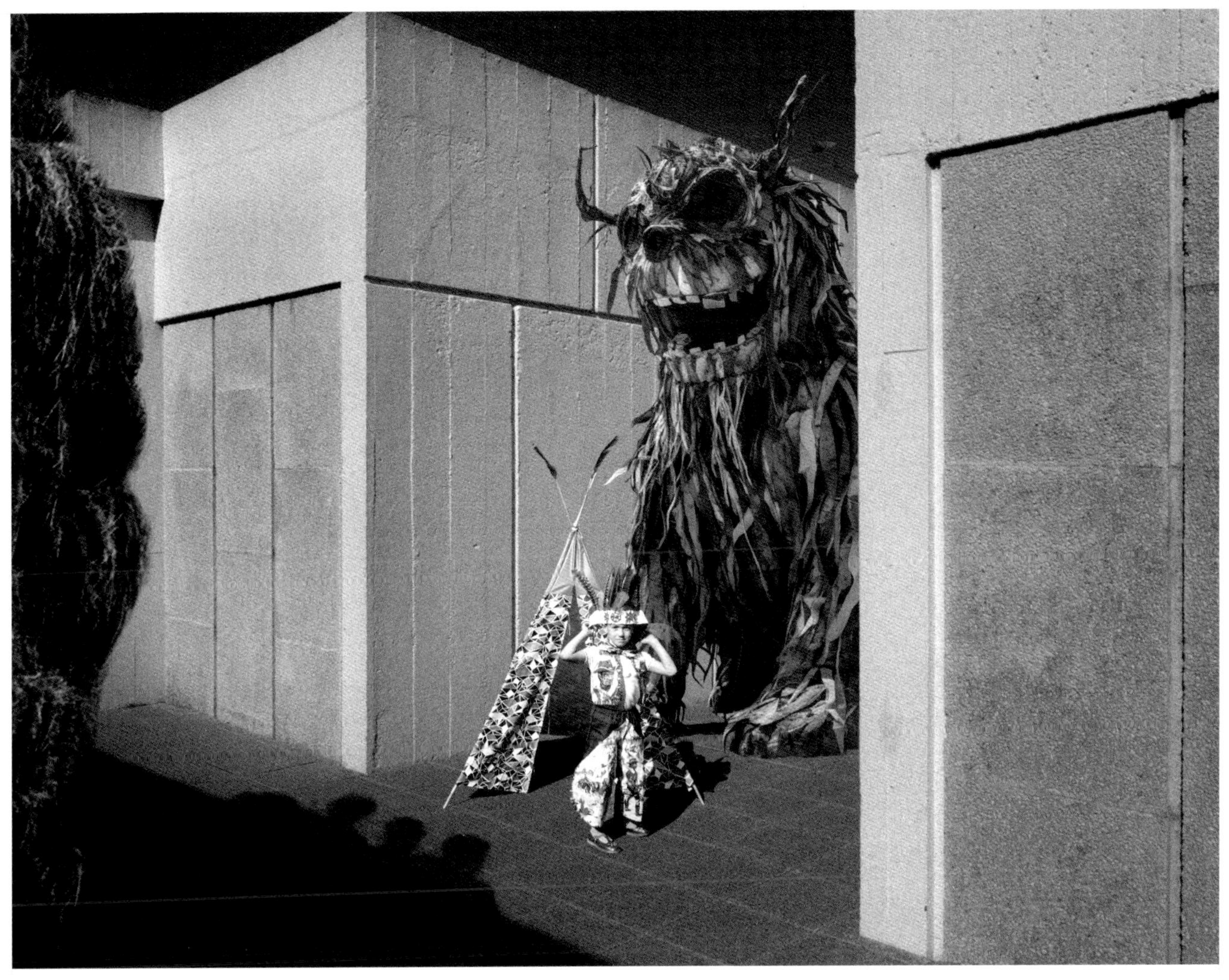

期许
Expectations, 2021–24
1000 × 800mm

拳击手
The Boxer, 2017–23
1000 × 800mm

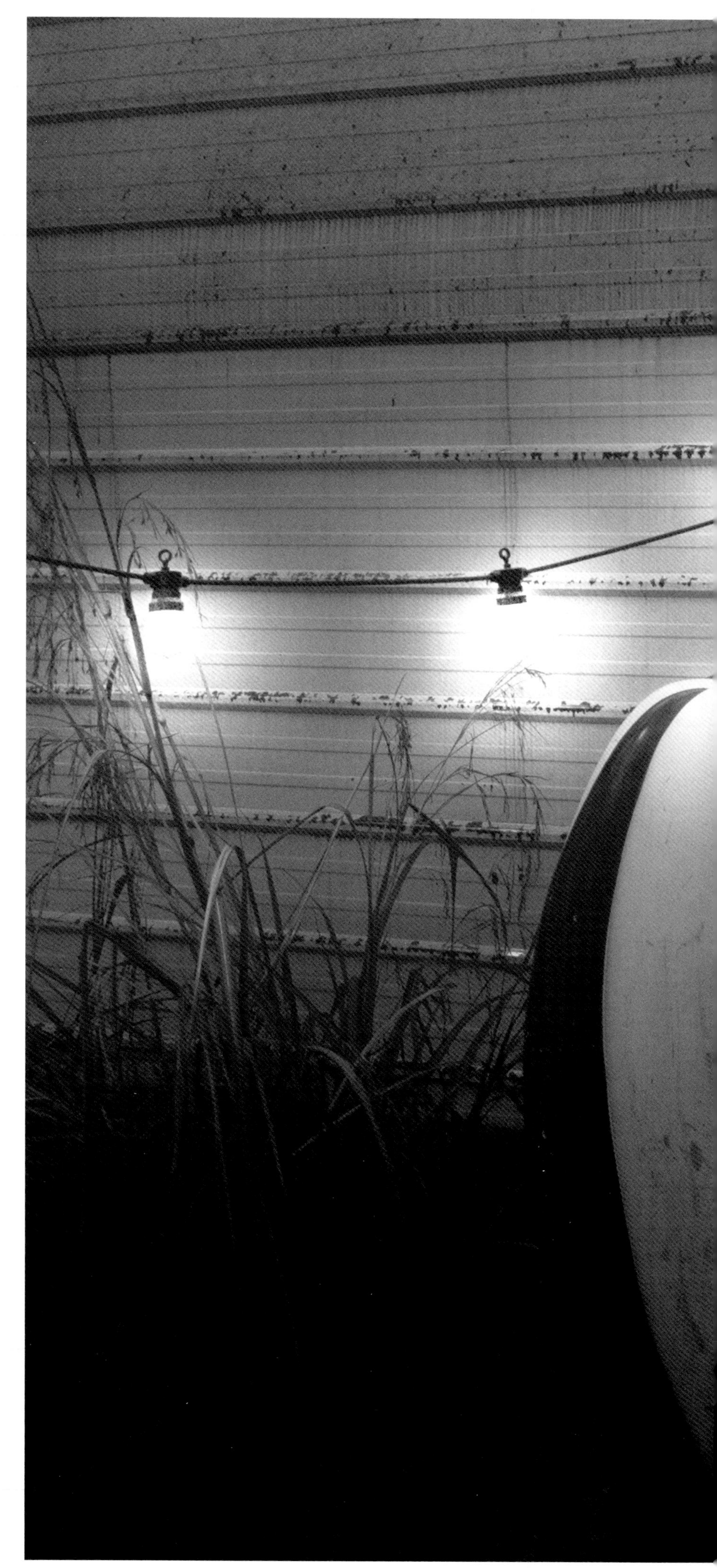

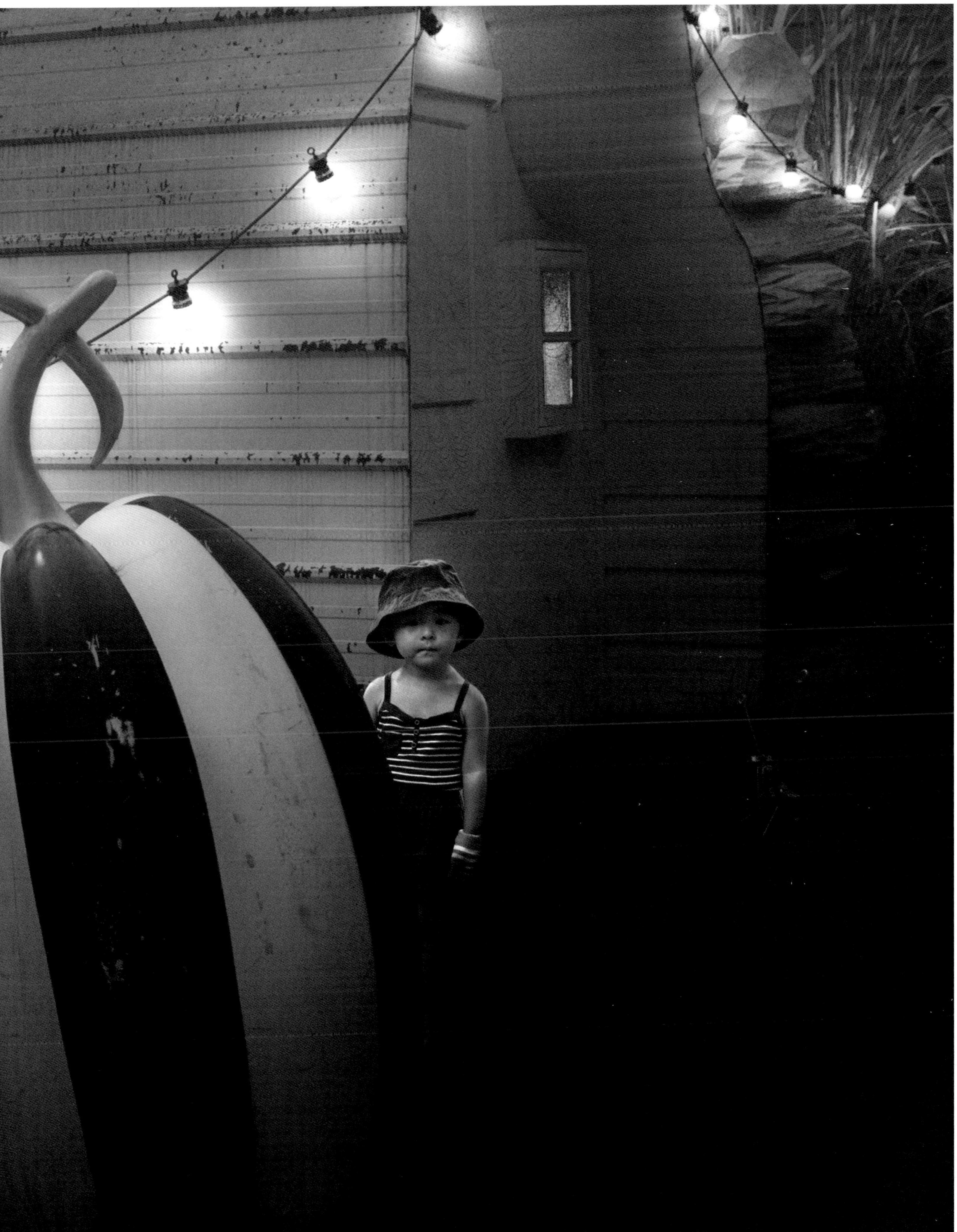

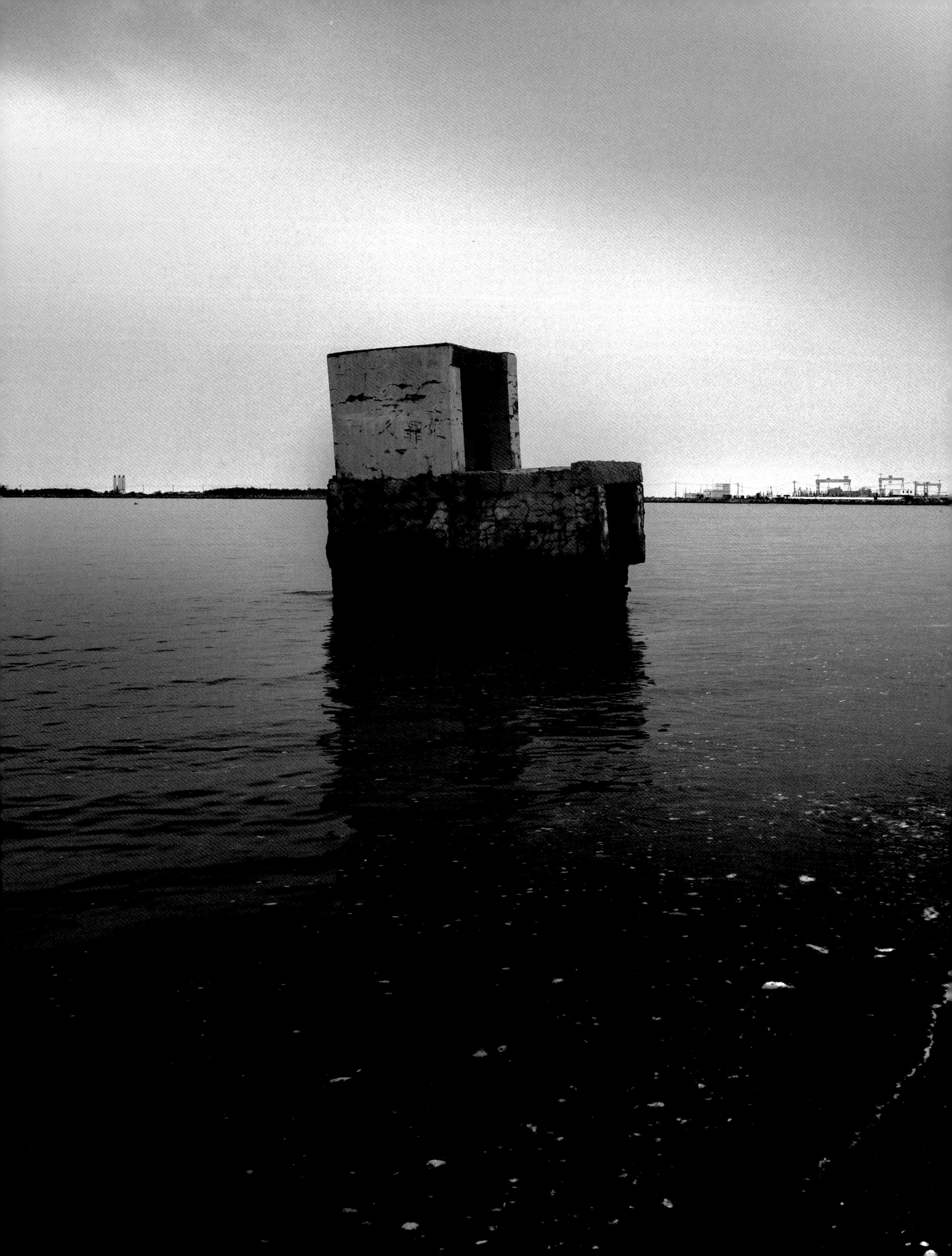

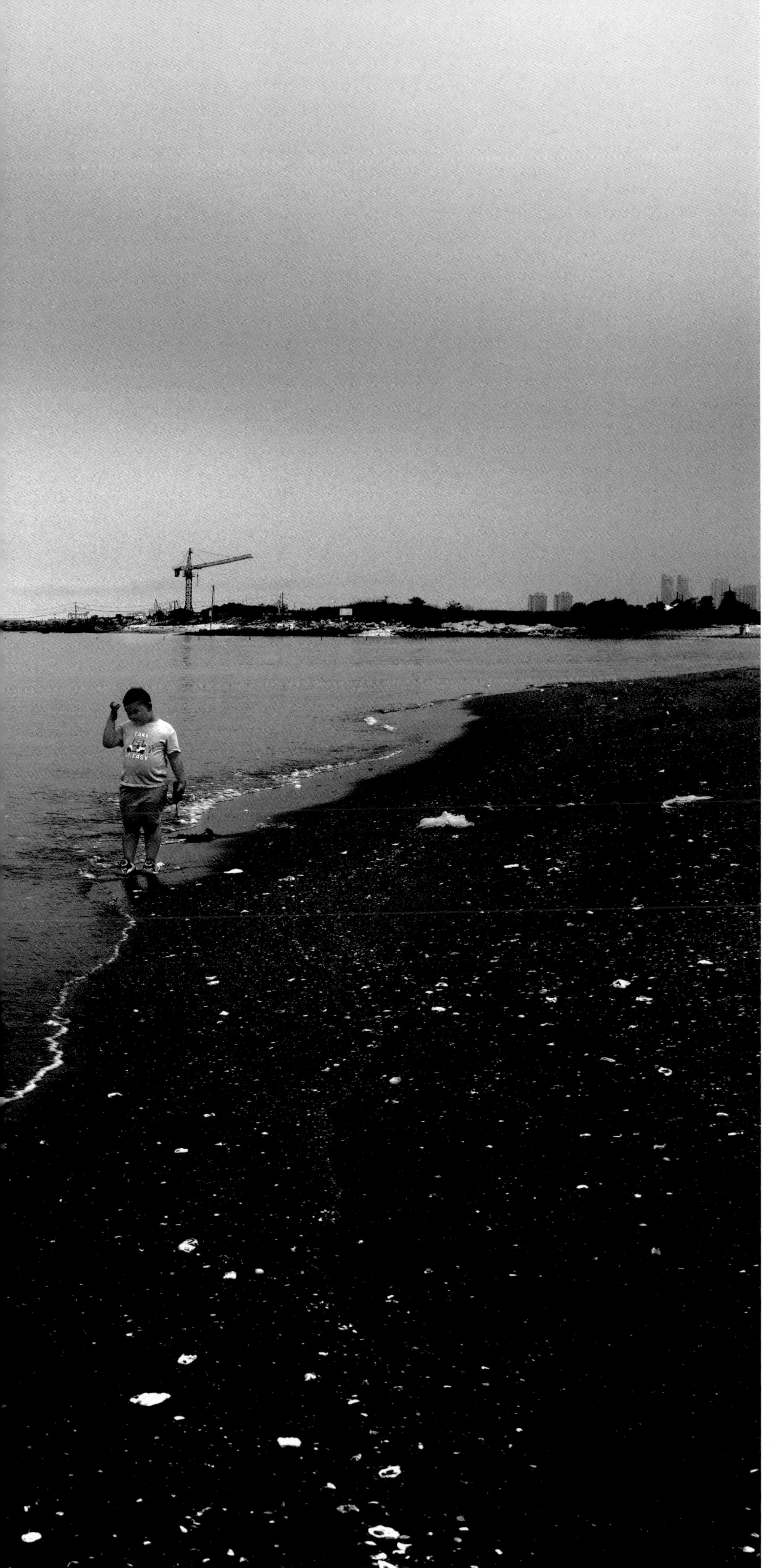

放轻松
Take It Easy, 2020
600 × 800mm

SECTION THREE

Multifaceted Dramas

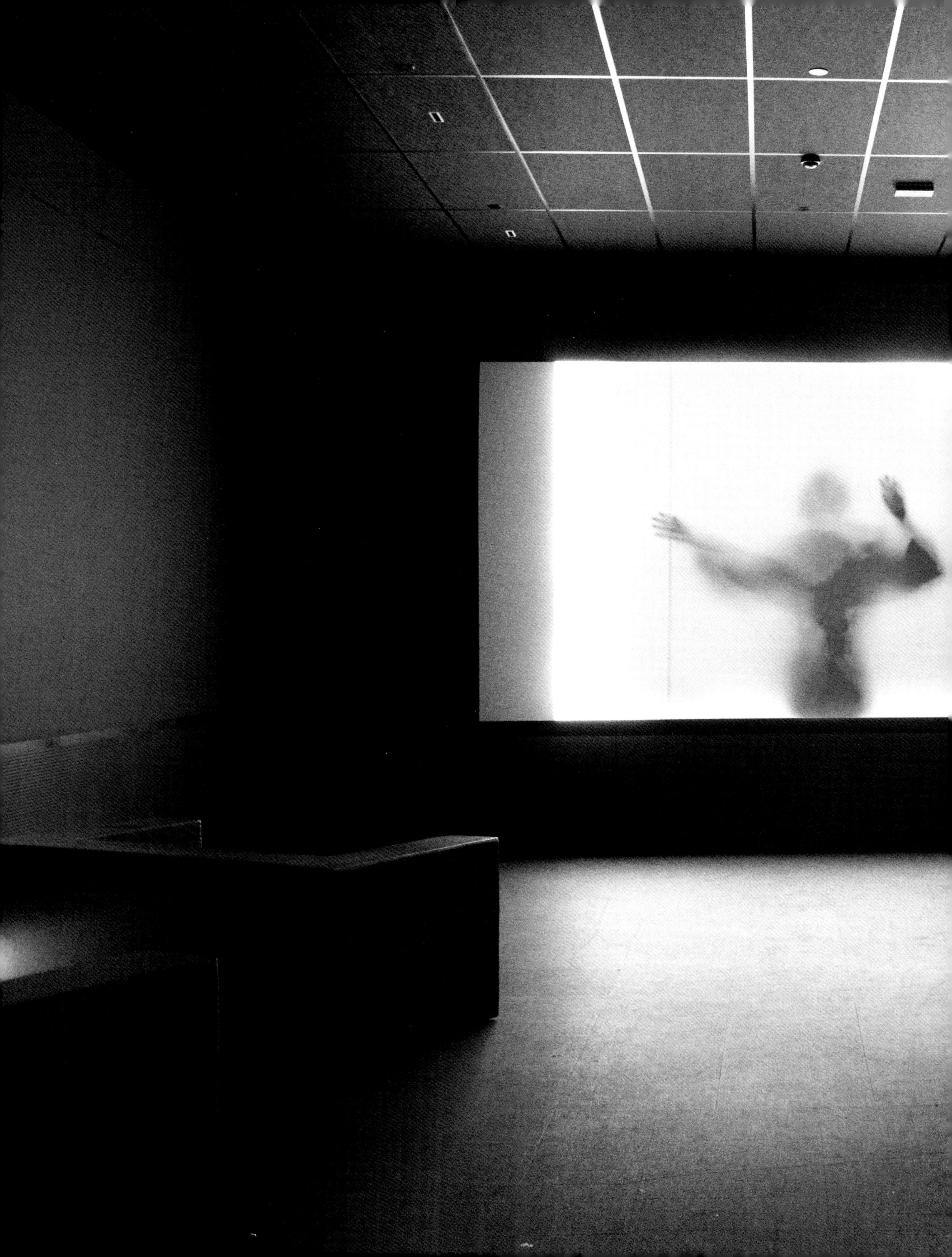

等待反馈
Waiting for Feedback,
2020–23
1000 × 800mm

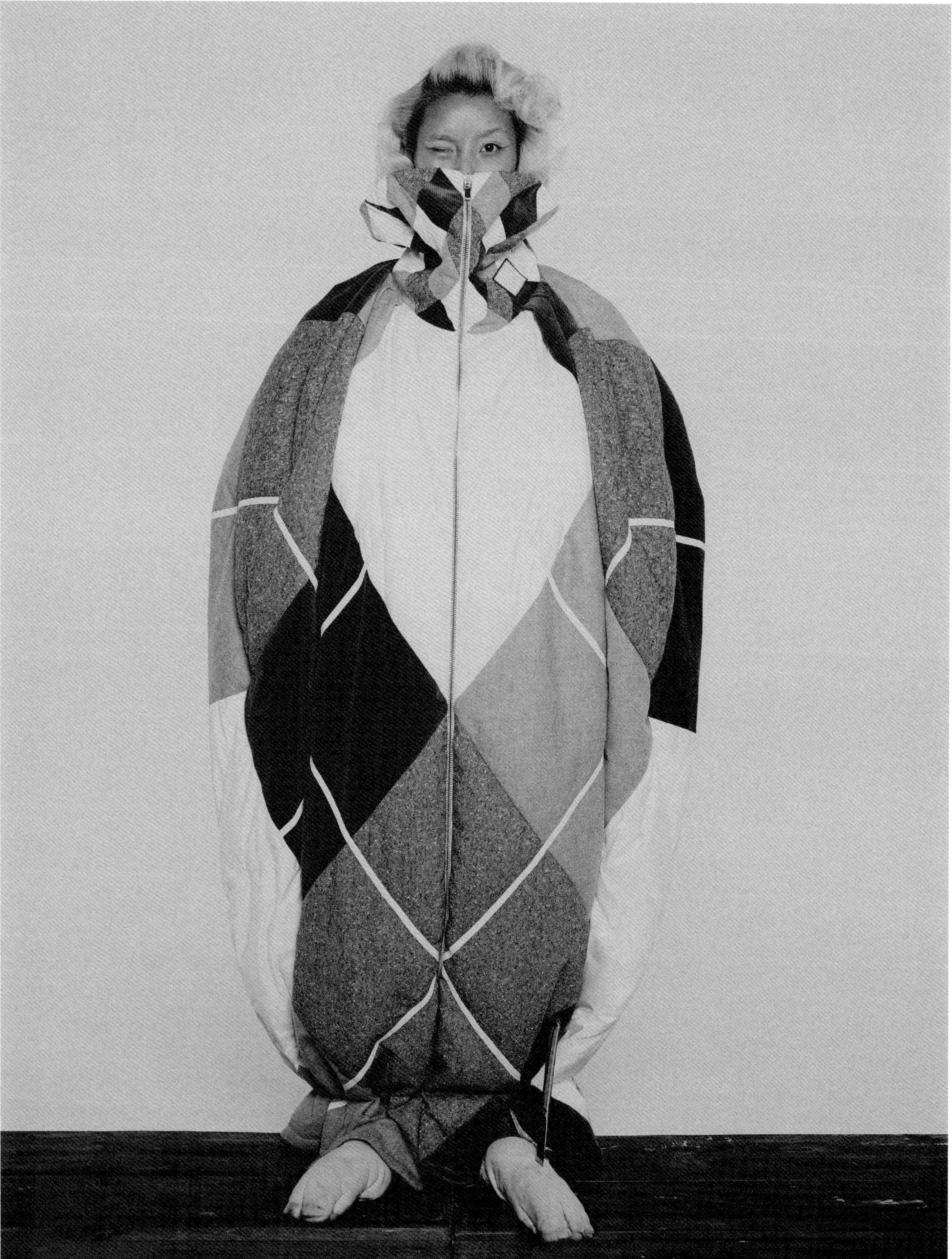

宰割
Be Slaughtered, 2017
600 × 800mm

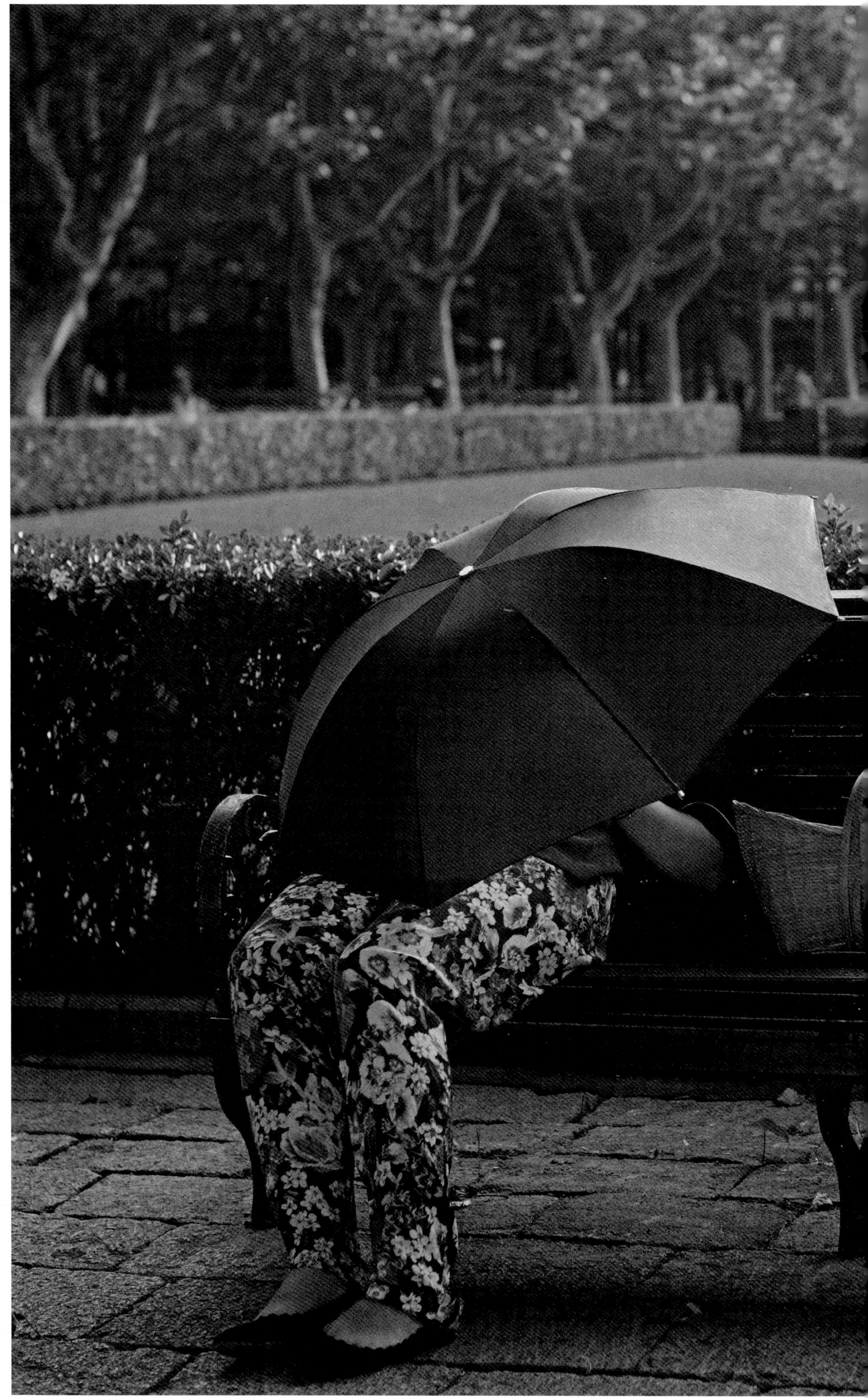

生活
Life, 2017
1000 × 800mm

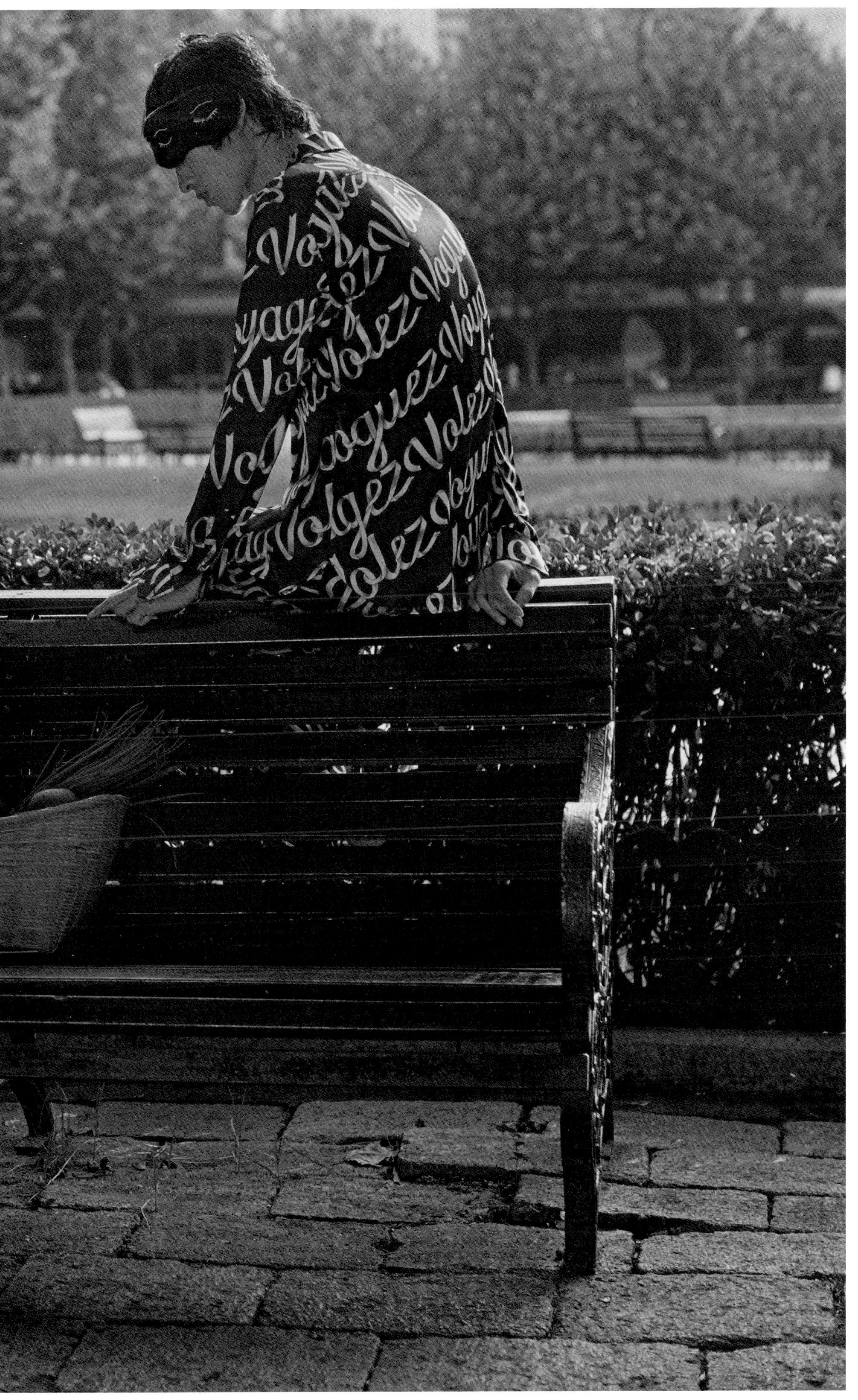
Volez

宠物
Pets, 2018
600 × 800mm

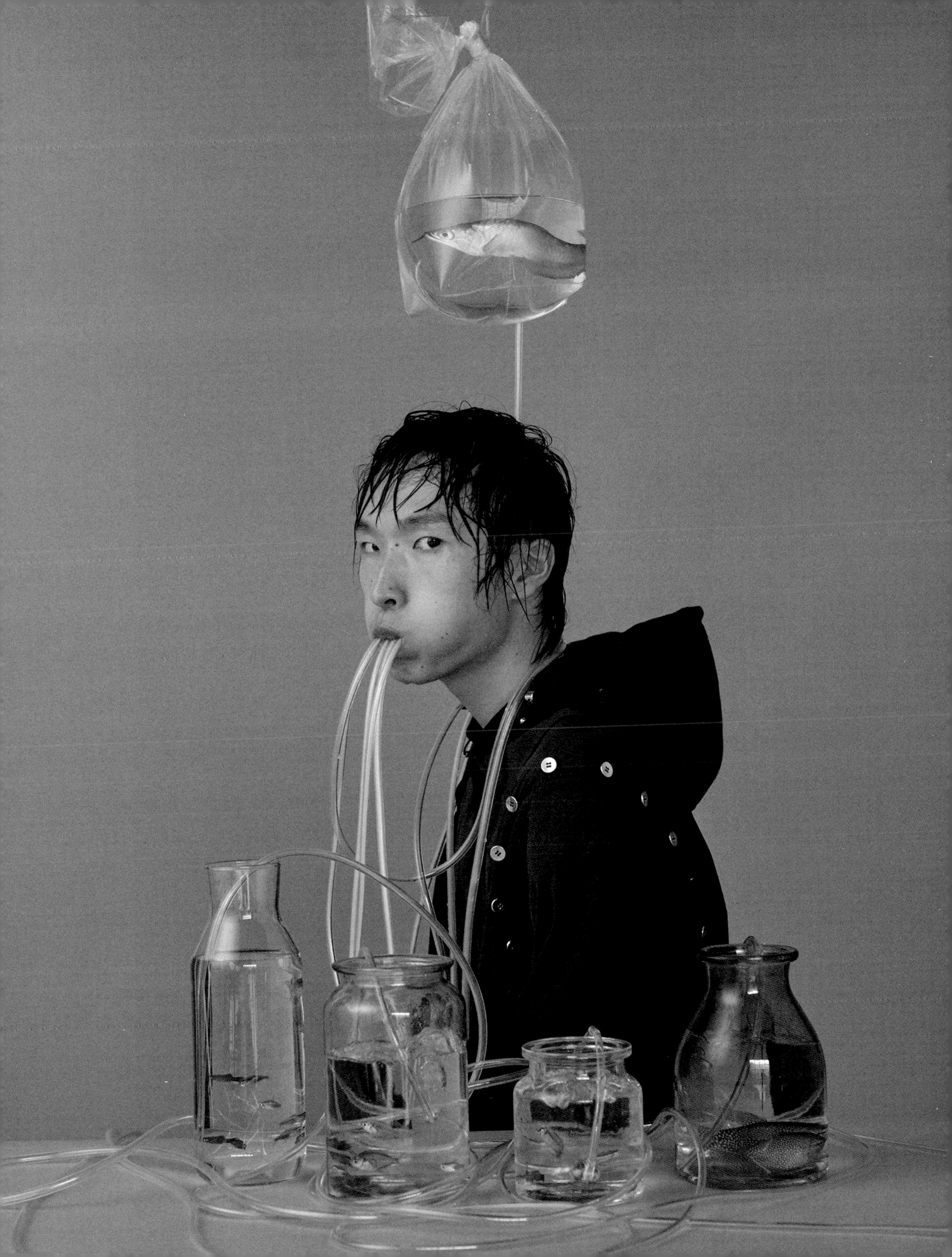

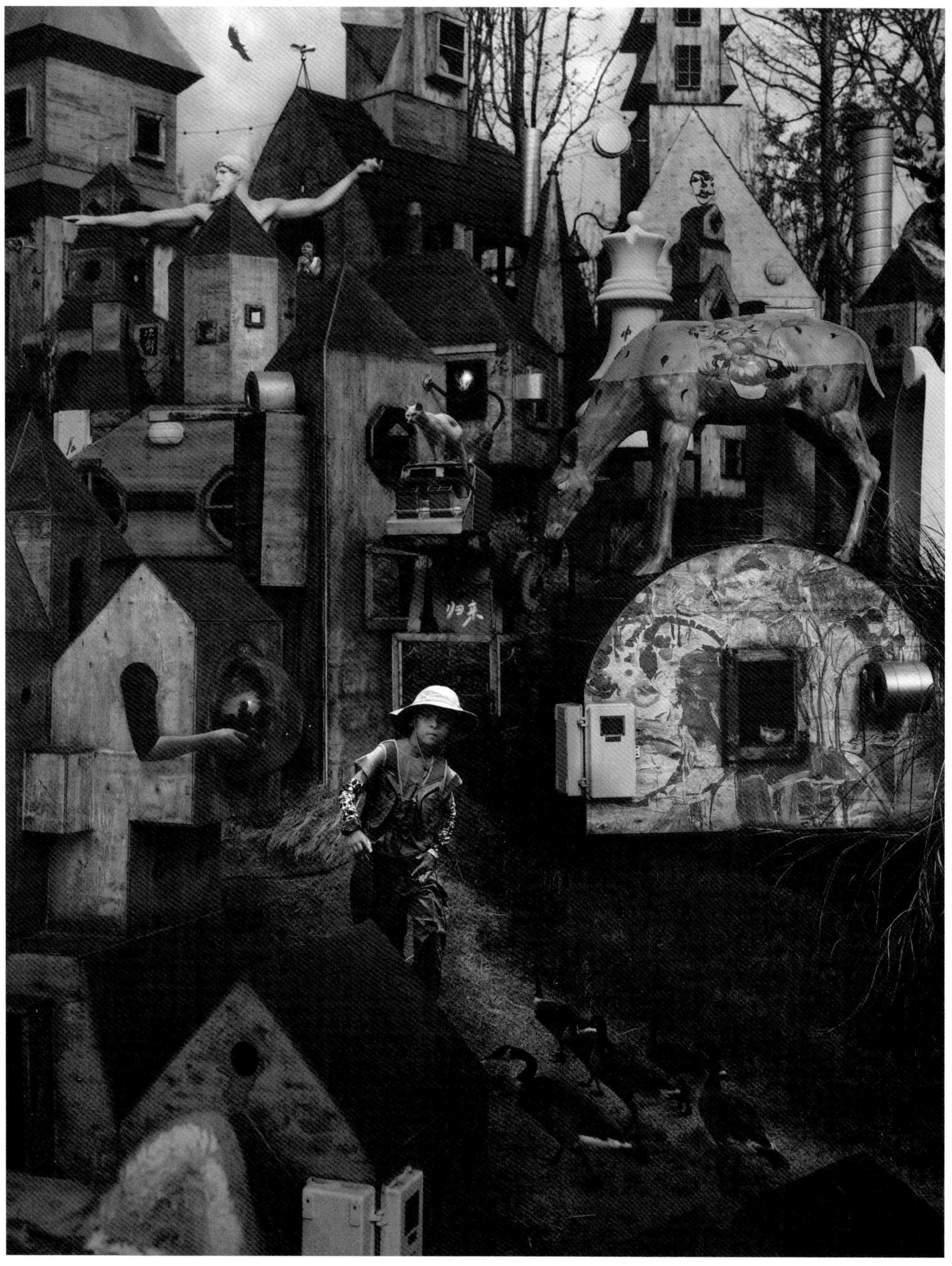

归来
Return, 2024
600 × 800mm

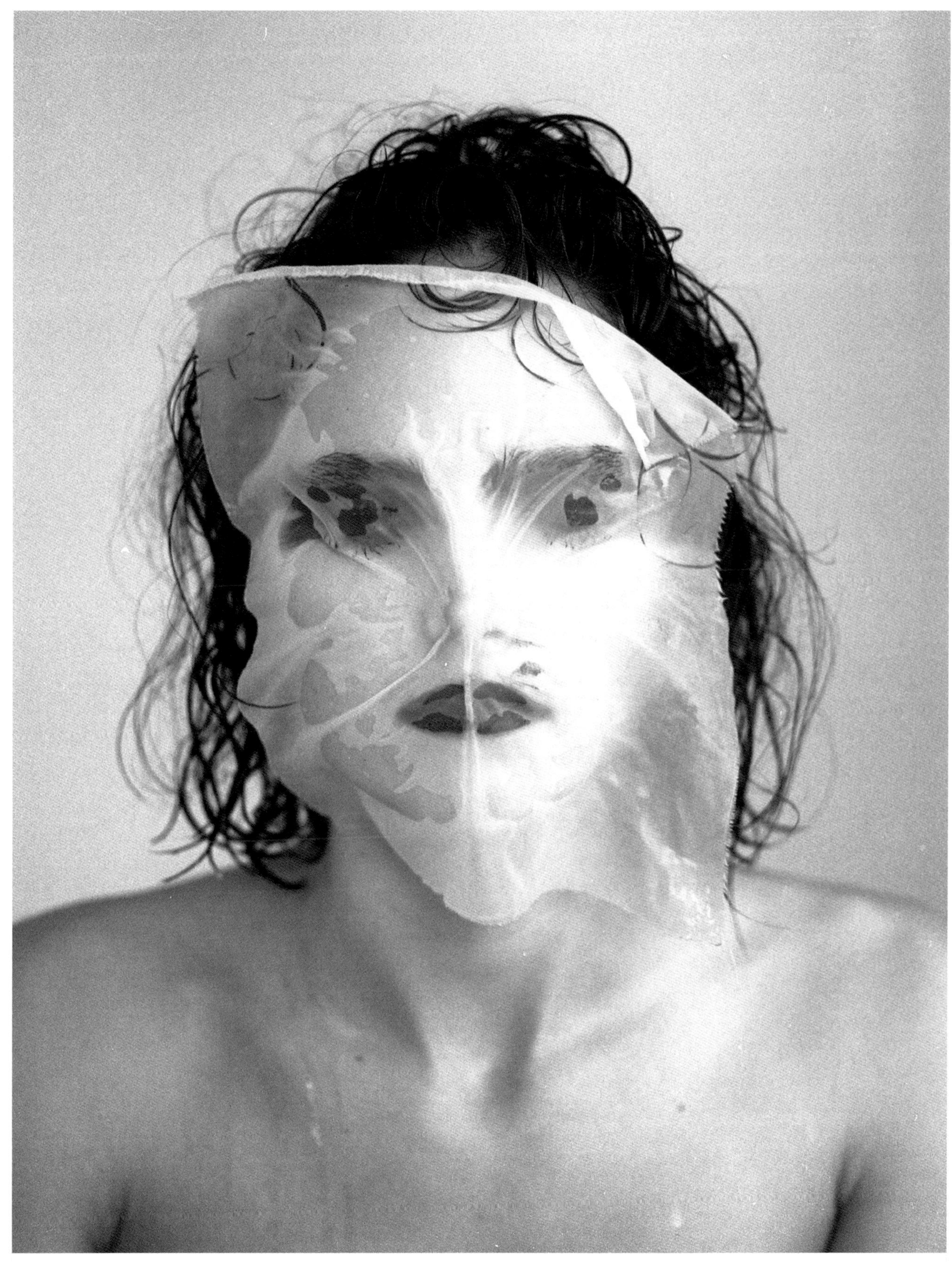

思念
Longing, 2012
600 × 800mm

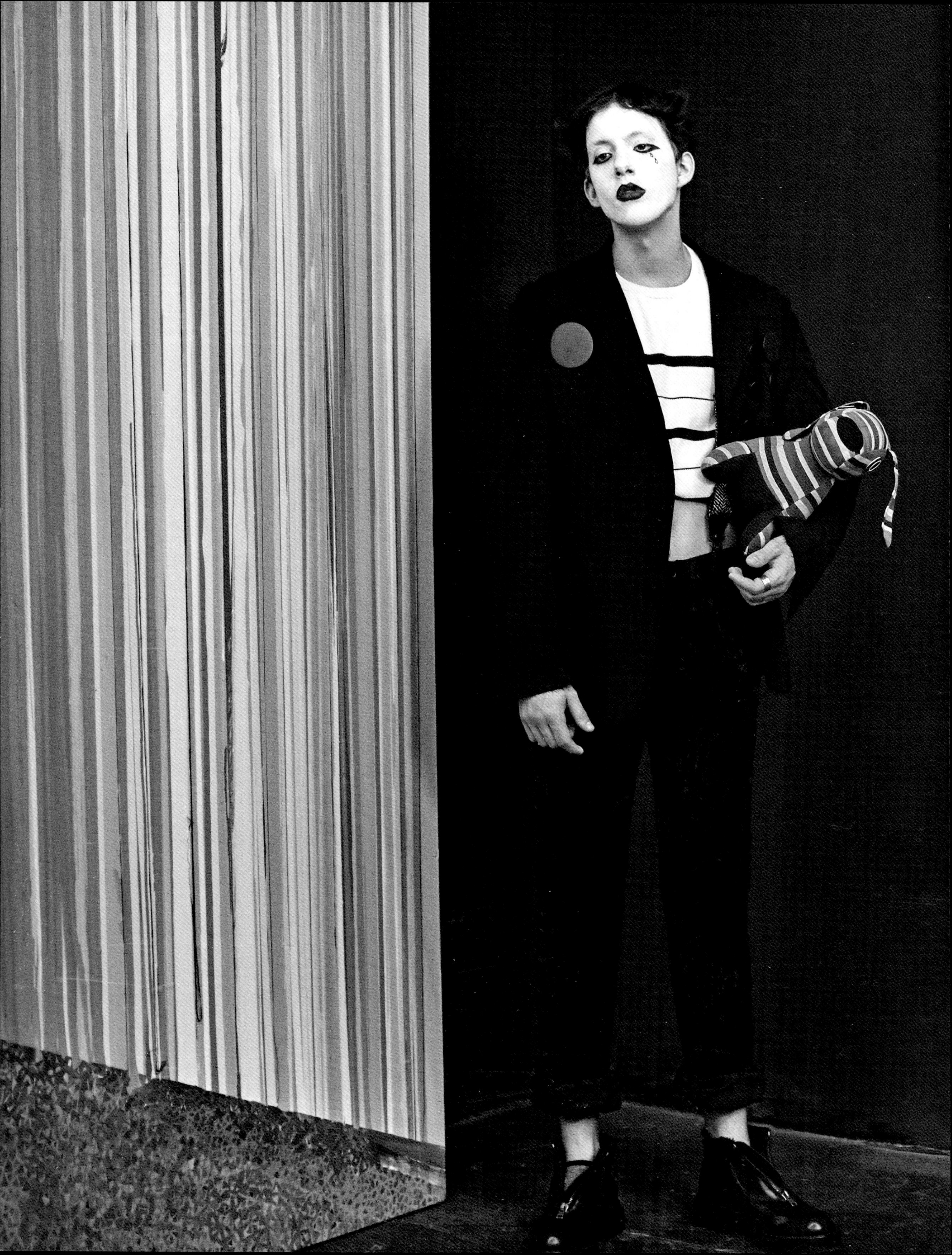

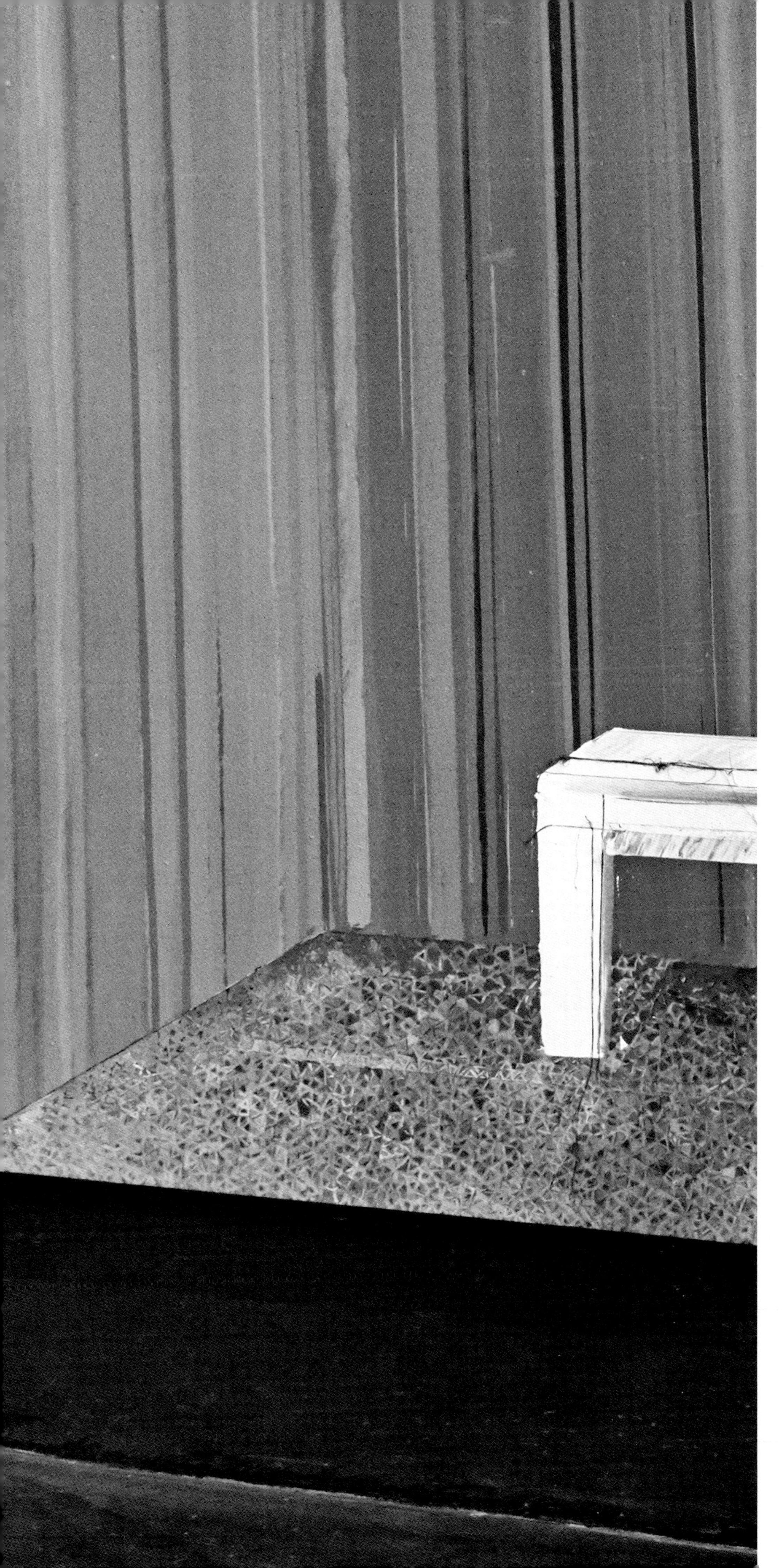

思念桃桃
Missing Peachy, 2015
1000 × 800mm

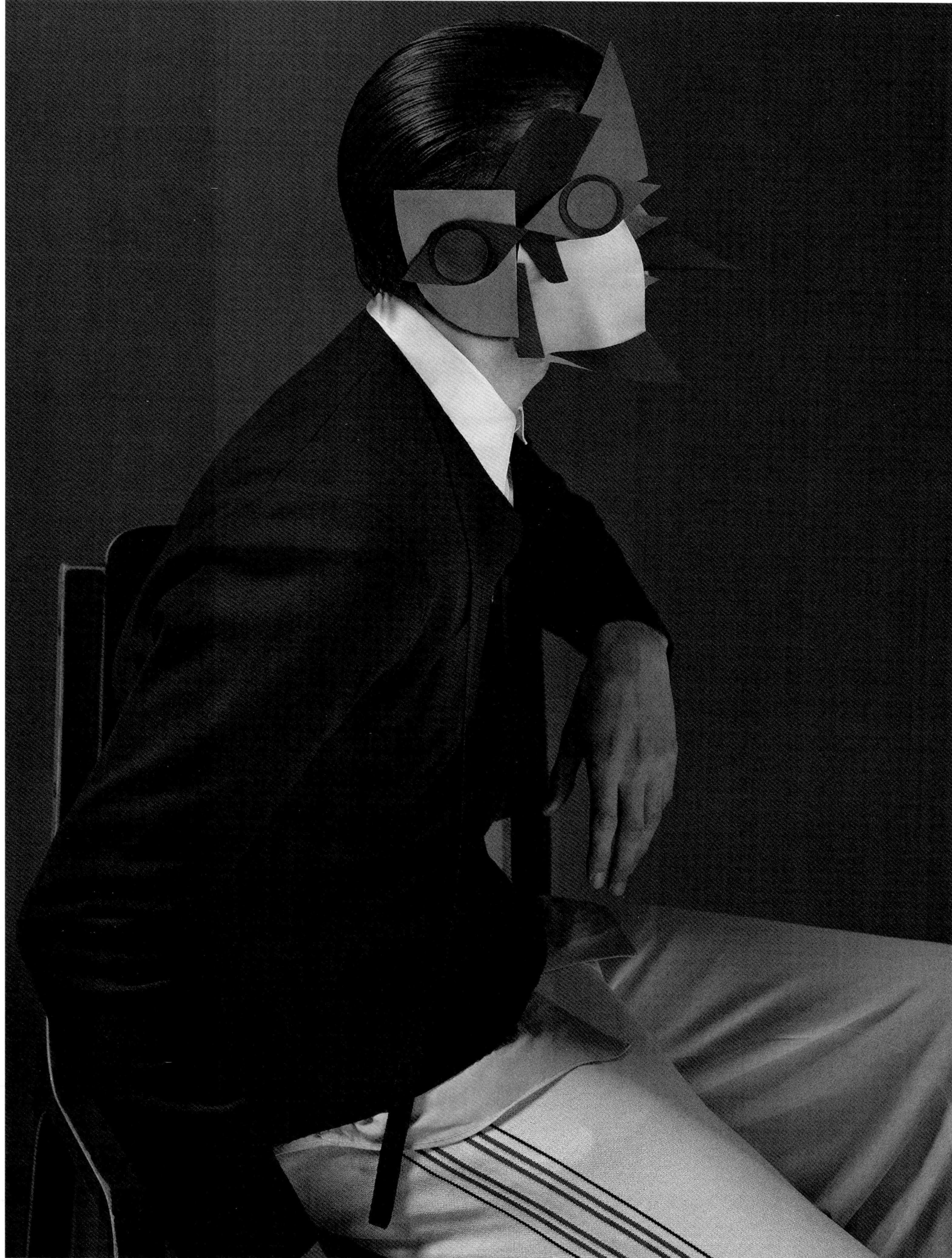

无厘头
Nonsense, 2018
600 × 800mm

谁不是谁的木偶
No-one is a Puppet, 2015
600 × 800mm

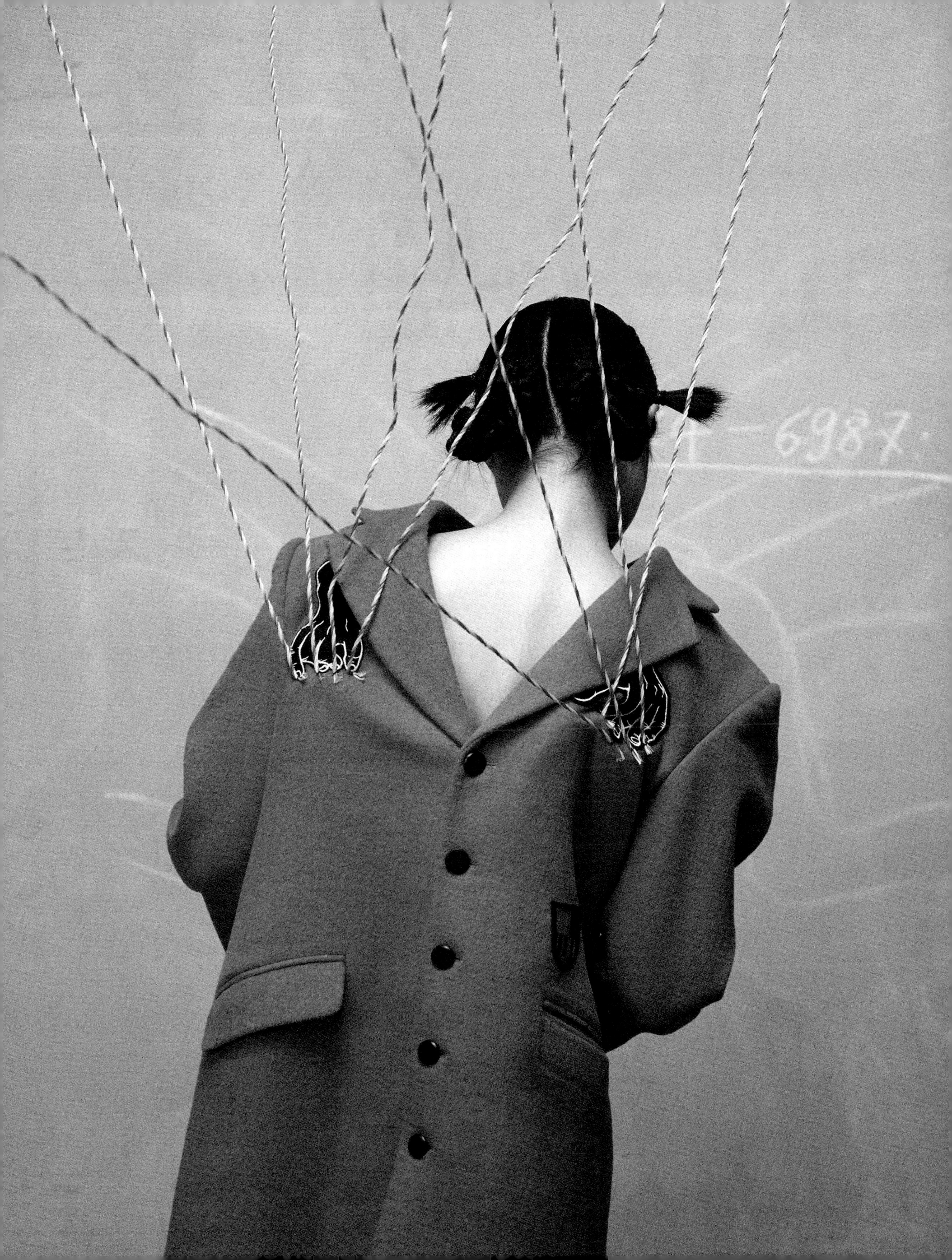
6987.

门卫大叔的梦想实现了
The Doorman's Dream Came True, 2018
600 × 800mm

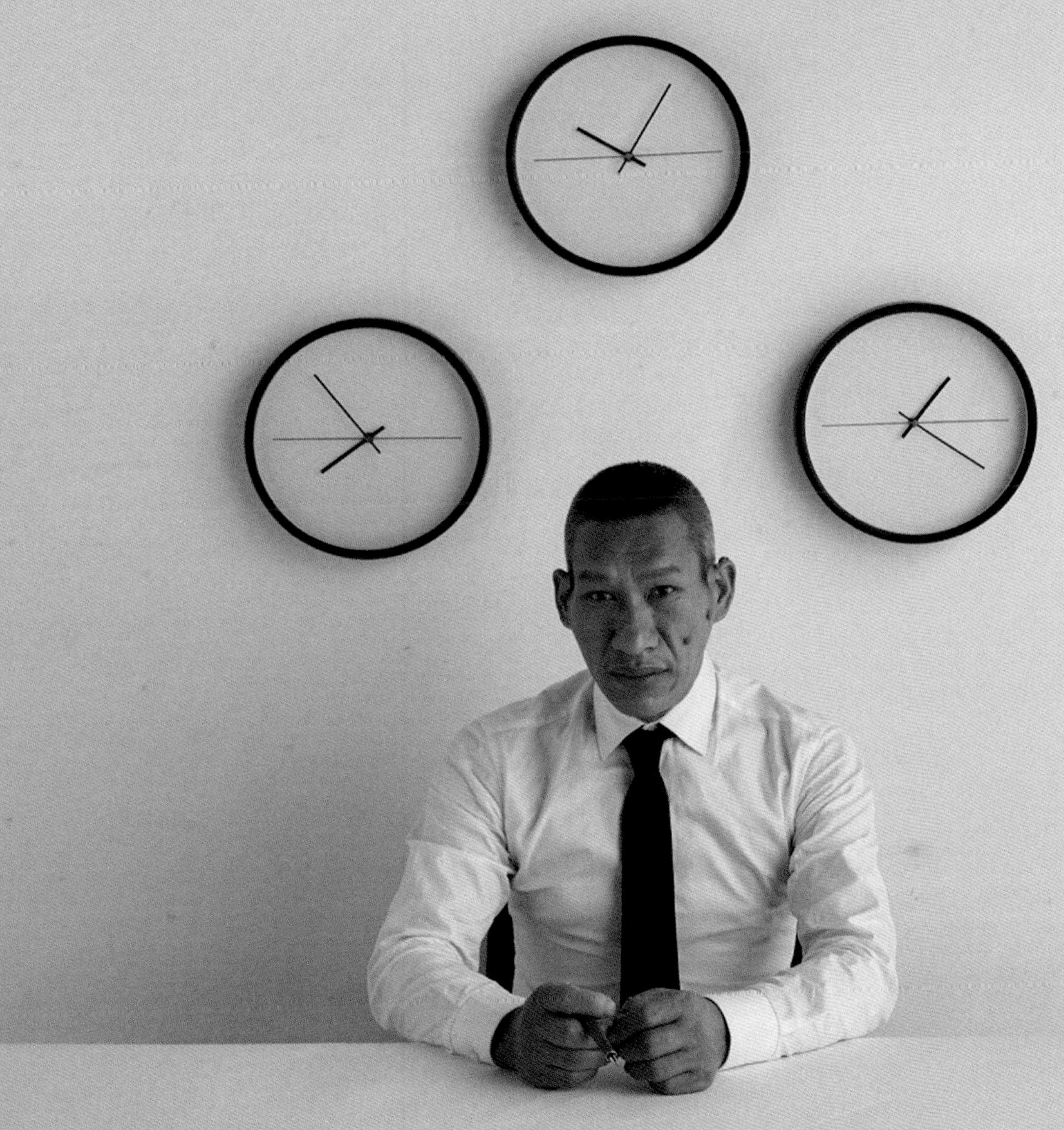

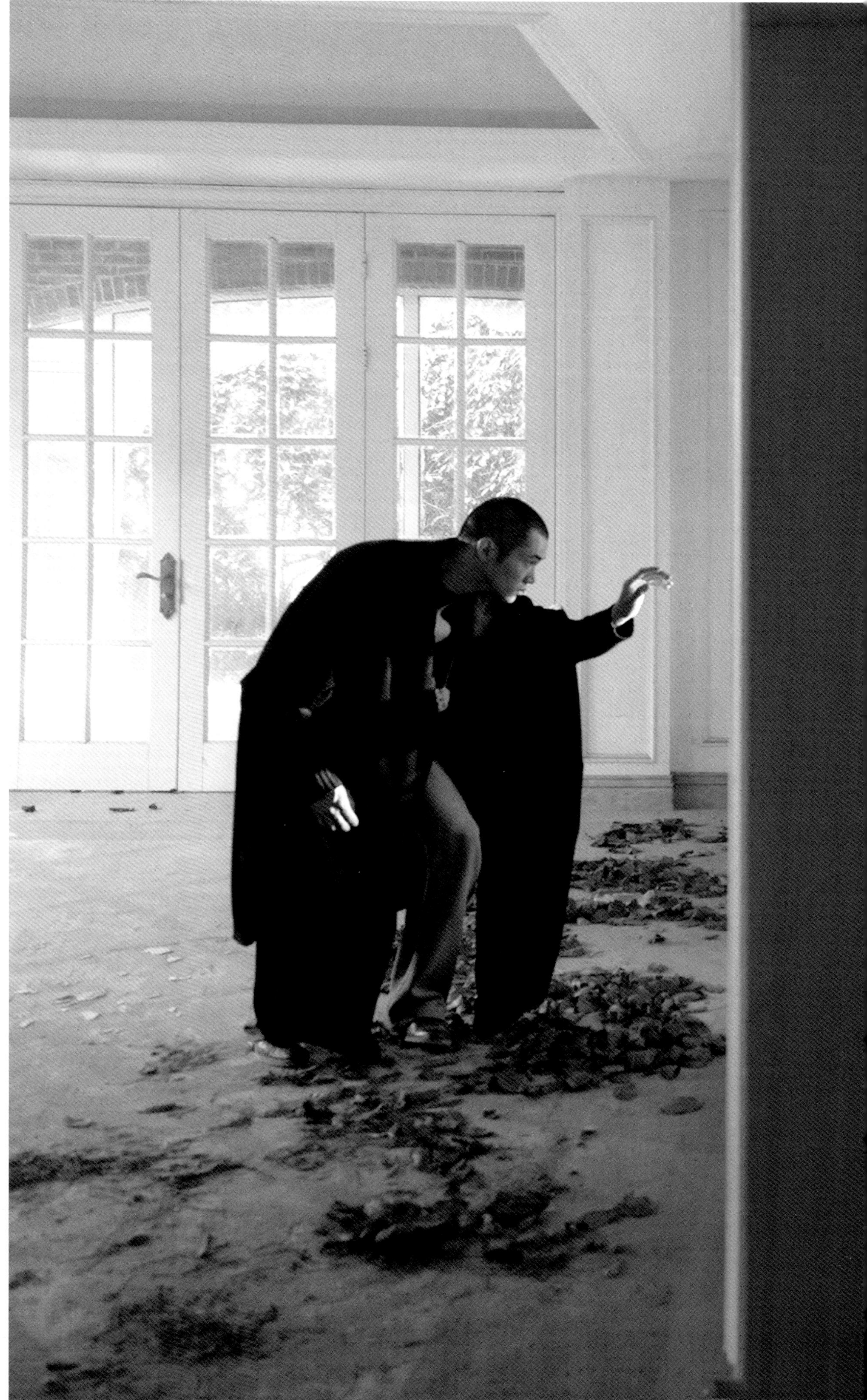

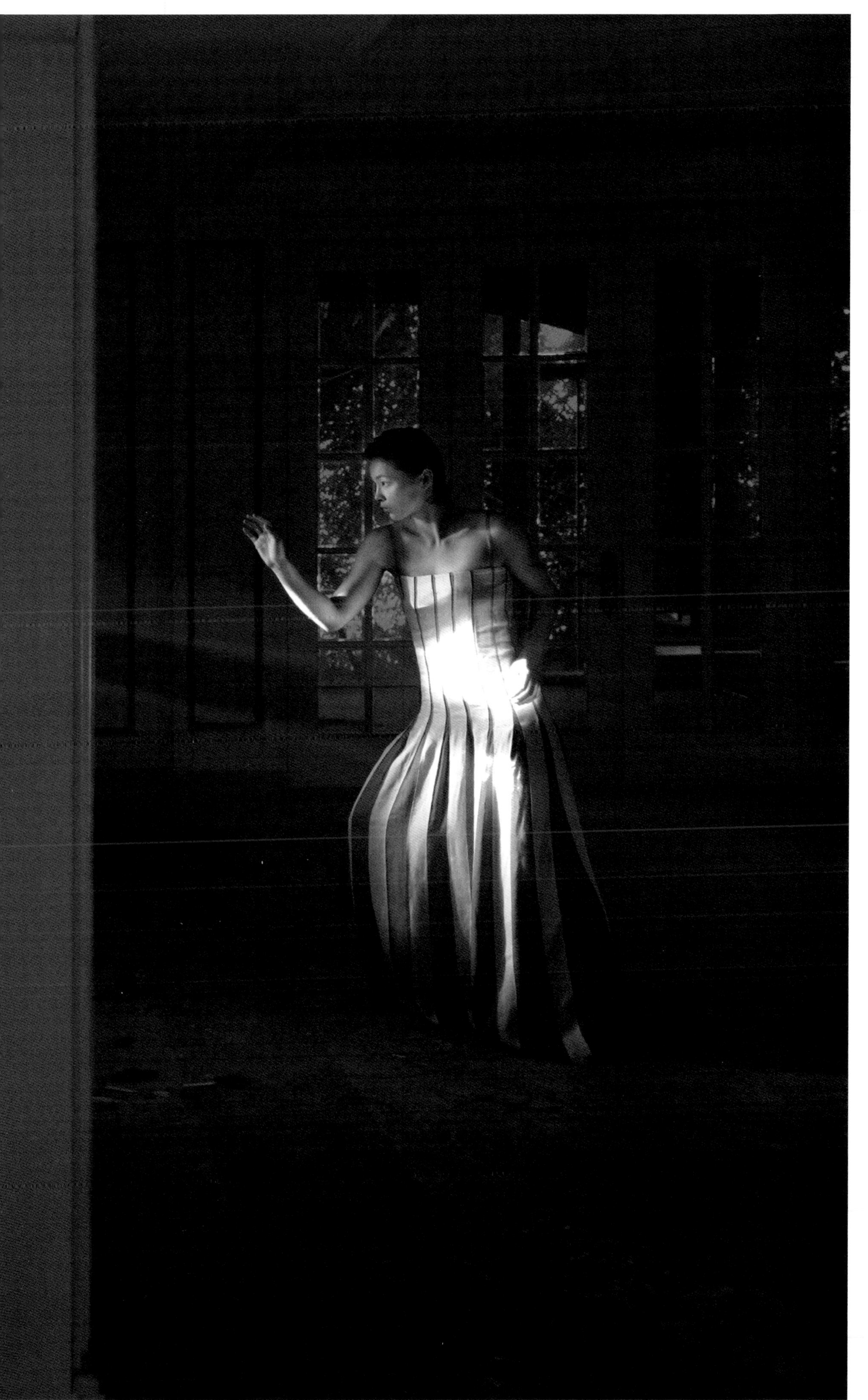

面对生长
Facing Growth, 2020
1000 × 800mm

搜寻
Search, 2024
600 × 800mm

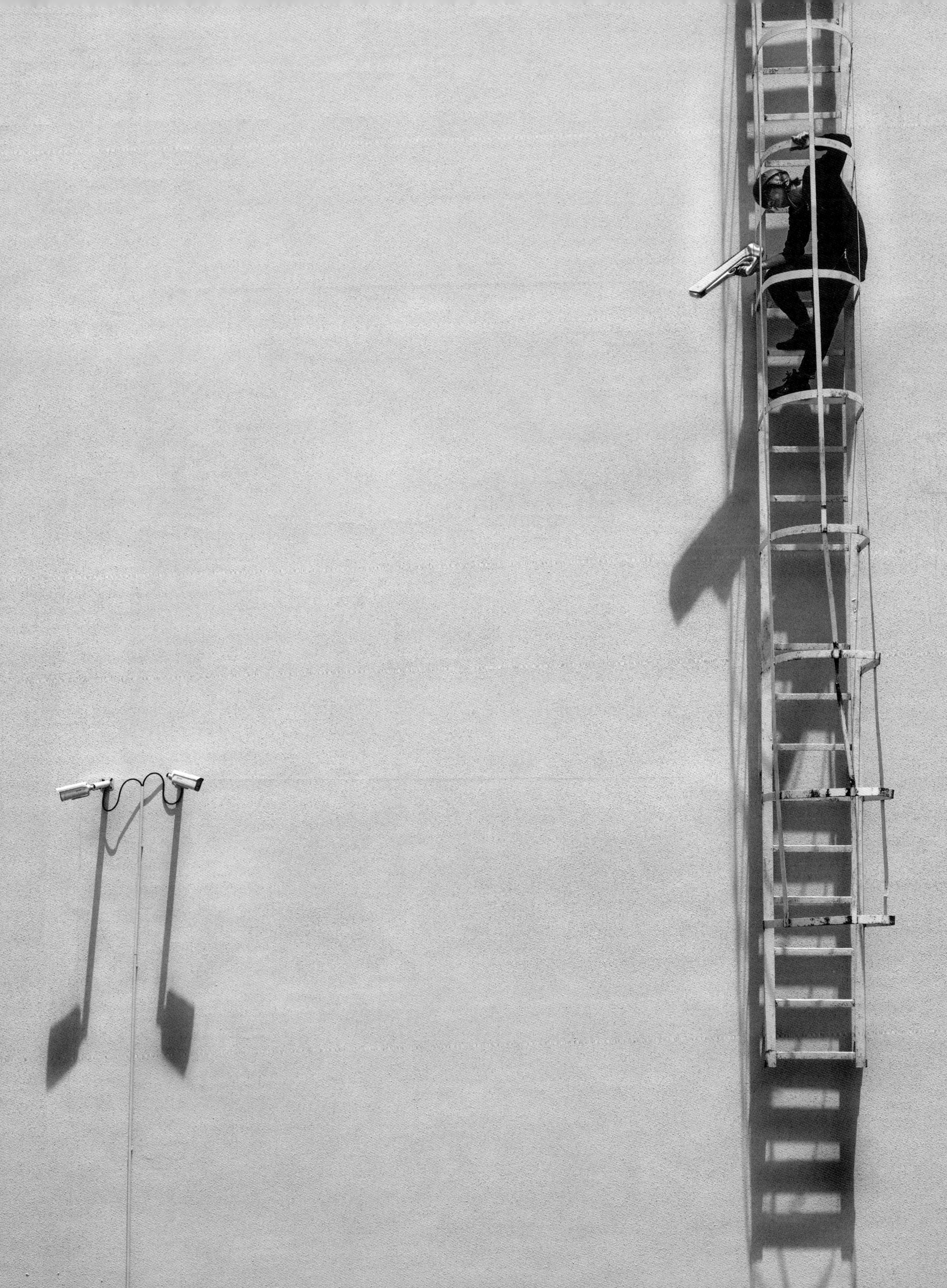

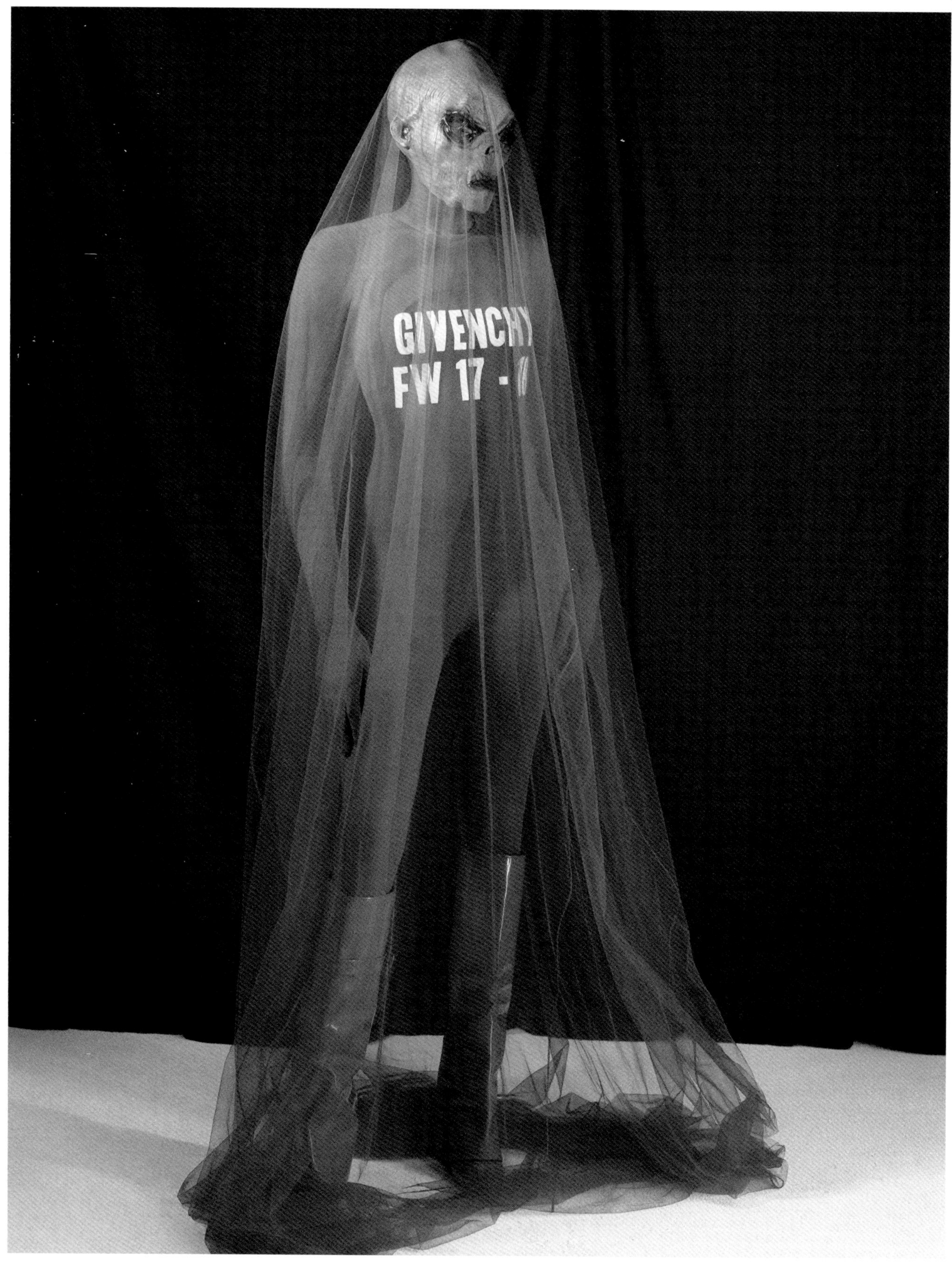

狂热纪梵希
Fanatical Givenchy, 2018
600 × 800mm

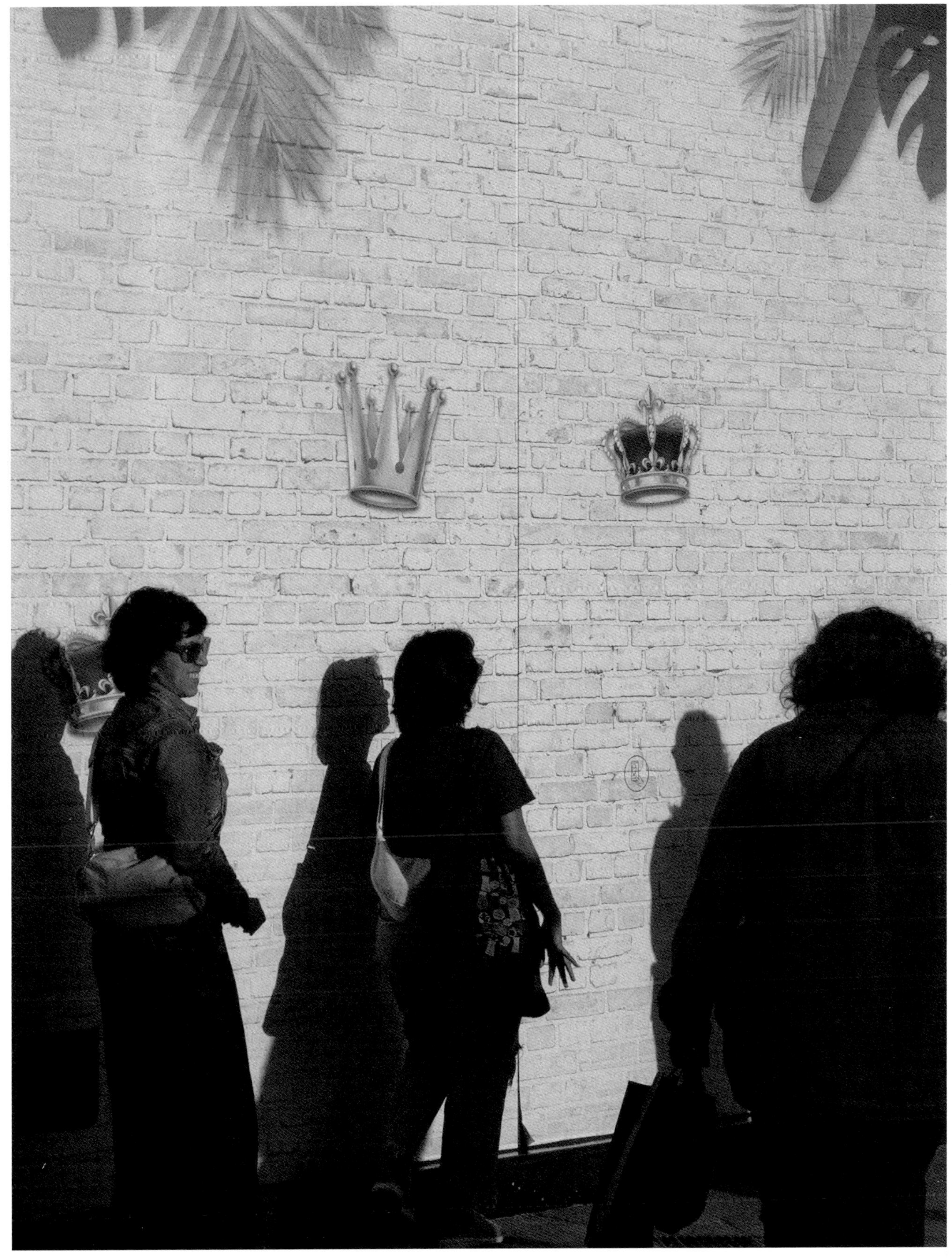

打卡时代
The Era of Punching In, 2024
600 × 800mm

镜中人
Man in Stained Glass, 2020
600 × 800mm

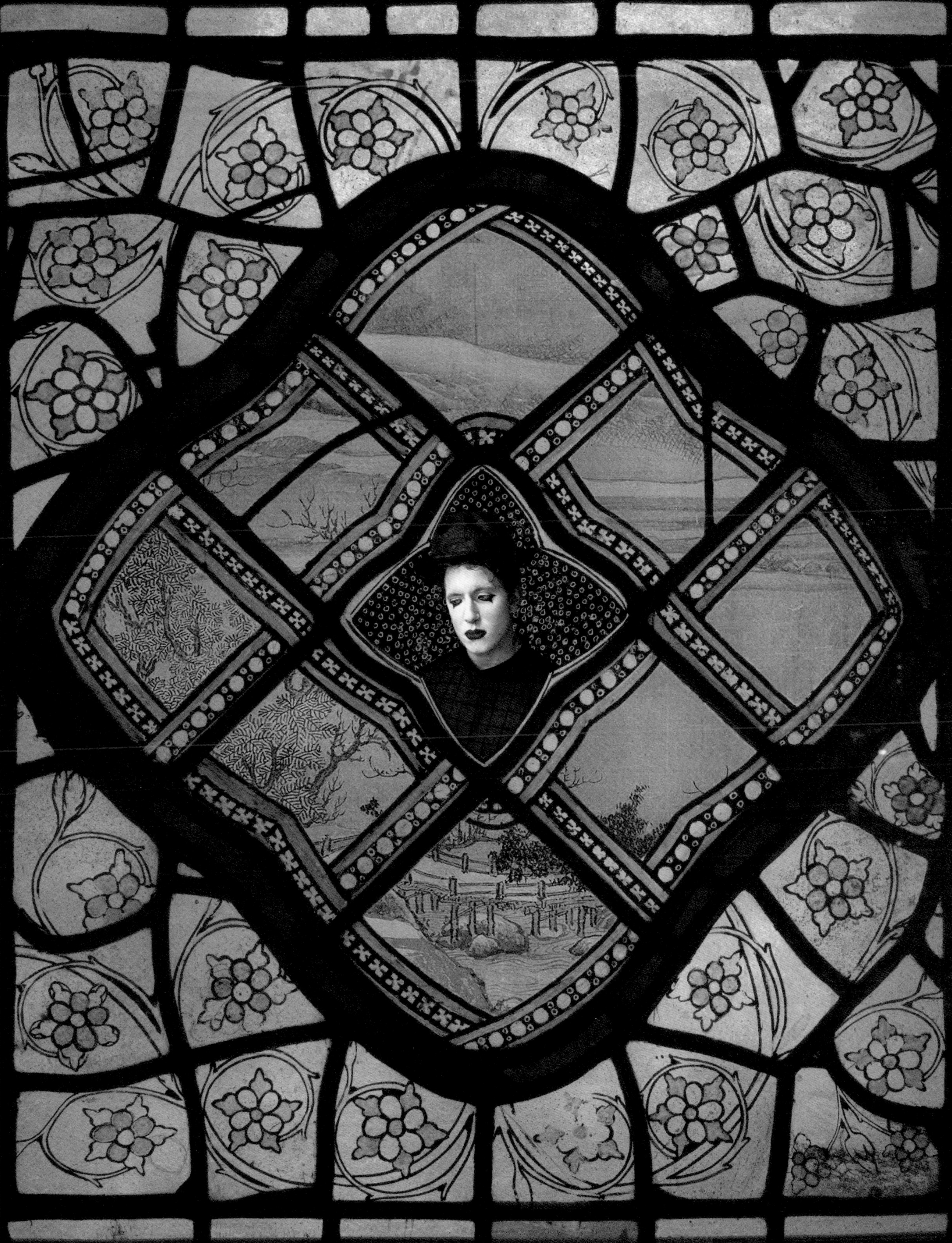

SECTION FOUR

The Rural Romance

我的王国
My Kingdom, 2022–24
600 × 800mm

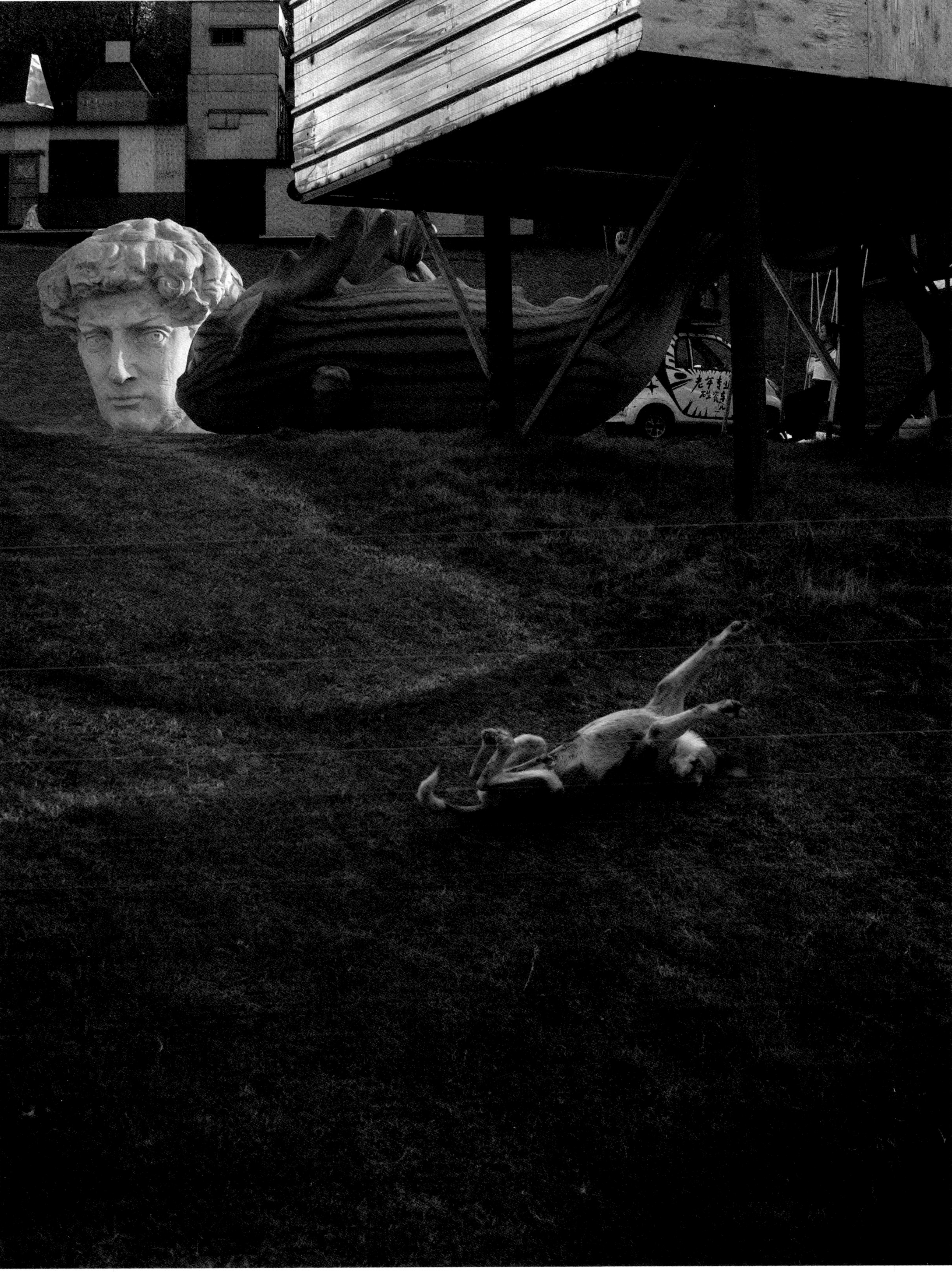

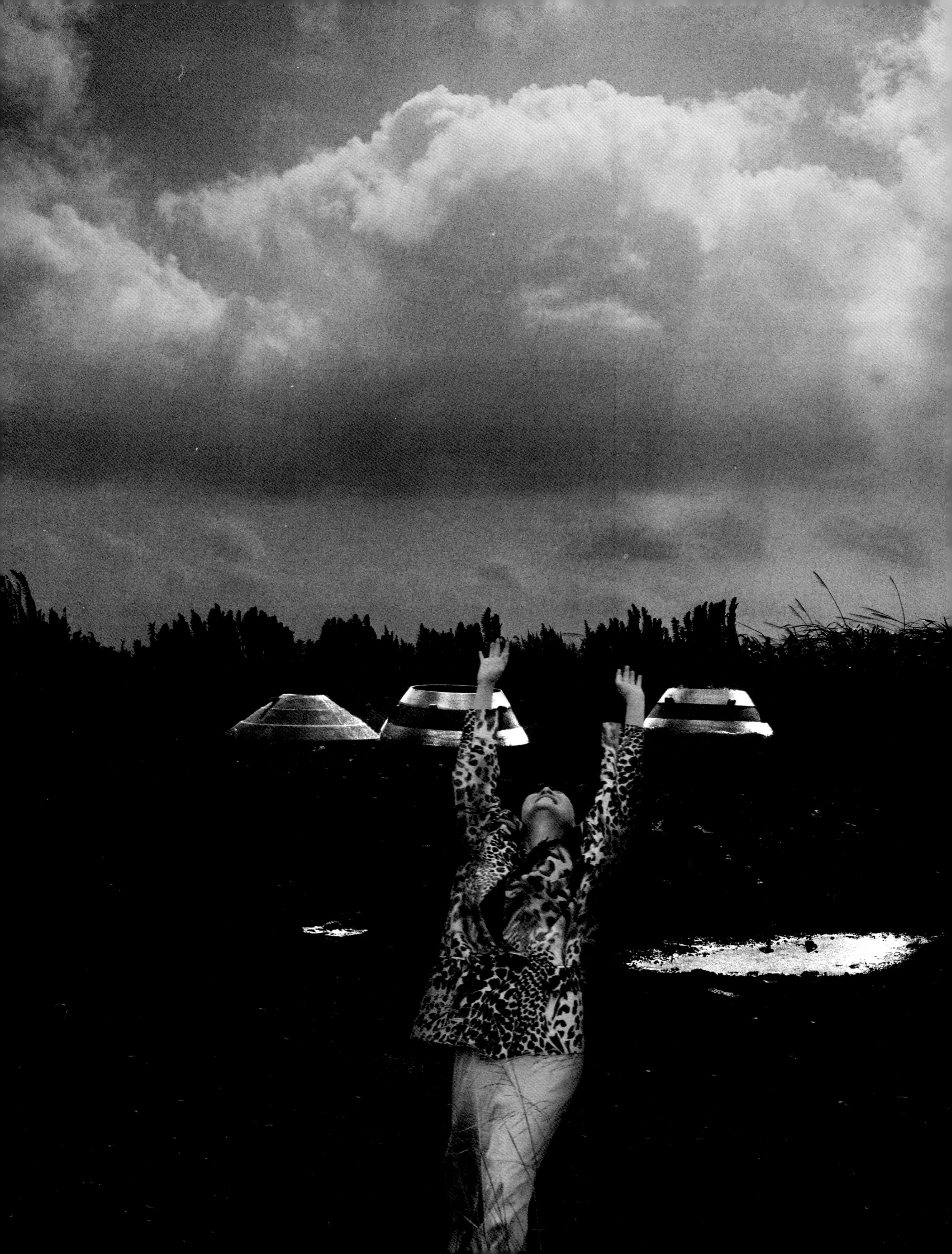

从哪里来的
Where Are They From, 2018–19
600 × 800mm

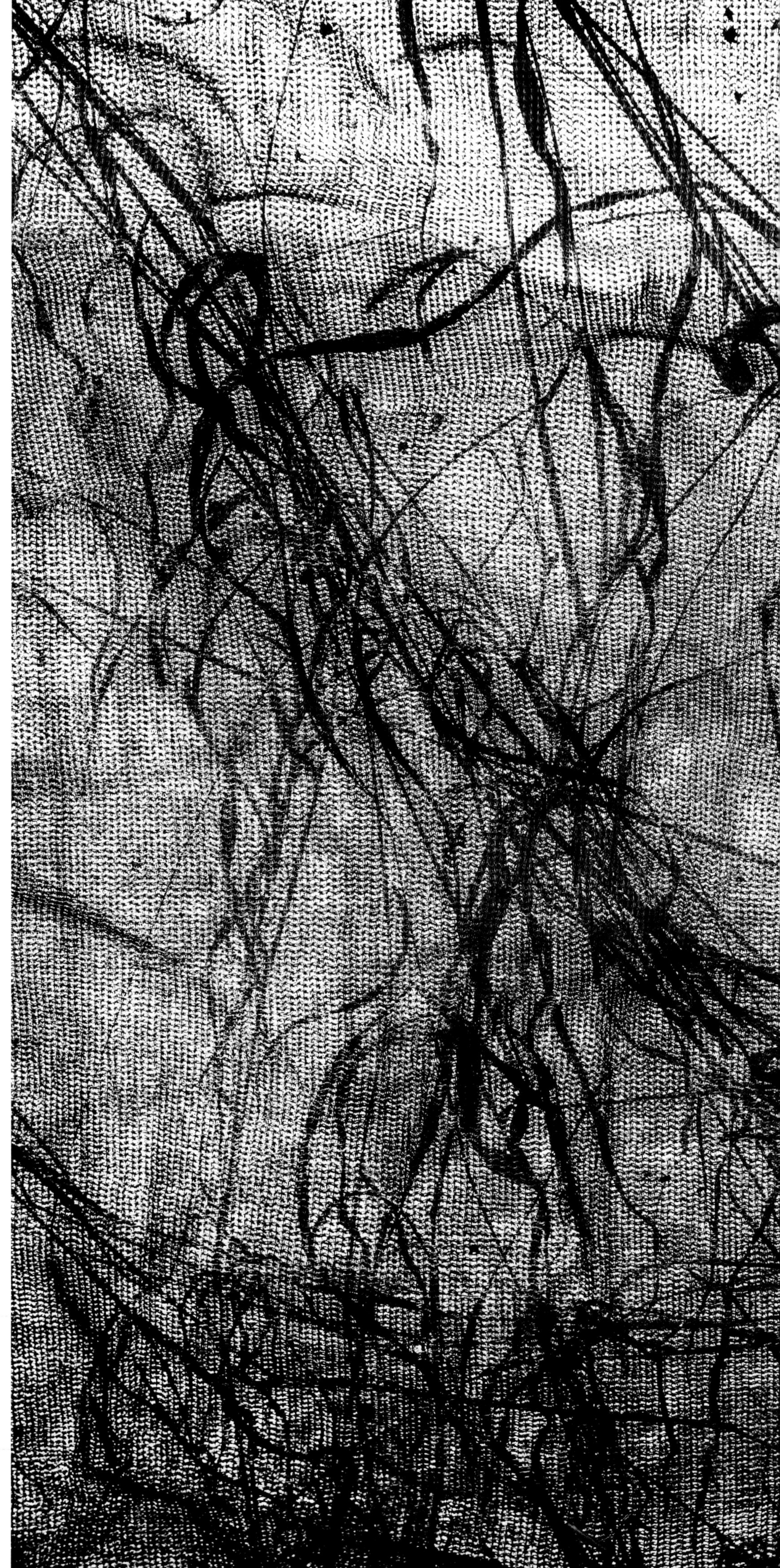

伯伯的作品
The Work by an Uncle, 2023
1000 × 800mm

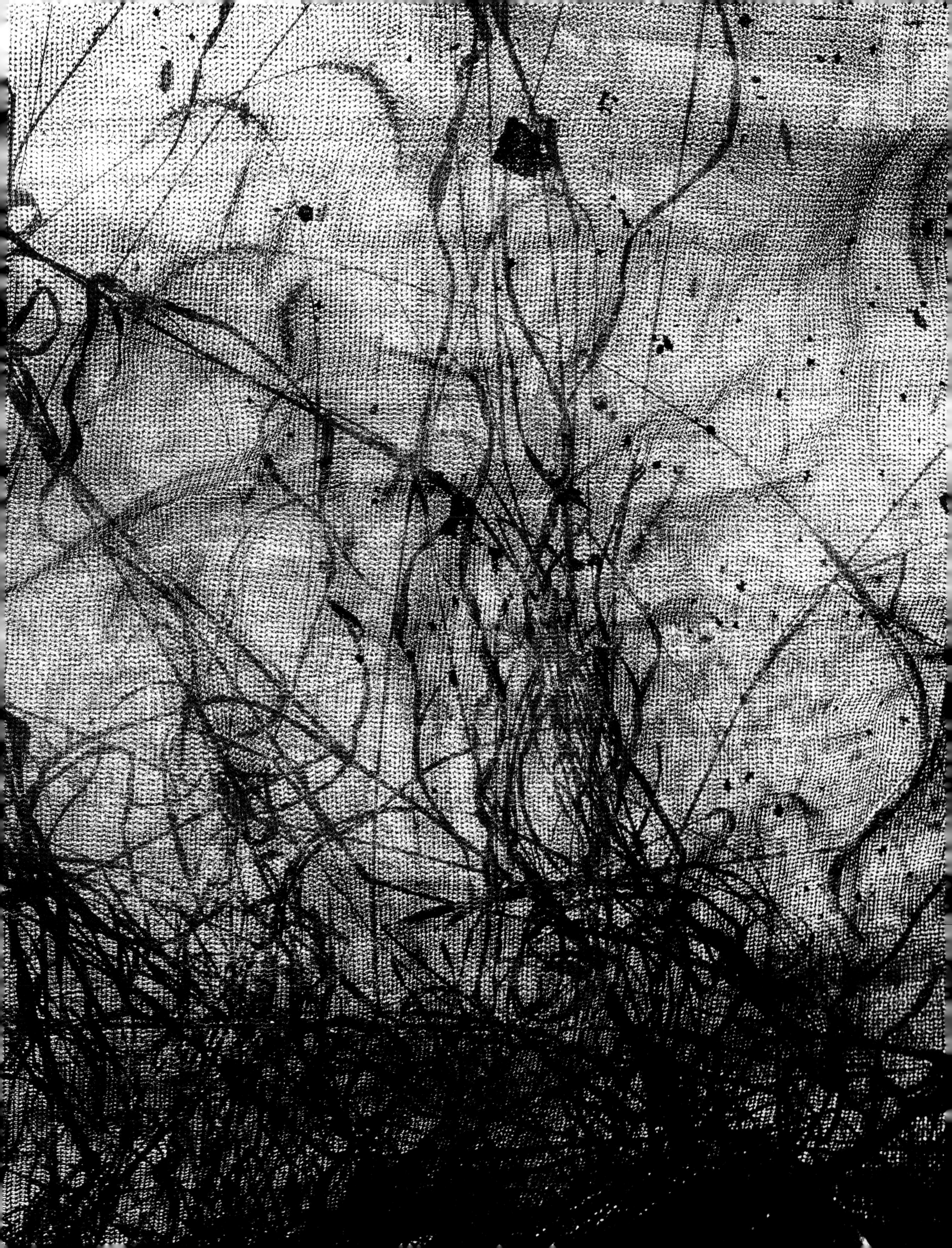

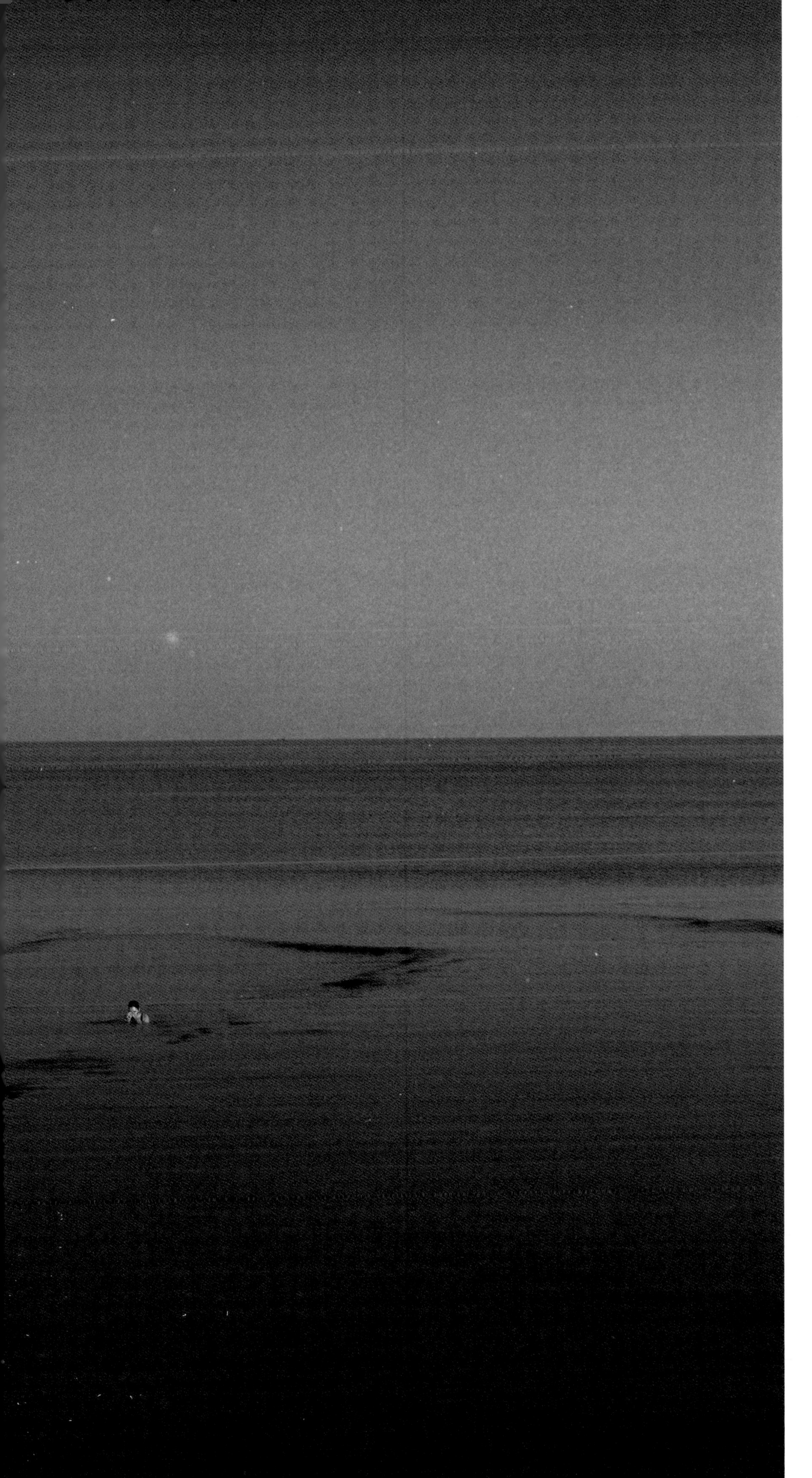

来救你了
Coming to Save You,
2017–23

1000 × 800mm

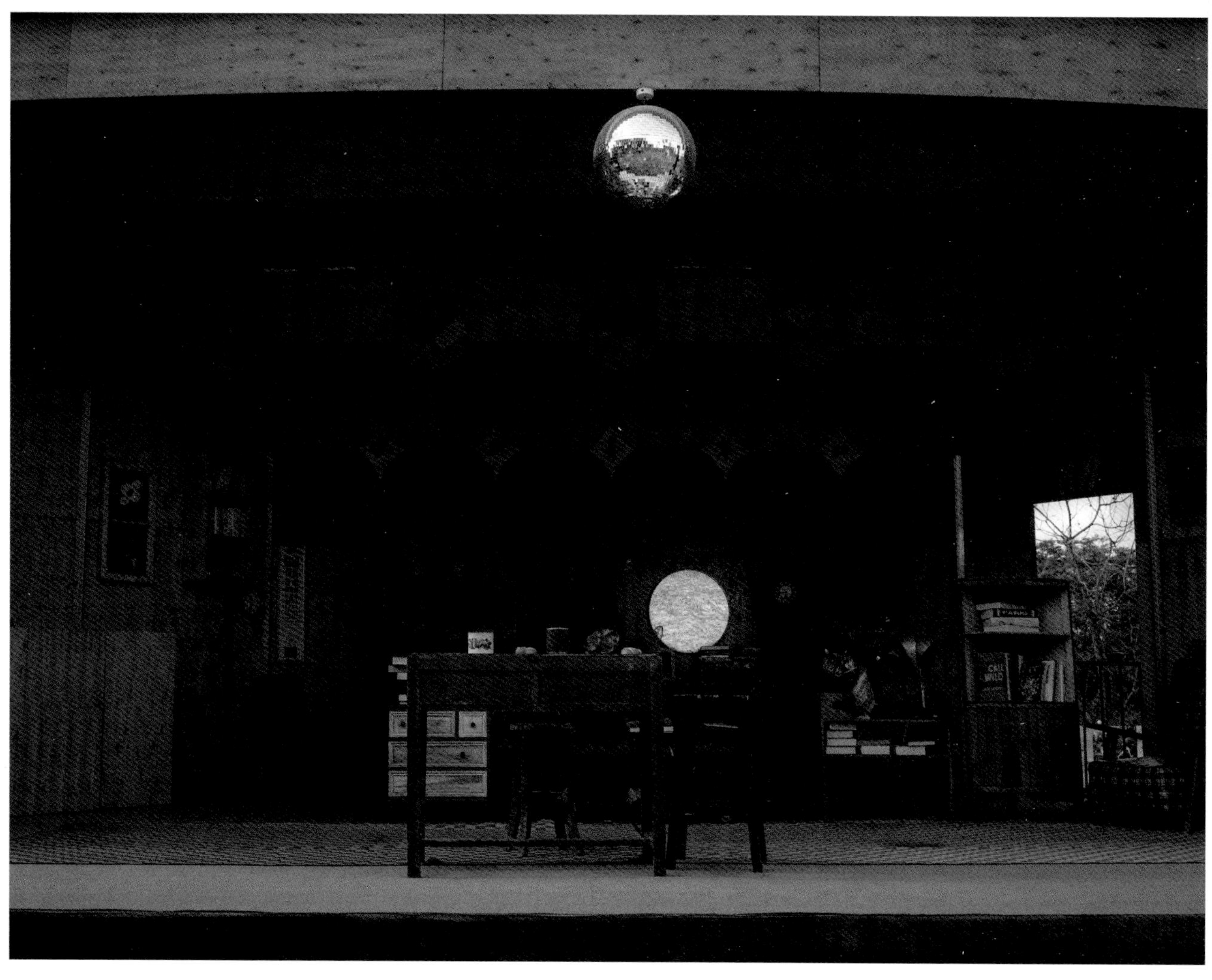

散光的眼睛需要一面镜子
Astigmatic Eyes Need a Mirror, 2024
1000 × 800mm

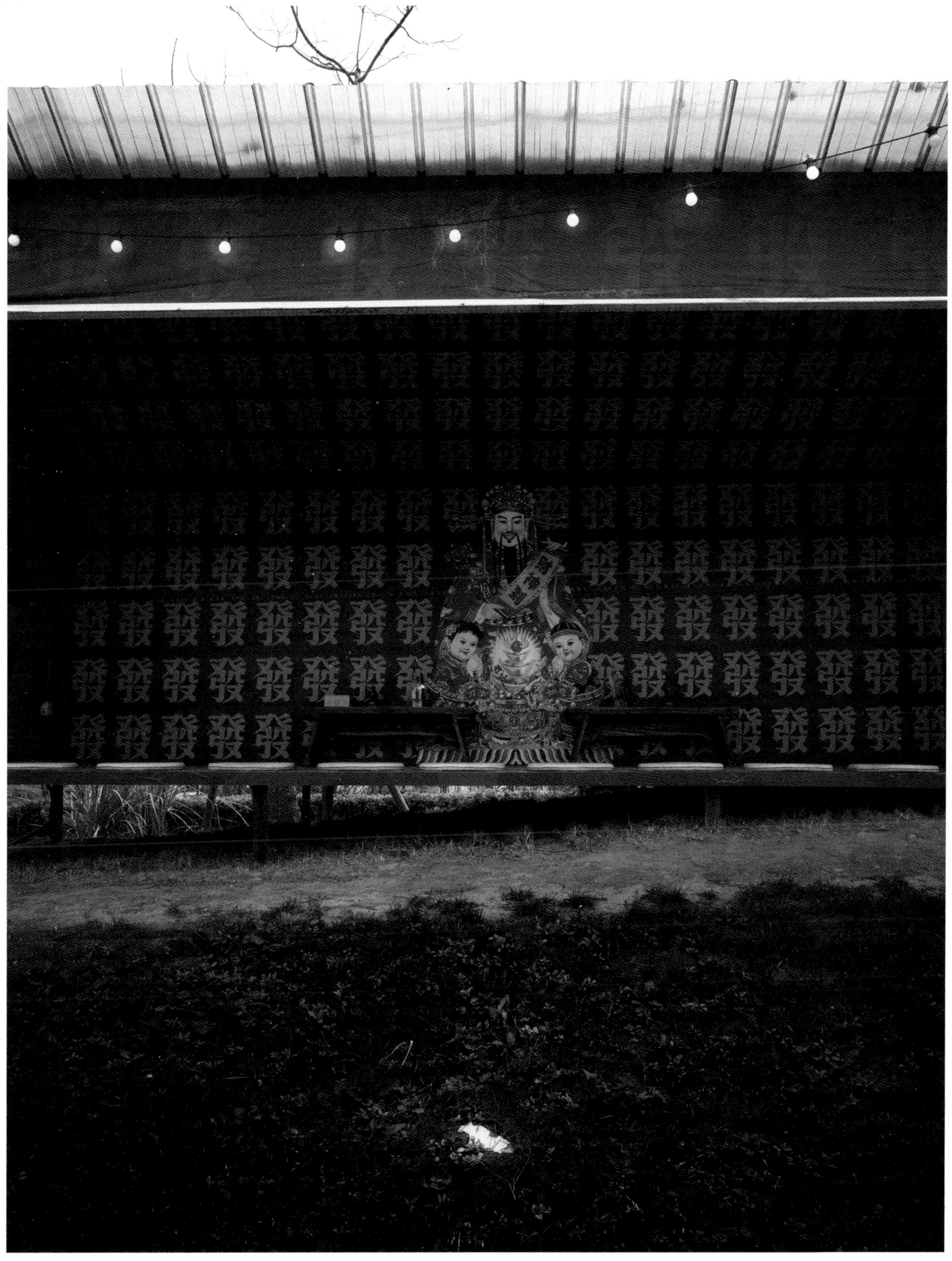

暴富的心一直在
The Desire to Get Suddenly Rich is Always There, 2024
1000 × 800mm

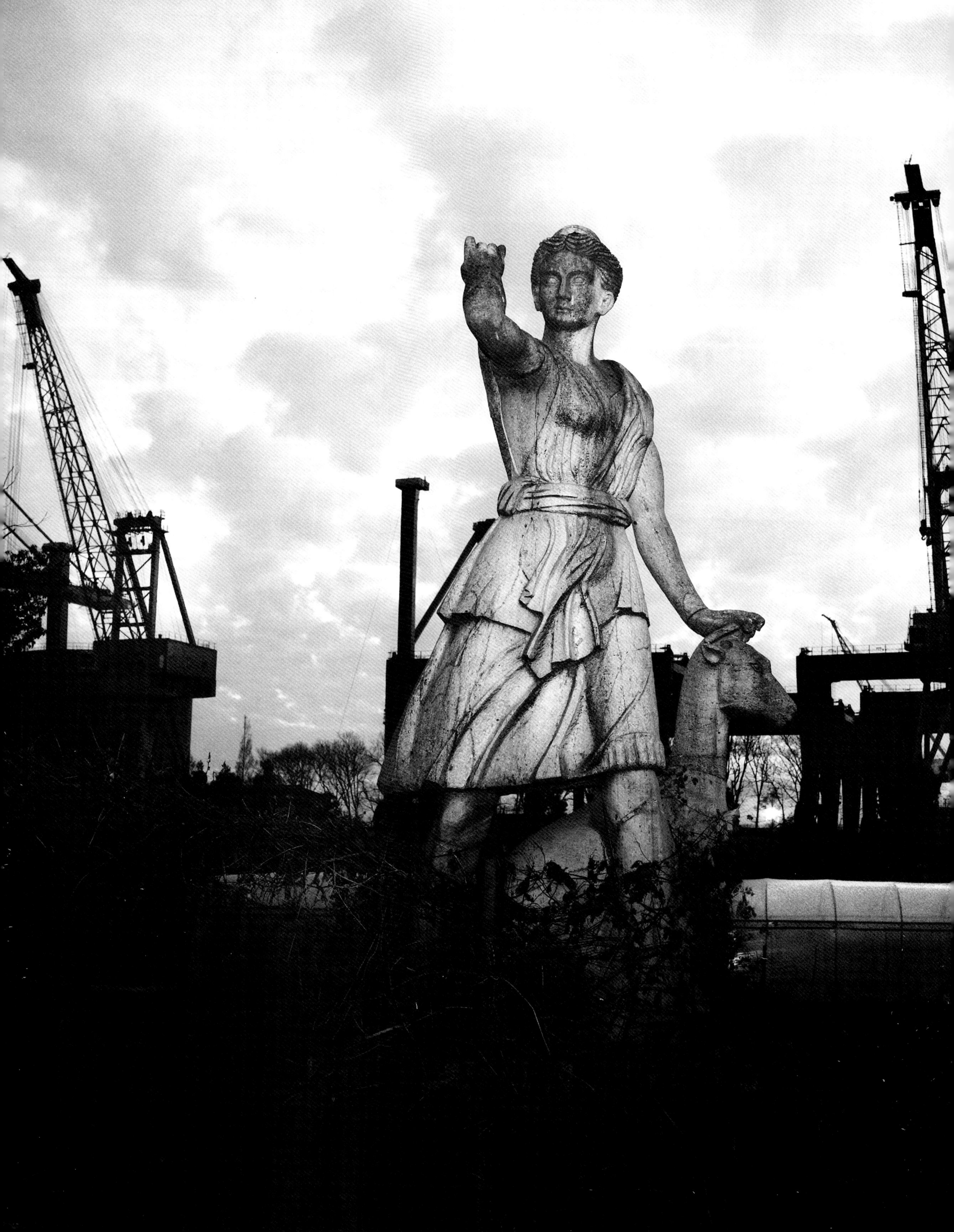

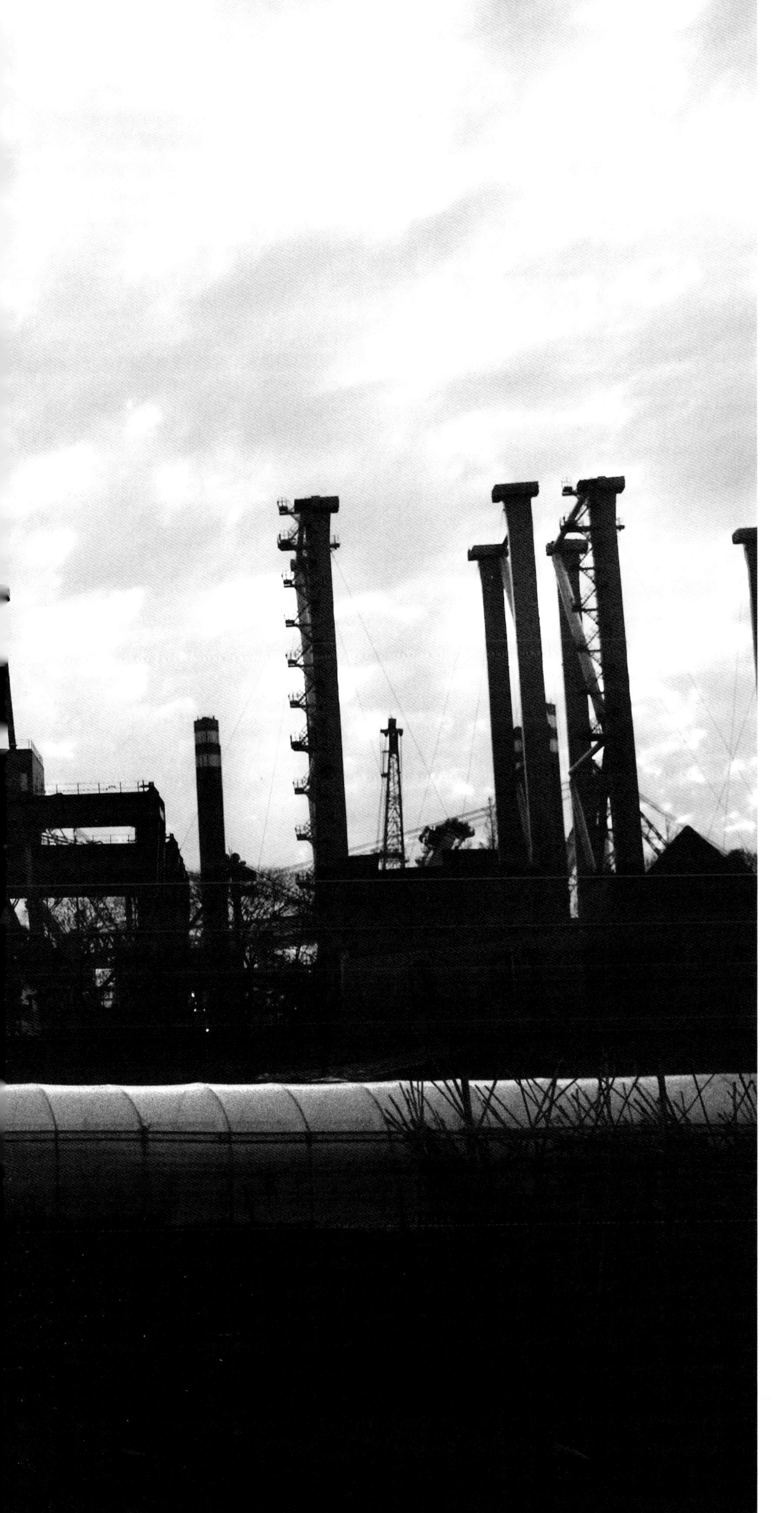

曾经的战场
The Battlefield of the Past, 2023
1000 × 800mm

暴裂无声
Burst Silently, 2024
600 × 800mm

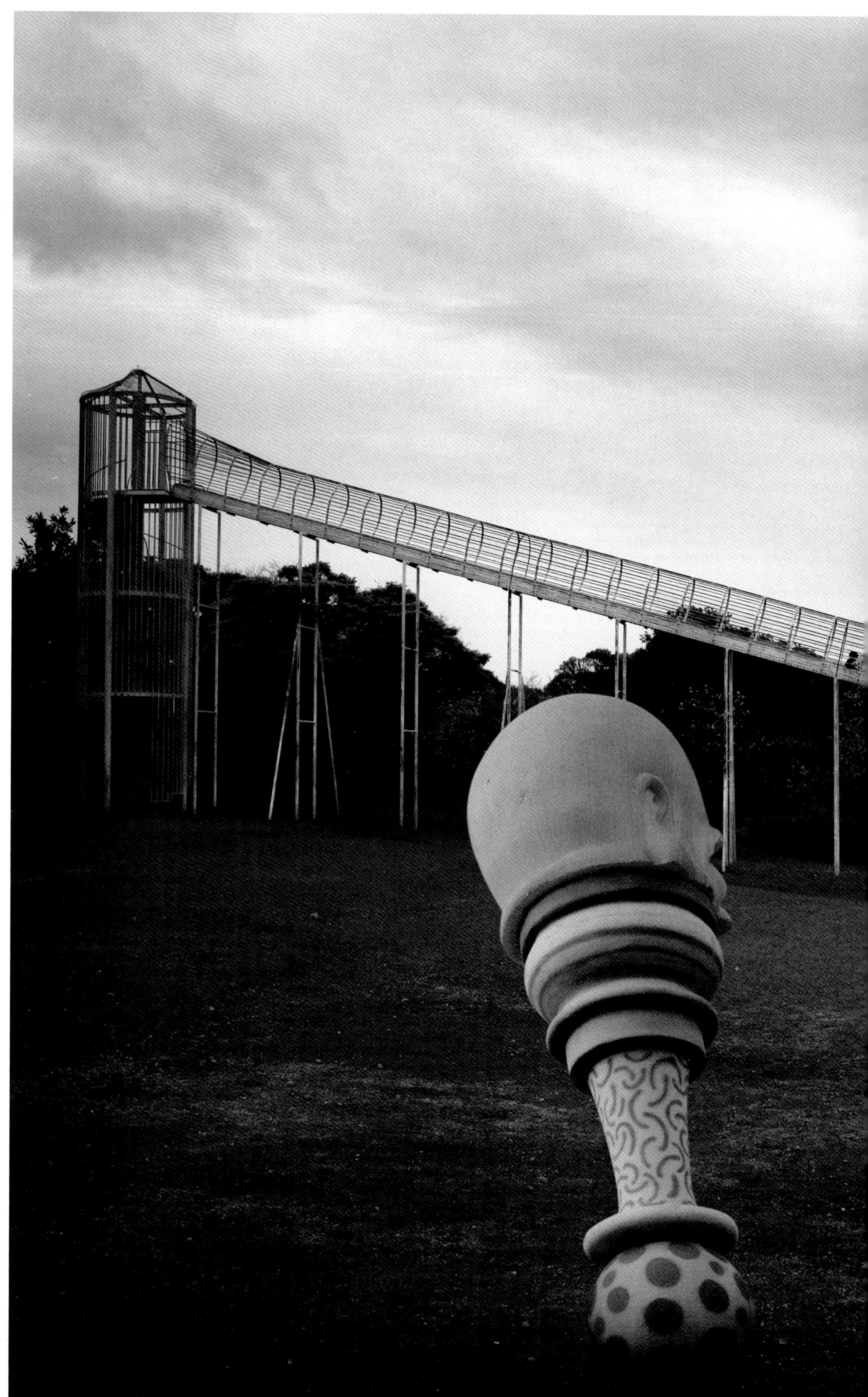

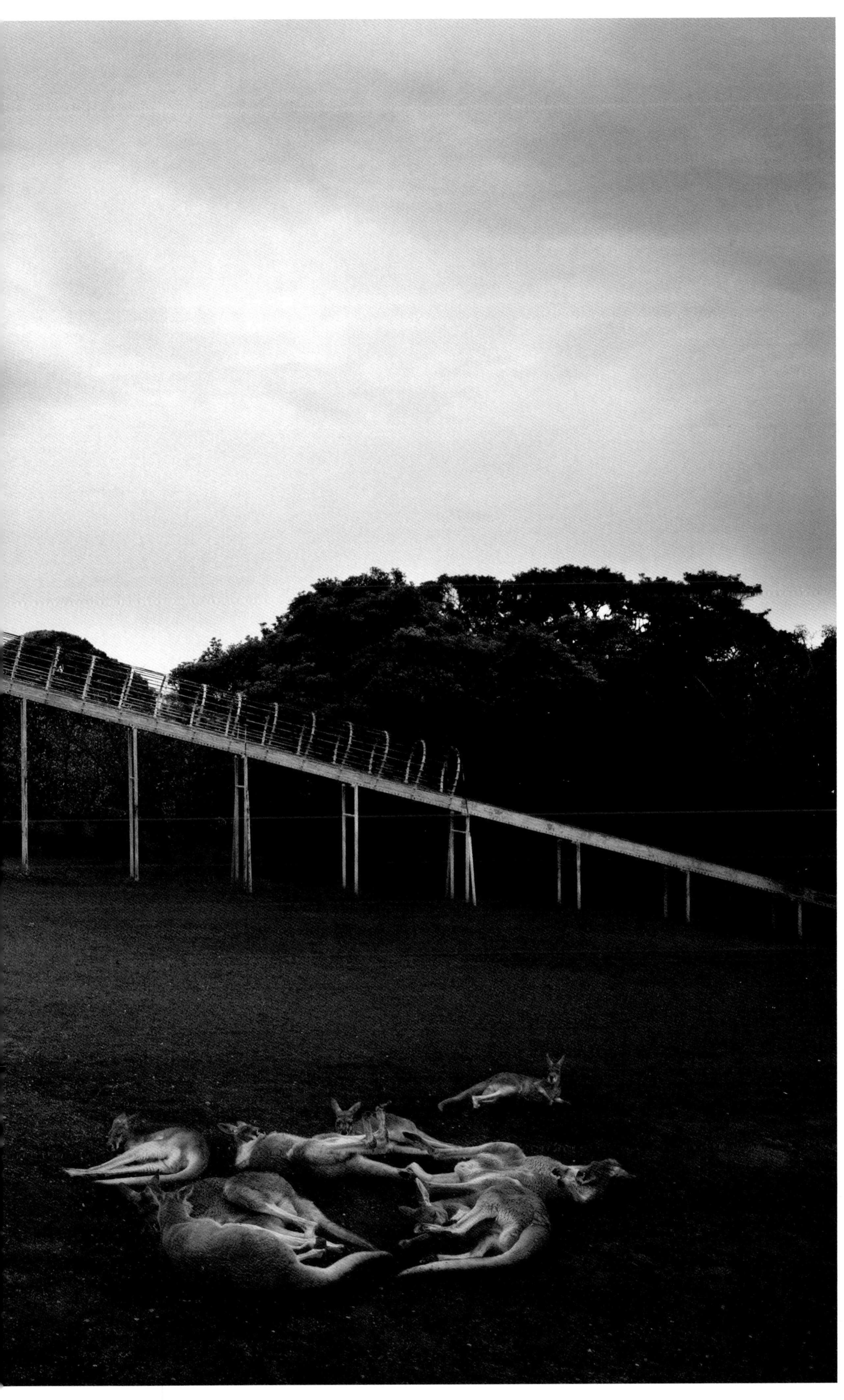

滑下来一定是仰着头
One Must Have Tilted One's Head When Slid Down, 2021–24
1000 × 800mm

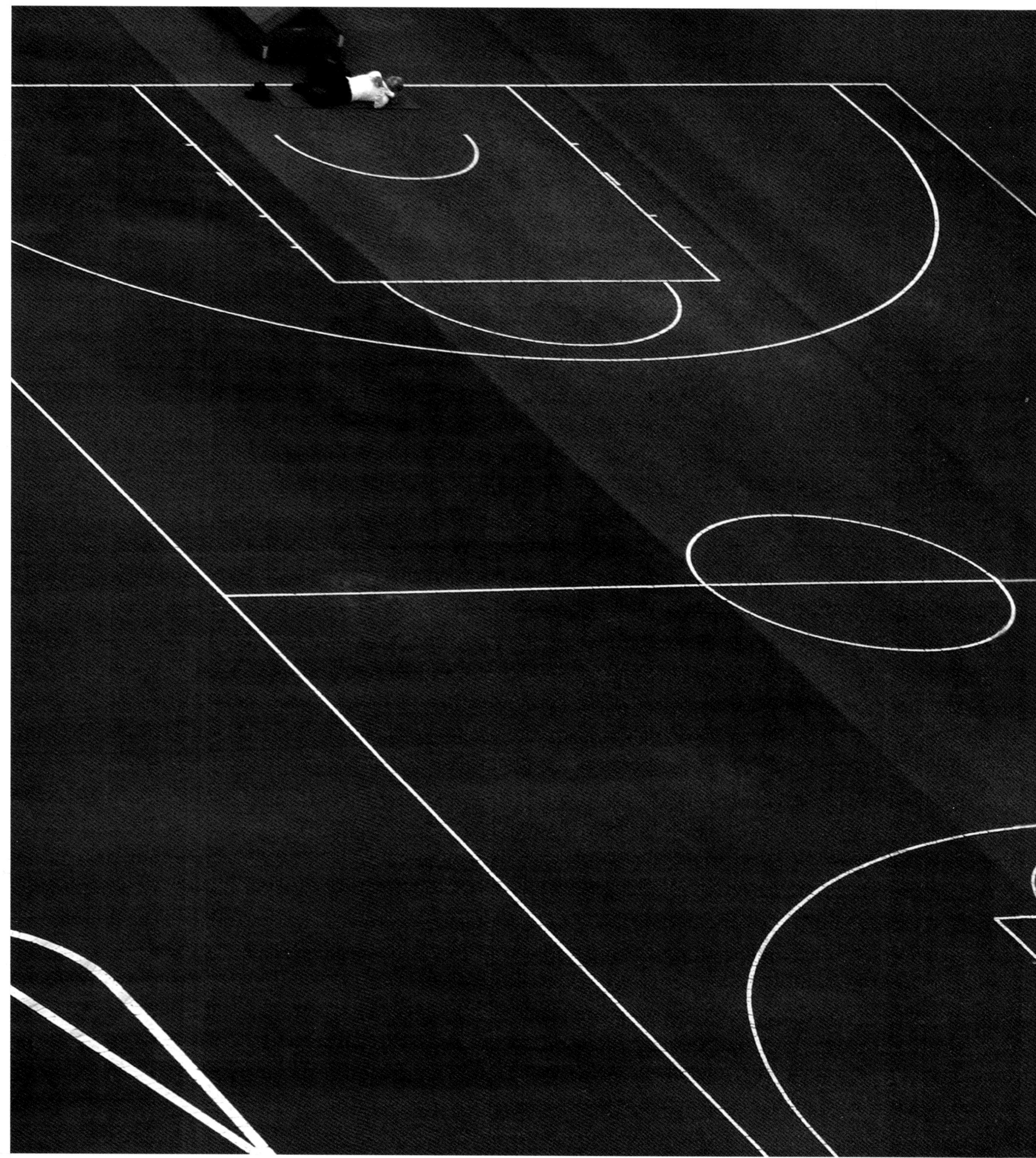

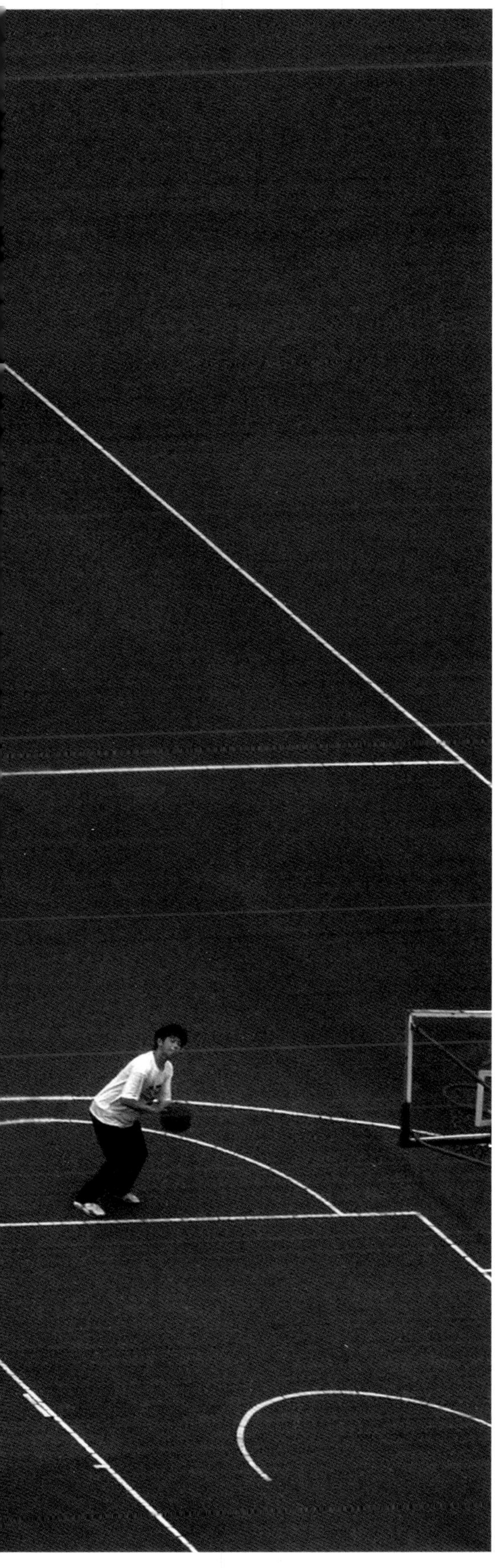

父与子
Father and Son, 2019
1000 × 800mm

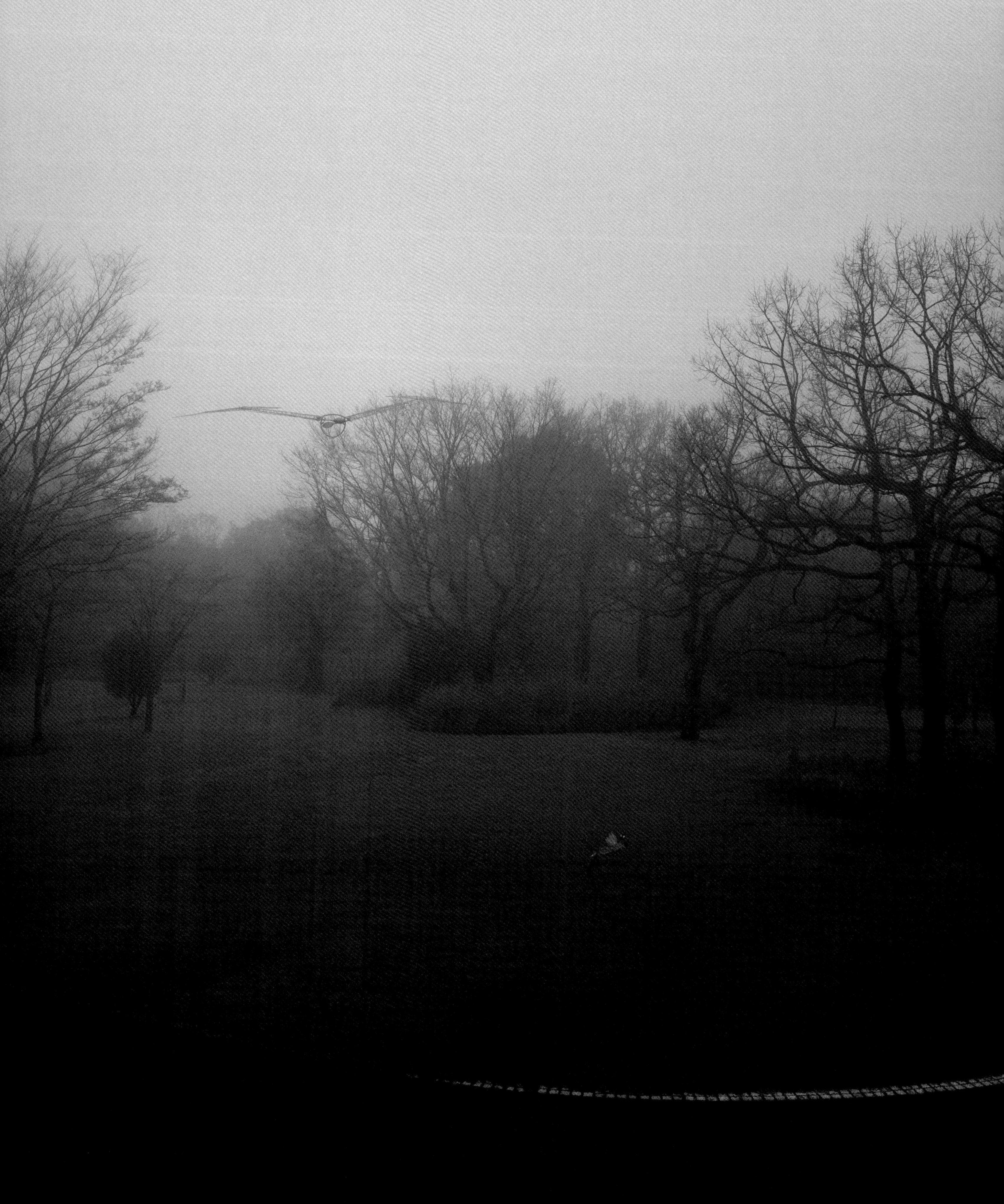

狩猎
Hunting, 2014–24
600 × 800mm

跳下来的时候会想什么
What Do We Think About When We Jump Down?, 2018–23
600 × 800mm

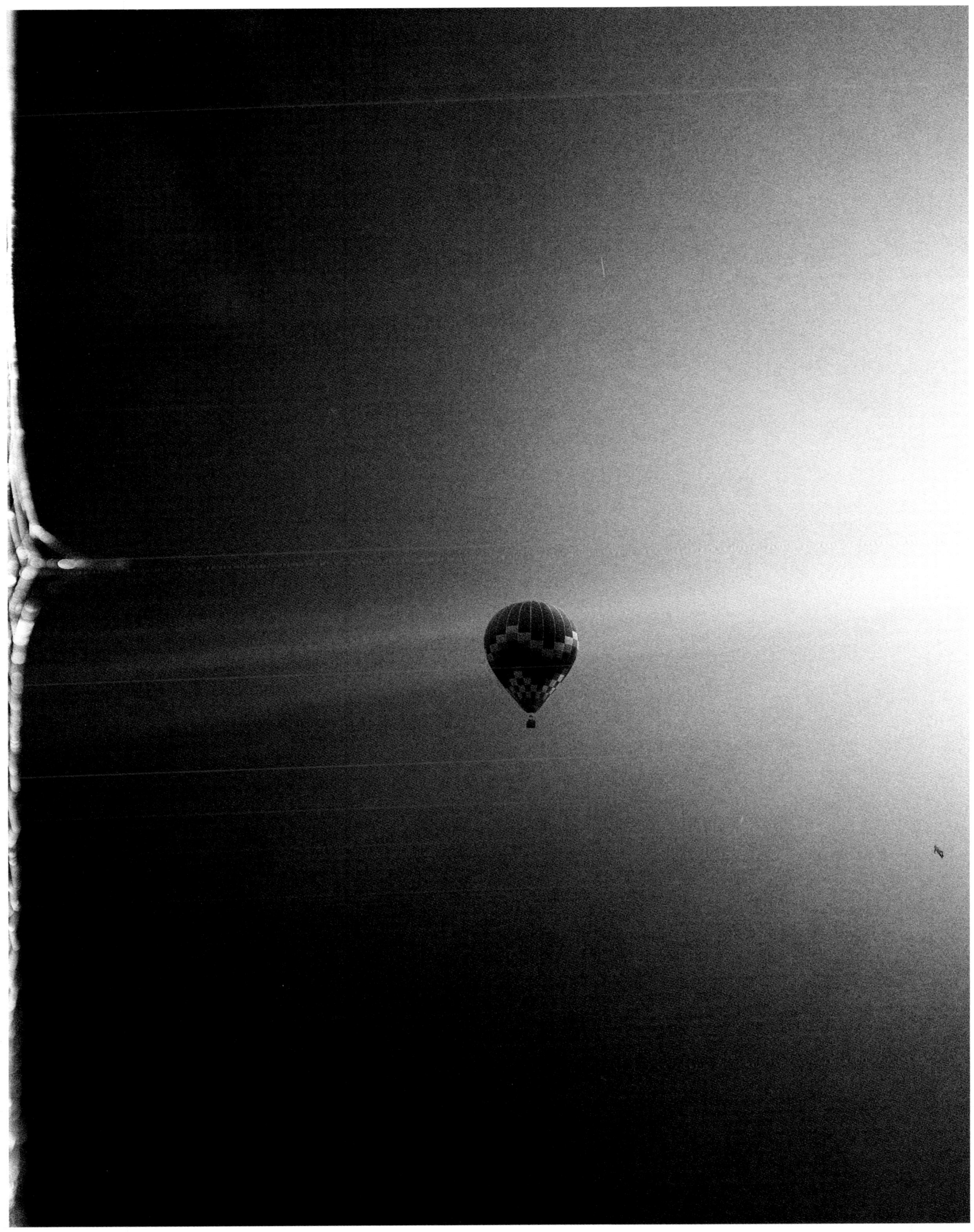

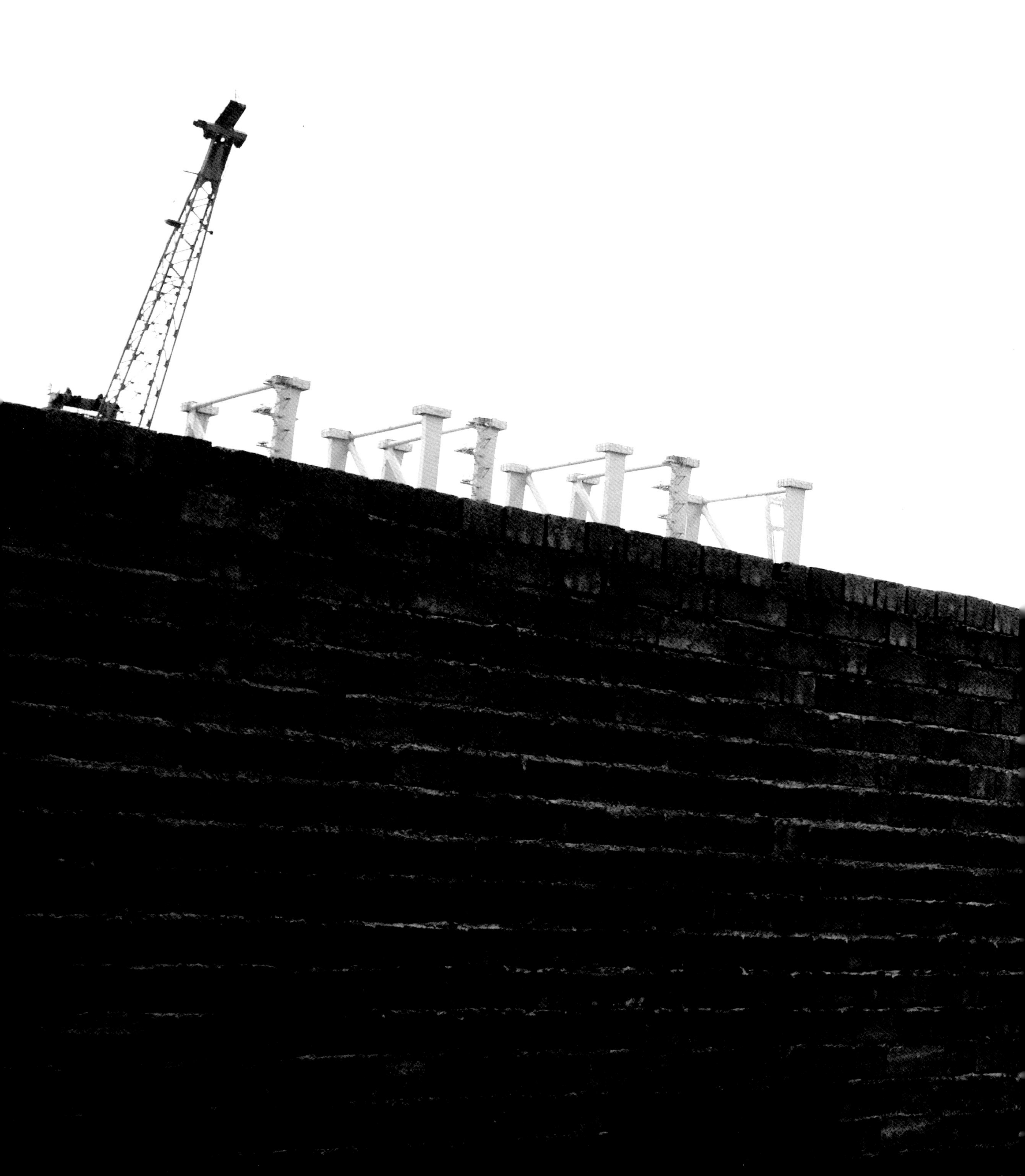

量力而行
Act Within Your Capabilities, 2023
1000 × 800mm

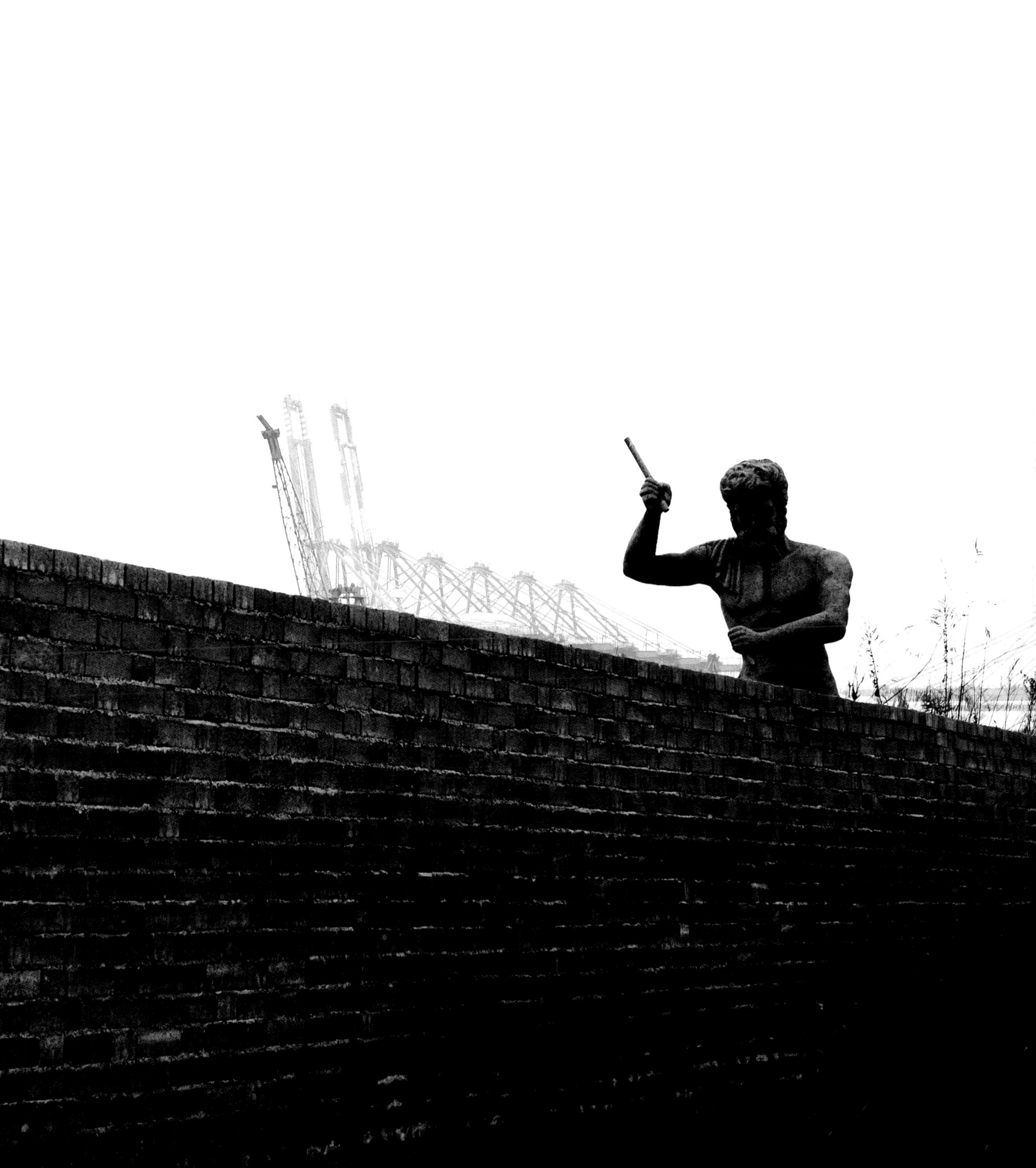

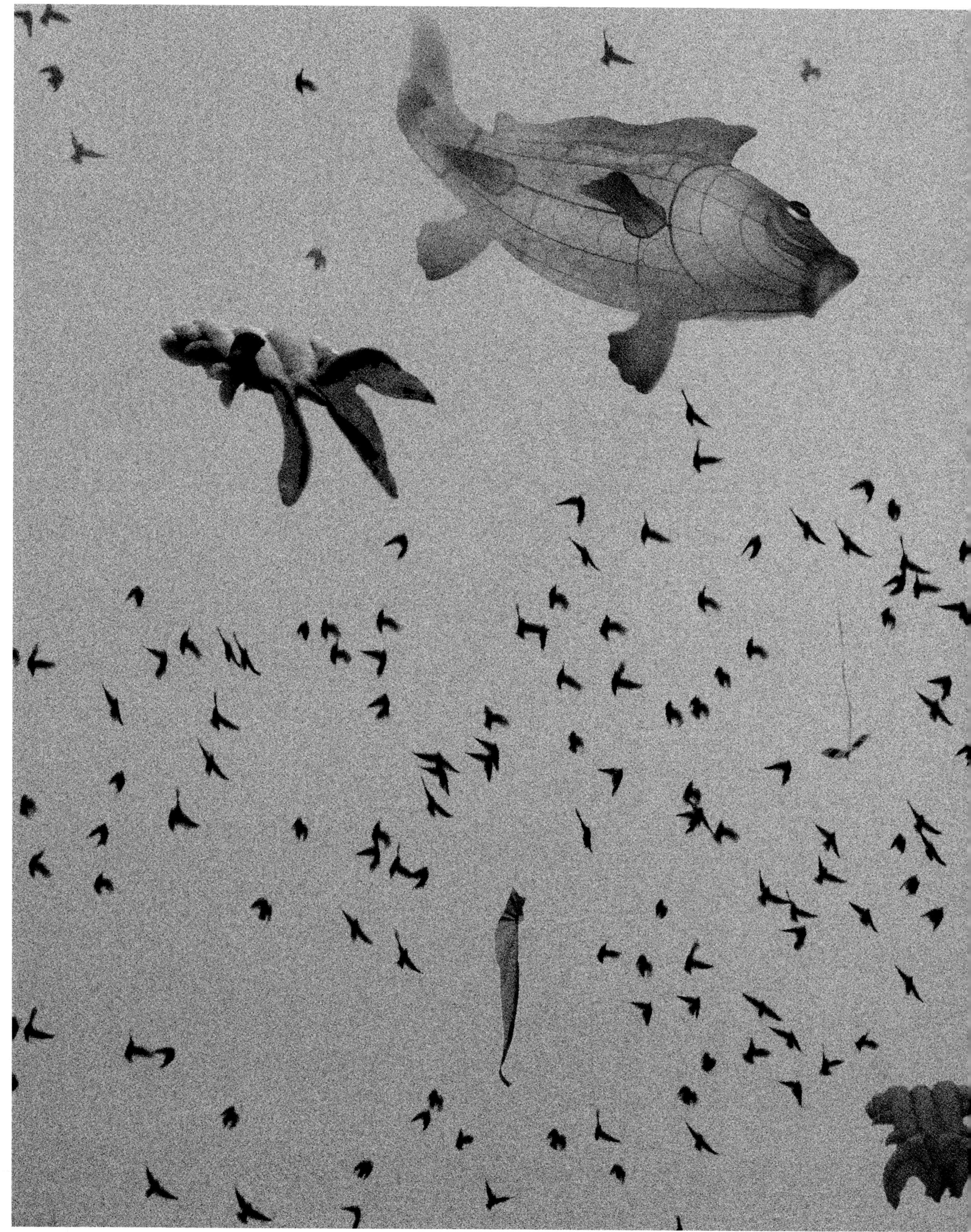

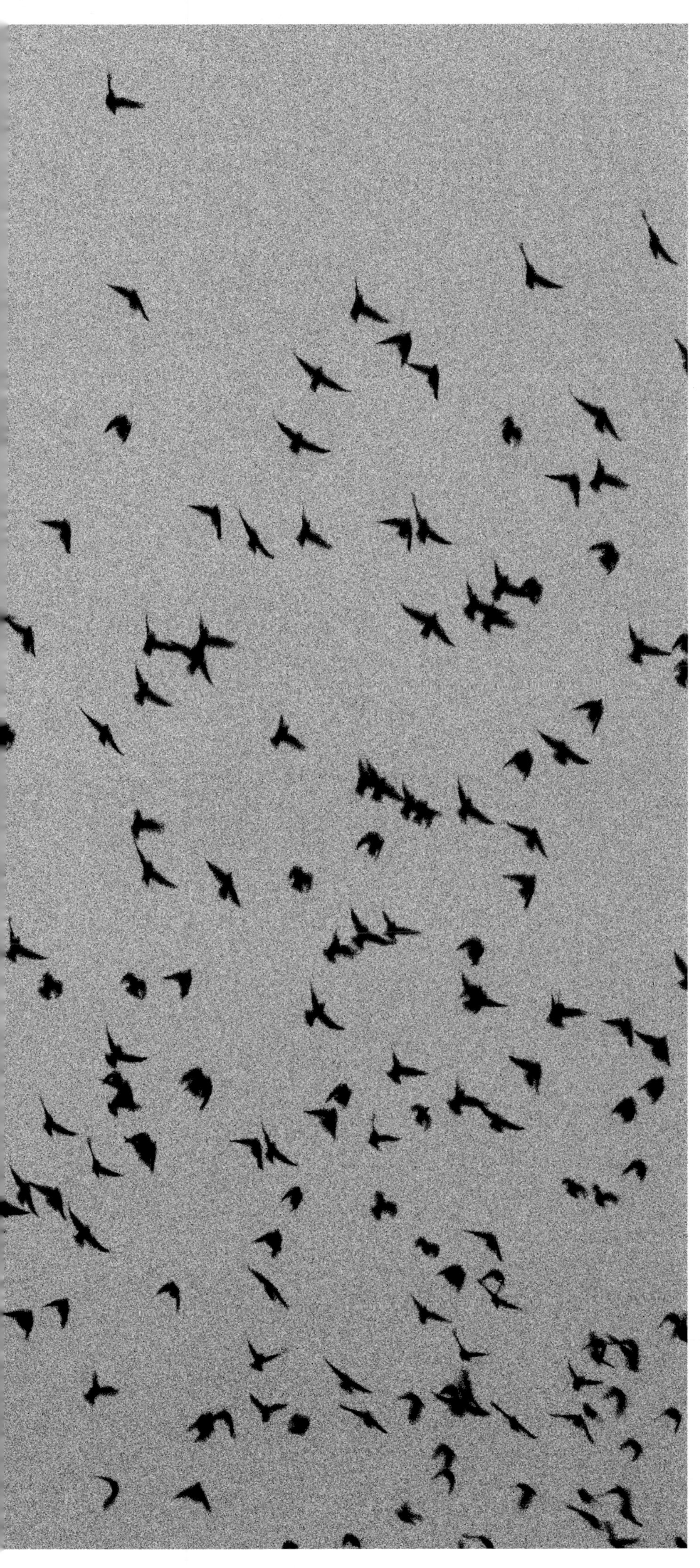

游心
Peaceful, 2020–21
1000 × 800mm

领地
Territory, 2023–24
600 × 800mm

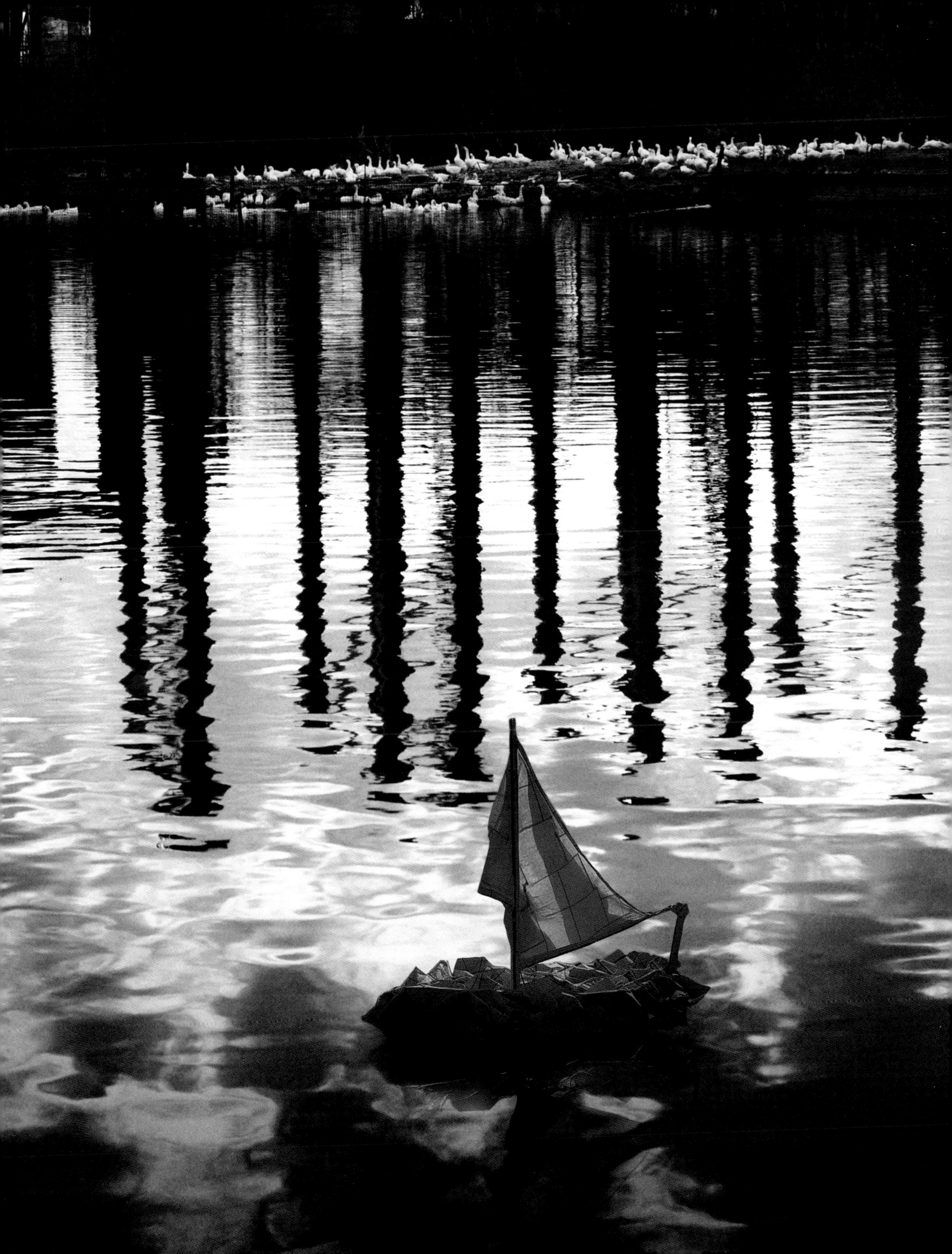

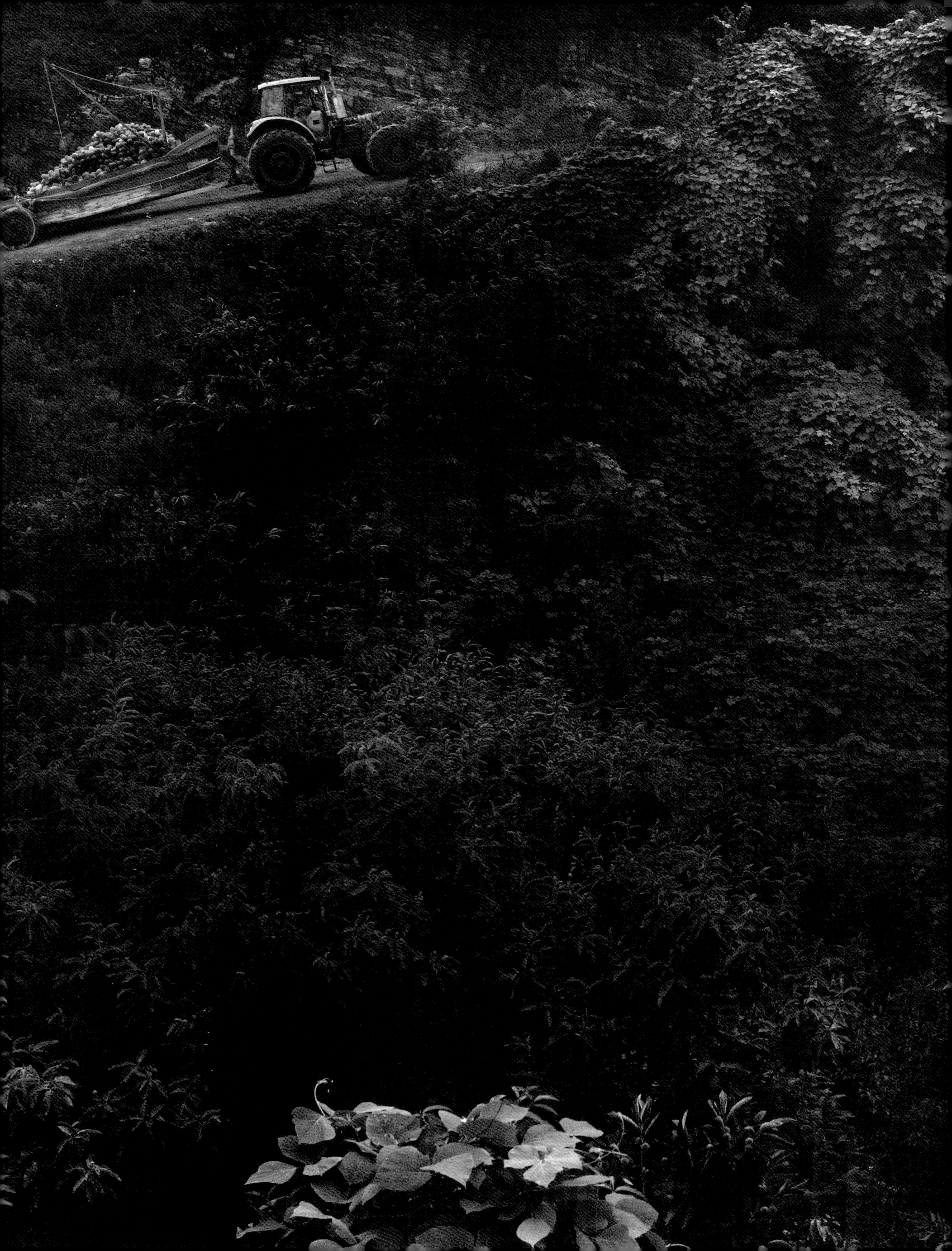

行路
On the Way, 2020
1000 × 800mm

围城之内
Within the Siege, 2020–24
600 × 800mm

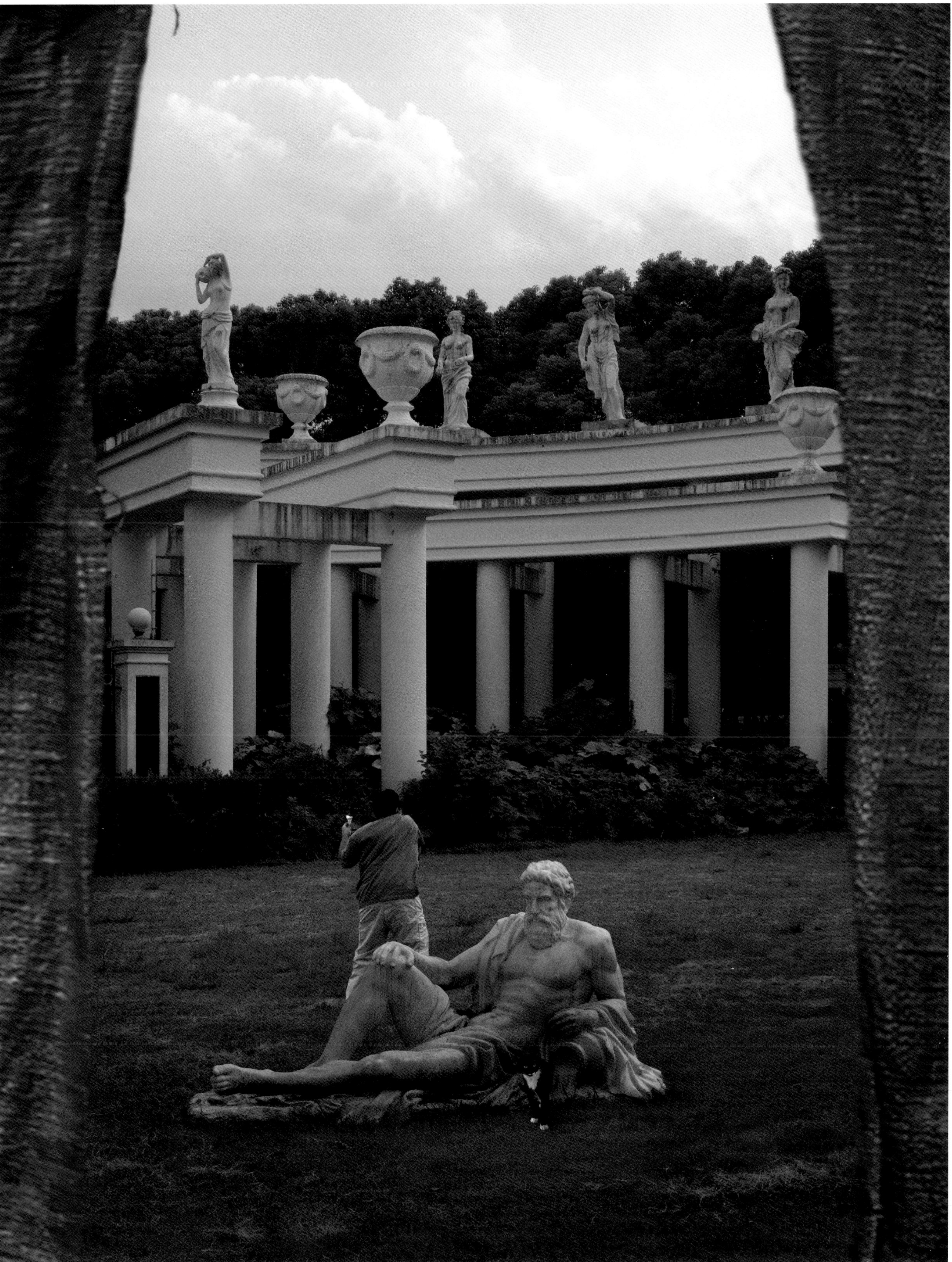

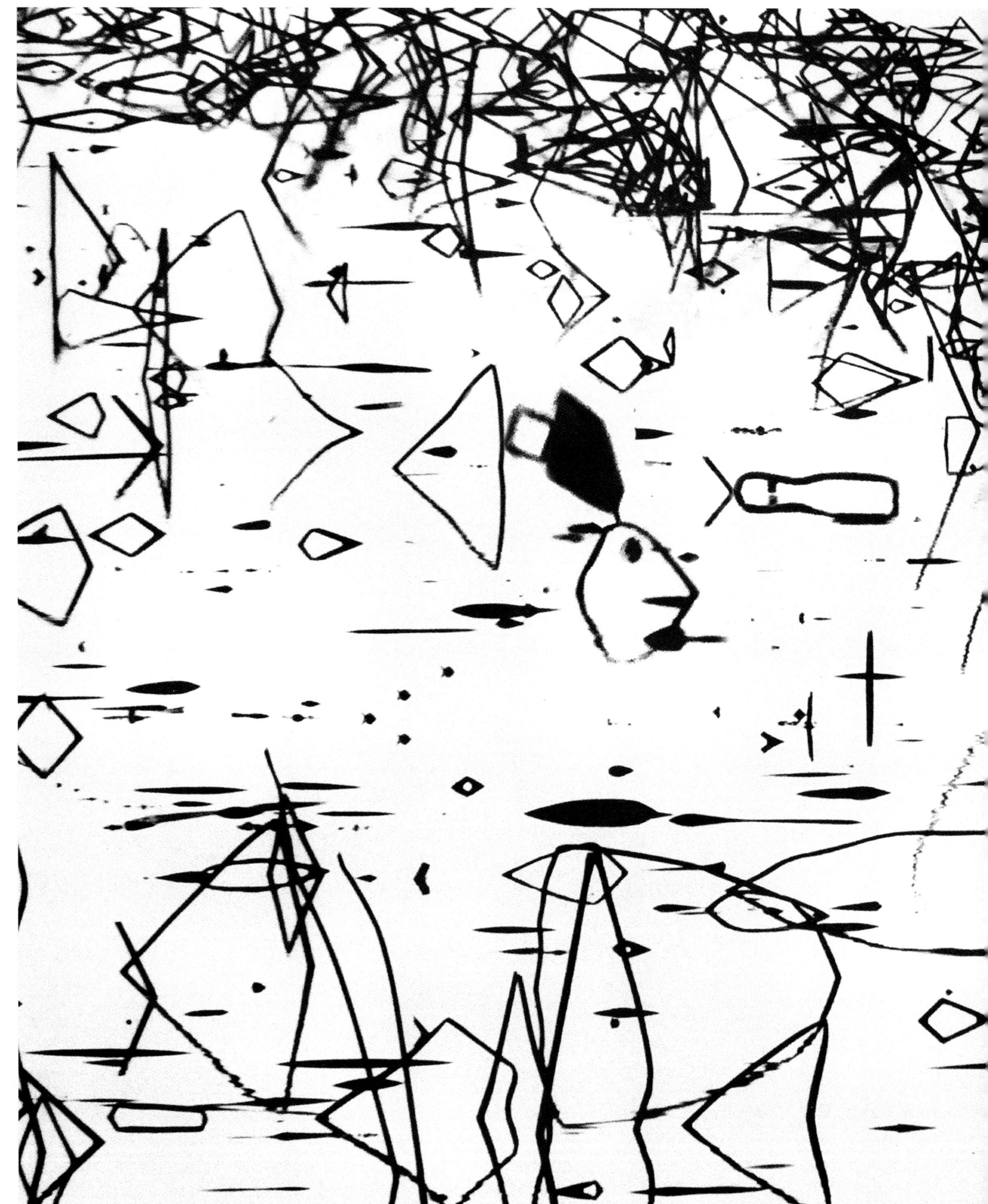

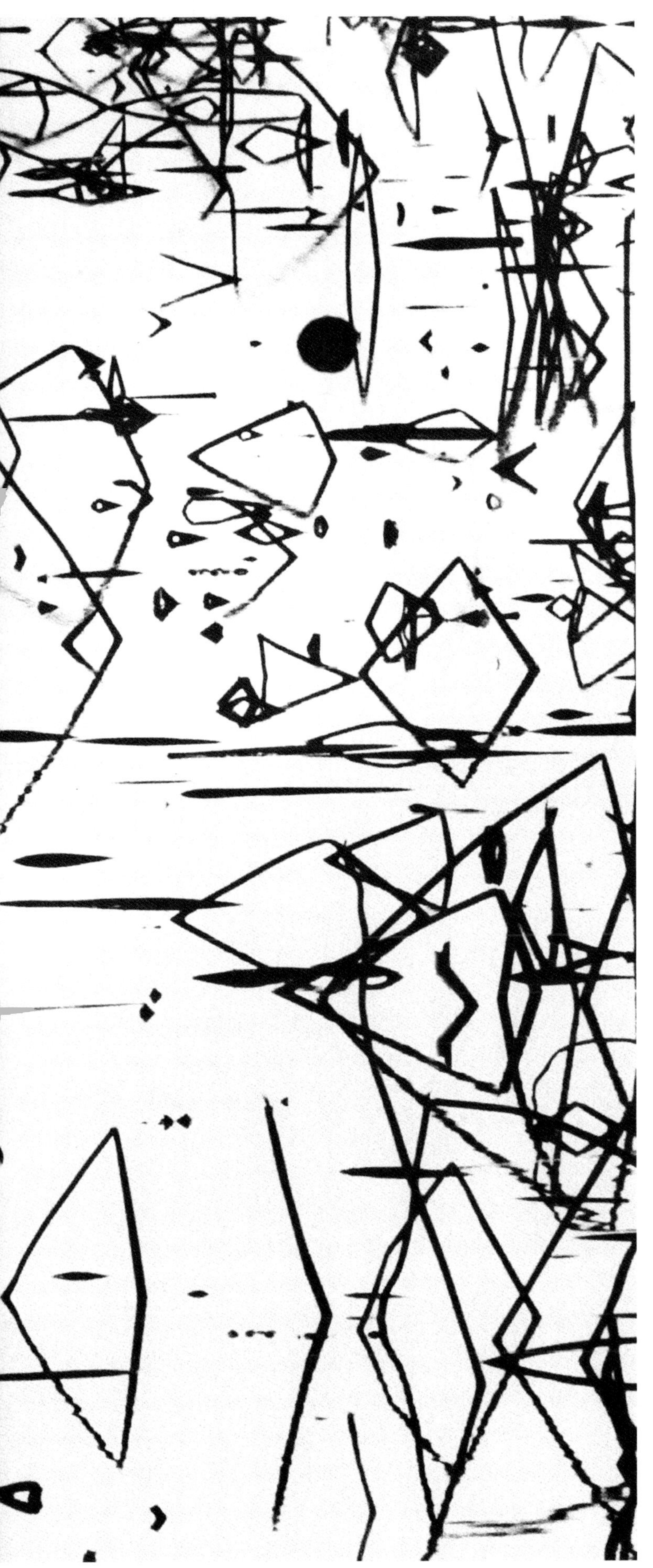

最后的倔强
The Last Stubbornness, 2020
1000 × 800mm

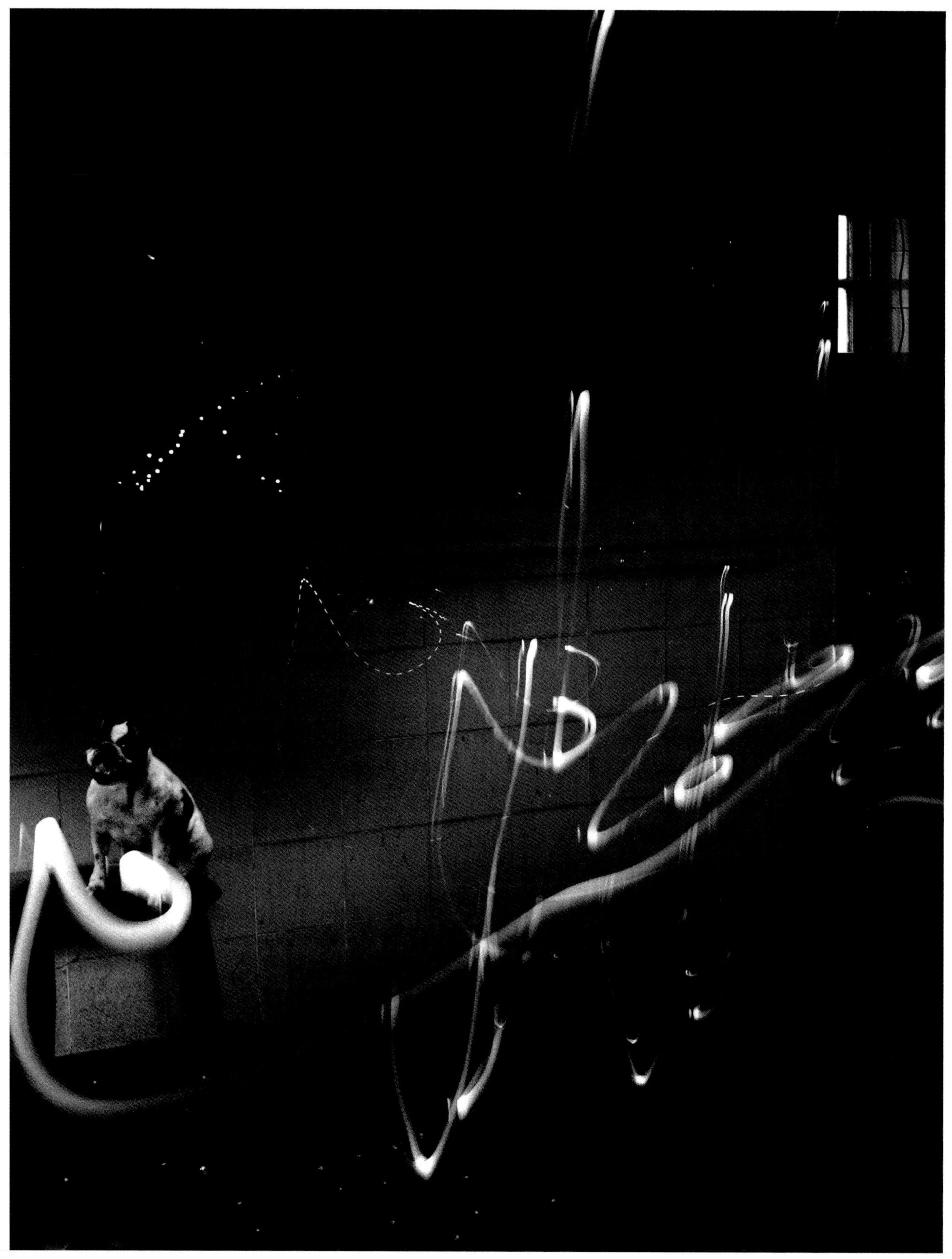

喊你的名字
Calling You, 2022
600 × 800mm

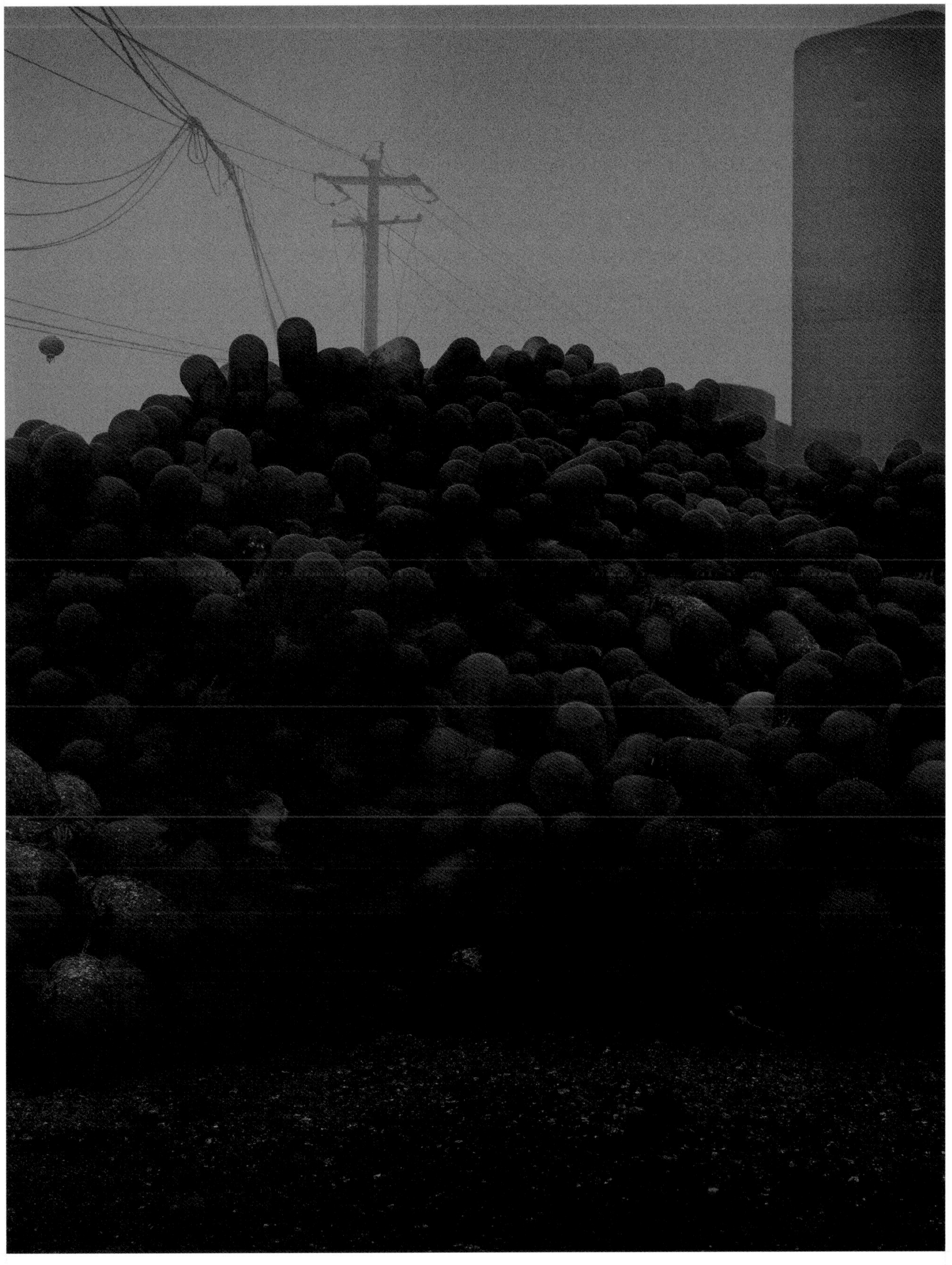

逃避
Evade, 2020
600 × 800mm

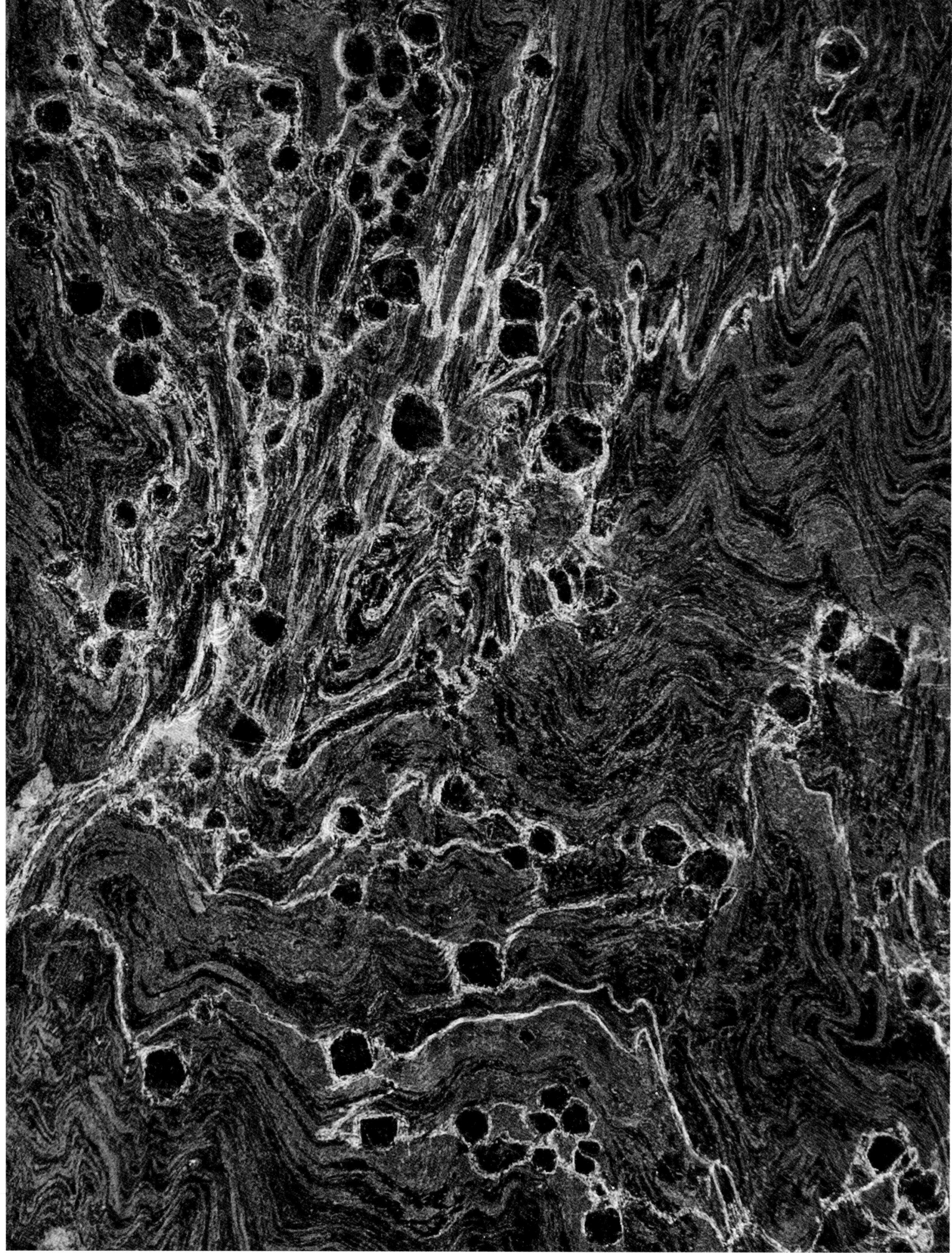

介入
Intervention, 2020
600 × 800mm

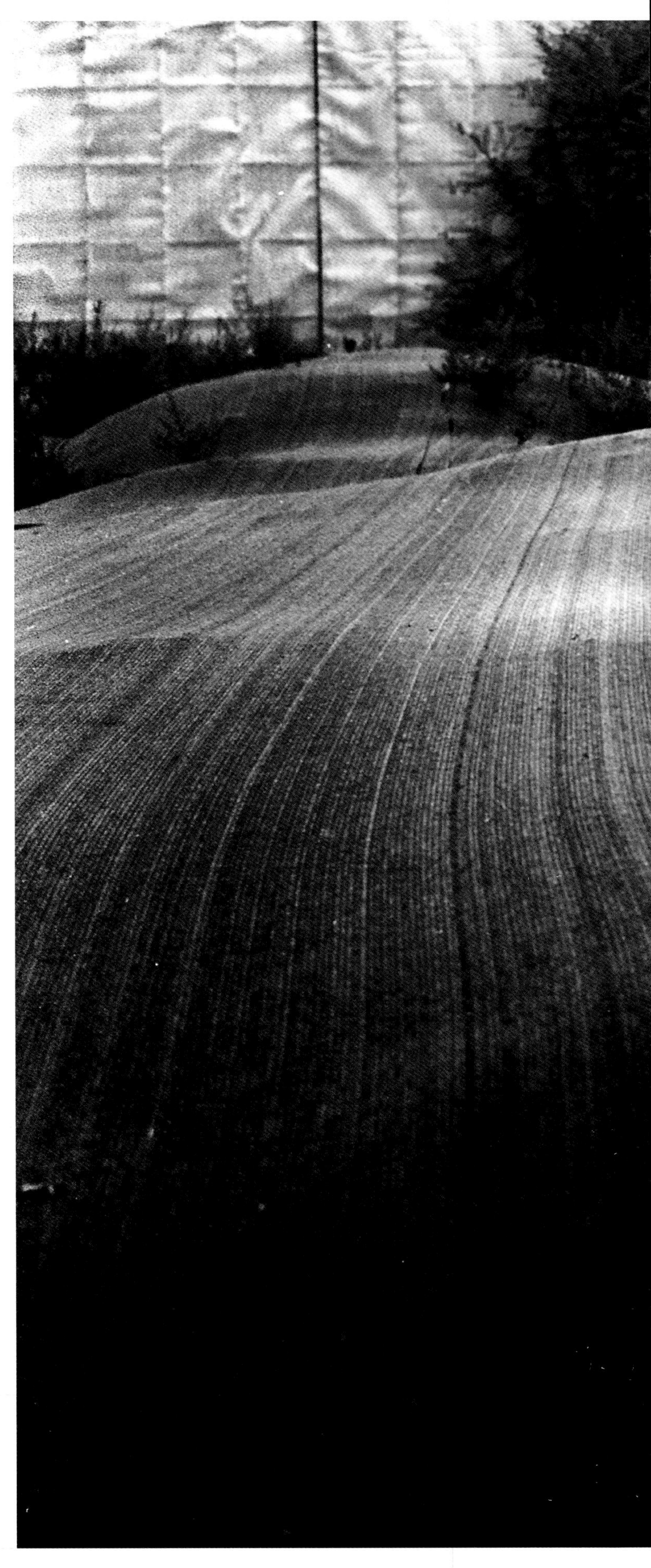

搁浅
Stranding, 2018–24
1000 × 800mm

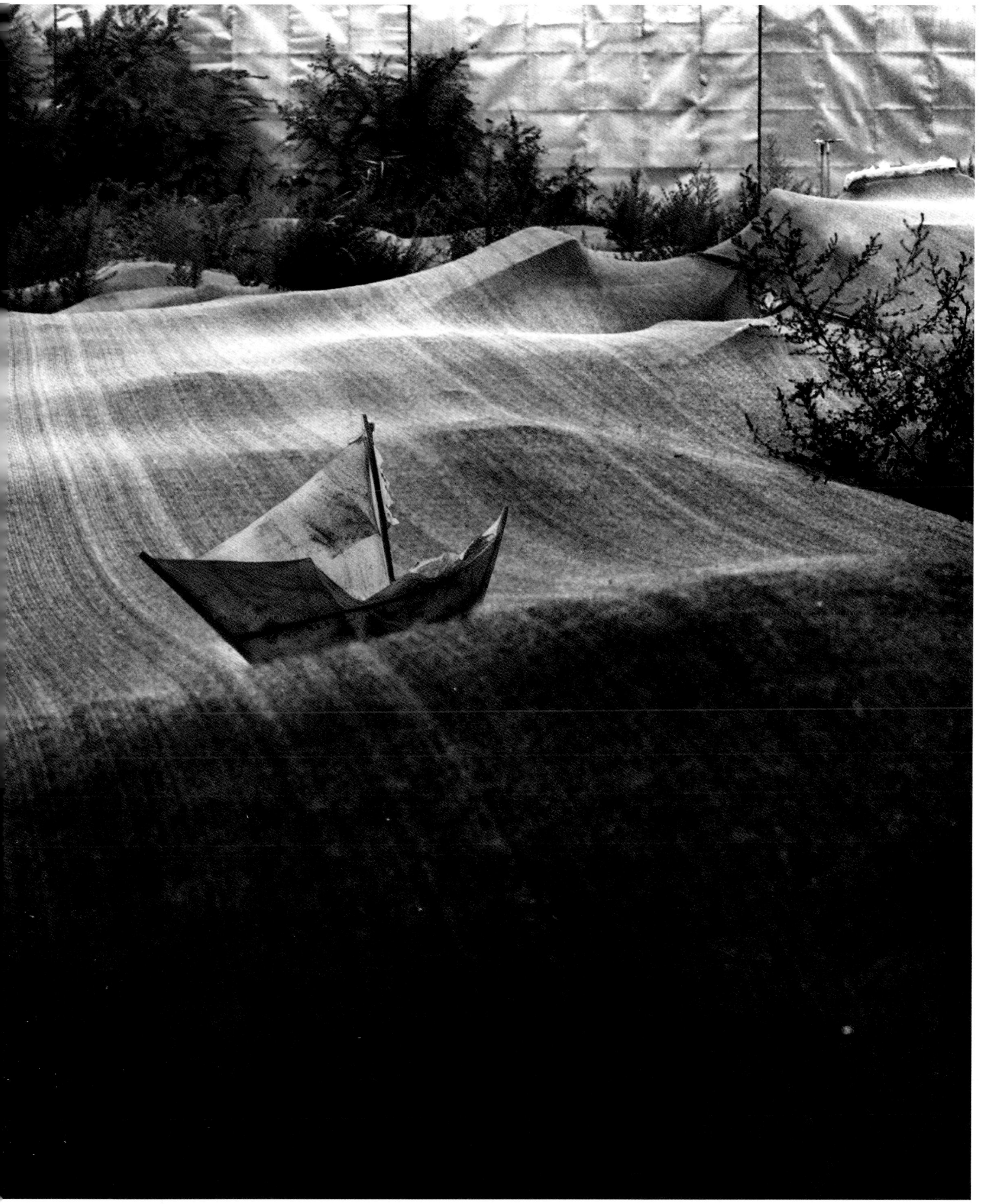

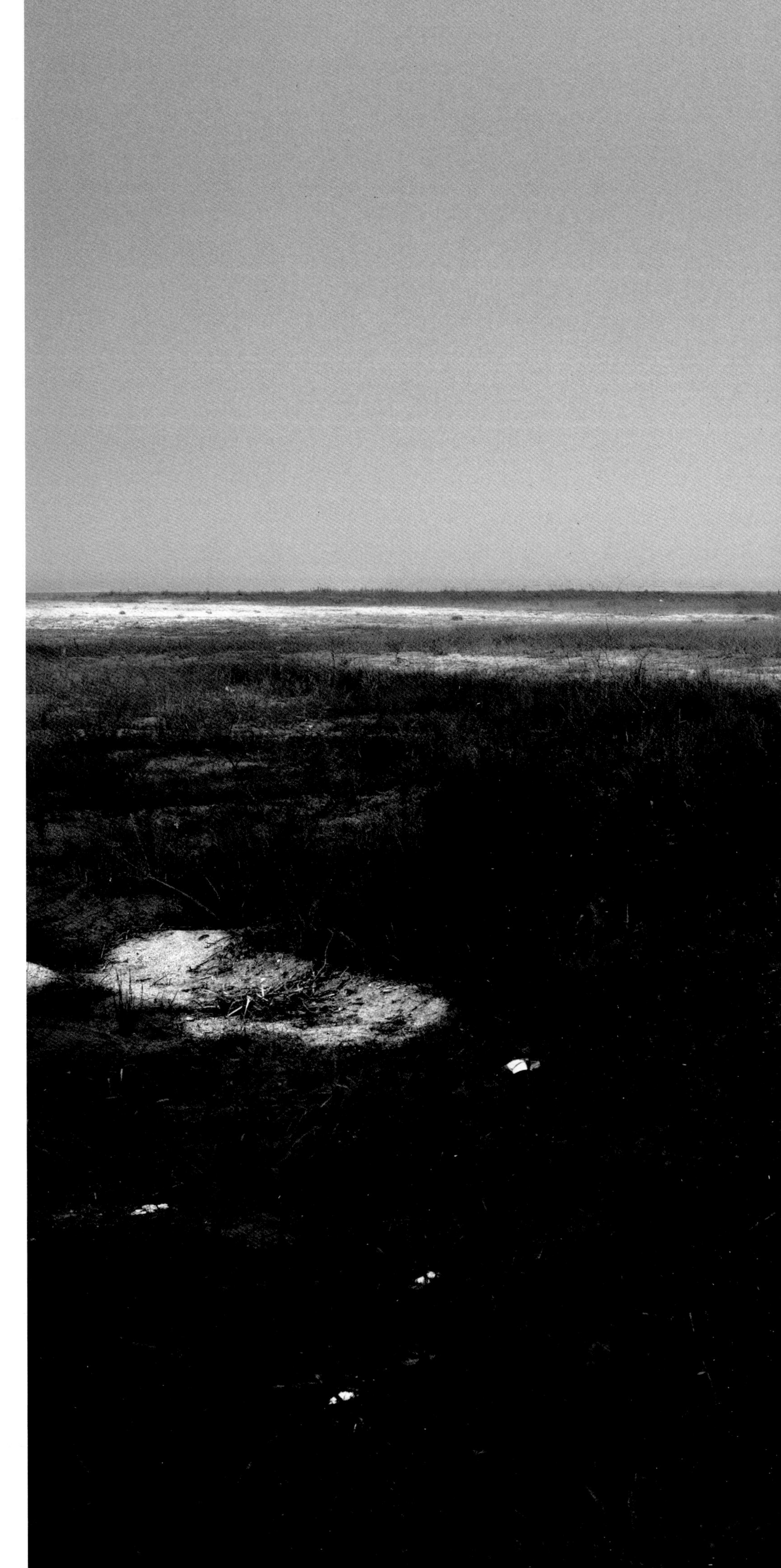

看海
See the Sea, 2020
600 × 800mm

影君子
A Shadowed Gentleman, 2020
600 × 800mm

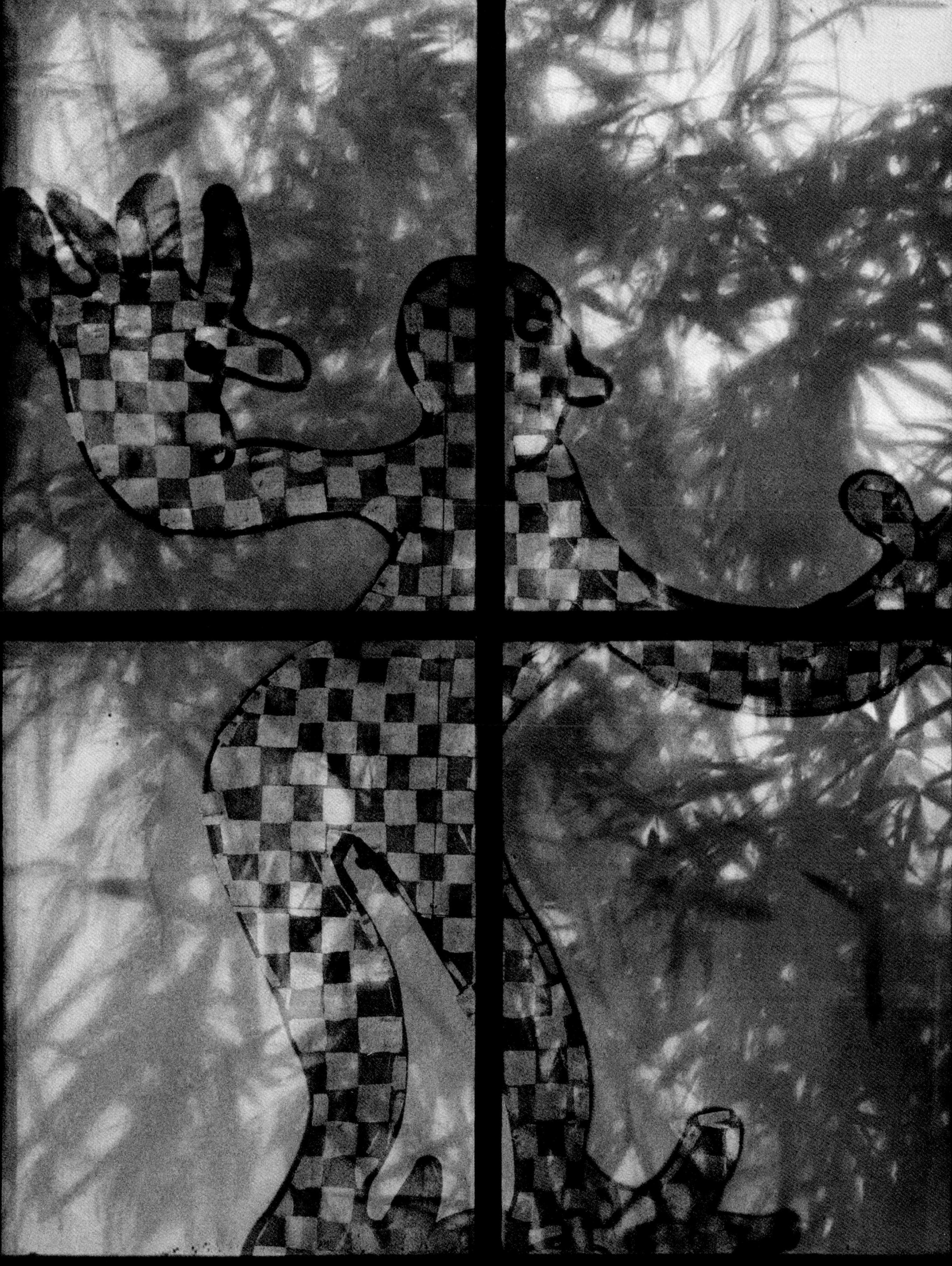

IMAGE CAPTIONS

p. 22
赶走那些闪光的虫子
Get Rid of Those Shiny Bugs, 2020
600 × 800mm

When the artist was a child, he was afraid of fireflies and felt they had the aura of death because fireflies usually appear in cold and damp places. When children are five or six years old, they have a view of life and death and instinctively resist things that symbolise death.

pp. 24–25
人类知道我们是怎么想的
Humans Know What We Think, 2018–21
1000 × 800mm

This is an abandoned American theme park scene in Shanghai. Animal figures are often used for entertainment, but humans may seem strange and amusing from their perspective.

p. 26
受排挤的竞争
The Outcast's Competition, 2019–23
600 × 800mm

This picture was taken during Shanghai Fashion Week. Although people are playing cards, there is still potential competition within. The round ball in the image represents the impact of external forces. Many people cannot adapt to the environment of the fashion industry and most often end up changing careers. This work records the moment of facing competitive pressure.

p. 29
大王叫我来巡山
The King of Bandits Asked Me to Patrol the Mountain, 2024
600 × 800mm

A scarecrow has become the king of a mountain. It is absurd. The painting was inspired by the story of the artist's grandfather. His grandfather was wounded on the Korean battlefield. Later, the government appointed the war hero to look after the public forests to prevent illegal tree felling.When he retired, this mountain became an abandoned place.

p. 30
快乐的灵魂
Happy Souls, 2024
600 × 800mm

For a while, the artist's eyes were blurry, and he didn't get enough sleep, so he thought he had a tumour. Later it was discovered that it was astigmatism and his worries were relieved. After getting his glasses, he happily crossed the street. Through the glass and the dim light, he secretly enjoyed the images of some people.

p. 32
水中的美人
Beauty in Water, 2022
600 × 800mm

Try using a scanner to process images, expressing an intuitive desire.

p. 33
生活中的各种想象就是想想
All Kinds of Imagination in Life are Just Some Simple Thoughts, 2017–23
600 × 800mm

The artist grew up in a small town. When he entered a big city, he found signal towers everywhere, which was very novel. But in an urban environment, this is everyday stuff. The distorted picture has little to do with ordinary people's lives.

p. 35
自始自终的认为人是外星人的宠物
I Have Always Believed that Humans are Pets of Aliens, 2023
600 × 800mm

The artist believes that human beings are controlled in the grand universe and that bigger monsters exist, with power beyond nature.

p. 36
囚舞
Prisoner Dance, 2020
600 × 800mm

p. 37
就这样静静地看着你
Just Looking at You Quietly, 2019
600 × 800mm

Love, moon, goddess Chang'e, and rabbit somehow blend into the Chinese fairytales about the moon.

pp. 38–39
隐秘在角落
Hidden in the Corner, 2020
1000 × 800mm

p. 40
礼物
The Gift, 2022–24
600 × 800mm

pp. 42–43
休憩
Recuperation, 2021
1000 × 800mm

pp. 46–47
徒有其表
Have a Good Appearance Only, 2022–23
1000 × 800mm

Many things that seem very lethal, such as rockets, are similar to balloons in the eyes of children, they are just sky-flying toys. The artist's hometown is on the seaside, separated from North Korea, South Korea and Japan by a sea. There
is a rocket launch station.

pp. 48–49
一直在找
Always Looking for Something, 2024
1000 × 800mm

A little girl kept choosing a goldfish, not knowing what fish she wanted. Many people in the world are the same. They are so busy that they are confused about their desires.

pp. 50–51

主宰的猪

The Pig is the Overlord, 2017–22

1000 × 800mm

The image is taken from the urban-rural integration area of Chongming, Shanghai. In times of rapid development, many people are idle and unable to adapt to foreign cultures. There are seemingly absurd things in the scenic spot, but they are real.

pp. 52–53

谁是曾经的征服者

Who Conquered this Place Before?, 2017–19

1000 × 800mm

With geological movement, the grassland became the ocean. This place is now ruled by humans. But the birth of human civilisation only occurred 10,000 years ago, and the ecological chain here was completely different before.

p. 54

外逃的灵魂

The Escaping Soul, 2014–22

1000 × 800mm

This is the studio of world-famous performance artist Zhang Heng. He enjoyed collecting coffin wood. The chanting music happened to sound at that time, making people feel like they were going to heaven.

p. 55

变强了他们就会怕

They Will Be Afraid When You Become Stronger, 2009–21

1000 × 800mm

This is a playground. There always seem to be cell towers at playgrounds. When people release happiness, they are constantly monitored to prevent disorder.

pp. 56–57

后院

The Backyard, 2020–24

1000 × 800mm

What the artist wants to express here is a person's relaxed state. When people want to relax, they can often try to take a step back. The backyard is the bottom layer of human memory.

p. 59

墙

Wall, 2023

600 × 800mm

This photo was taken in a large science and technology museum. There was a person blocking the door at that time. In addition to the man-made physical wall, the person himself is also a wall.

p. 60

发财的梦却被一个大锅盖给毁了

The Dream of Getting Rich was Ruined by a Big Pot Lid, 2010–20

600 × 800mm

The image is taken from Songjiang, Shanghai, where a billboard with a TV tower is behind it. That place is very unique. No buildings or radiation are allowed; only chickens and ducks can be raised.

p. 62

远离伪装者

Stay Away From Pretenders, 2012–23

1000 × 800mm

It represents a type of people in contemporary society who have split personalities and are good at lying.

p. 63

曾经的兄弟

Former Brothers, 2016–23

1000 × 800mm

The combination of friends in the college dormitory and the wasteland scene shows the changes in the relationship between people. We used to be very good college friends, but they went their separate ways after graduation, and we don't keep in touch as frequently as before.

pp. 64–65

拷问

Torture, 2018

1000 × 800mm

pp. 66–67

白日焰火

Fire During the Day, 2017–18

1000 × 800mm

This image was taken in Qinghai, and the fireworks celebration is quite absurd. Traditionally, in Qinghai, people do not use fireworks to celebrate. People from other places may be coming, but what they celebrate needs to be clarified.

pp. 68–69

通缉

List as Wanted, 2022–23

1000 × 800mm

pp. 70–71

那天的婚礼

The Wedding on that Day, 2016–23

1000 × 800mm

In an abandoned paradise, there is a traditional Chinese wedding scene with ancient Egyptian statues.

pp. 72–73

面对难题

Facing Problems, 2012–15

1000 × 800mm

In the urban-rural fringe, the demolition here shows that there are many things that people in China do not want to face.

p. 74

众神之宴

The Feast of the Gods, 2020

600 × 800mm

p. 76

天外天

Beyond Heaven, 2020–23

1000 × 800mm

p. 77
期许
Expectations, 2021–24
1000 × 800mm

pp. 78–79
拳击手
The Boxer, 2017–23
1000 × 800mm

pp. 80–81
放轻松
Take It Easy, 2020
600 × 800mm

pp. 84–85
等待反馈
Waiting for Feedback, 2020–23
1000 × 800mm

In the Long Museum, the artist heard the audience whispering in front of his video works. Artists want to be recognised, which also expresses common human nature. People want to be loved, noticed and praised.

p. 86
宰割
Be Slaughtered, 2017
600 × 800mm

Pigs' trotters are a metaphor for the status of young Chinese people willing to work overtime.

pp. 88–89
生活
Life, 2017
1000 × 800mm

Avoiding responsibility and doing something else (or not doing anything at all), people today have different reactions to exploitation at a social level.

p. 91
宠物
Pets, 2018
600 × 800mm

p. 92
归来
Return, 2024
600 × 800mm

p. 93
思念
Longing, 2012
600 × 800mm

With the masking on, the portrait resembles Michael Jackson.

pp. 94–95
思念桃桃
Missing Peachy, 2015
1000 × 800mm

p. 96
无厘头
Nonsense, 2018
600 × 800mm

p. 99
谁不是谁的木偶
No-one is a Puppet, 2015
600 × 800mm

p. 101
门卫大叔的梦想实现了
The Doorman's Dream Came True, 2018
600 × 800mm

The janitor uncle always wanted to be the general manager. However, no matter how he dressed and surrounded himself, his inner temperament remained that of a janitor.

pp. 102–03
面对生长
Facing Growth, 2020
1000 × 800mm

p. 105
搜寻
Search, 2024
600 × 800mm

p. 106
狂热纪梵希
Fanatical Givenchy, 2018
600 × 800mm

p. 107
打卡时代
The Era of Punching In, 2024
600 × 800mm

p. 108
镜中人
Man in Stained Glass, 2020
600 × 800mm

p. 113
我的王国
My Kingdom, 2022–24
600 × 800mm

The cars here have 'Elders as Professional Scammer' written on them. These images appear in a scene that is both humorous and harmonious.

p. 114
从哪里来的
Where Are They From?, 2018–19
600 × 800mm

We don't know the reason why many things exist.

pp. 116–17
伯伯的作品
The Work by an Uncle, 2023
1000 × 800mm

This image is based on a grassland, with thatch on the net forming the picture.

pp. 118–119
来救你了
Coming to Save You, 2017–23
1000 × 800mm

p. 120
散光的眼睛需要一面镜子
Astigmatic Eyes Need a Mirror, 2024
1000 × 800mm

p. 121
暴富的心一直在
The Desire to Get Suddenly Rich is Always There, 2024
1000 × 800mm

pp. 122–23
曾经的战场
The Battlefield of the Past, 2023
1000 × 800mm

This place used to be a battlefield, but now the idle land is fully utilised by people to ferment chicken manure. So the combination of things here seems inconsistent.

p. 124
暴裂无声
Burst Silently, 2024
600 × 800mm

On New Year's Eve, there was a sudden light, and after pressing the shutter, the sound came belatedly. Because of the development of internet technology, the way the Spring Festival is celebrated in rural areas has also changed.

pp. 126–27
滑下来一定是仰着头
One Must Have Tilted One's Head When Slid Down, 2021–24
1000 × 800mm

The artist accidentally saw the image. He didn't expect kangaroos to lie down and sleep like humans.

pp. 128–29
父与子
Father and Son, 2019
1000 × 800mm

p. 130
狩猎
Hunting, 2014–24
600 × 800mm

What I want to express here is a process of hunting.

p. 132
跳下来的时候会想什么
What Do We Think About When We Jump Down?, 2018–23
600 × 800mm

pp. 134–35
量力而行
Act Within Your Capabilities, 2023
1000 × 800mm

China has experienced very rapid development during its reform and opening up. People and places are swept along by the tide of time. As things continue to be built, things continue to be abandoned. What is expressed here is the state brought about by the era of high industrialisation.

pp. 136–37
游心
Peaceful, 2020–21
1000 × 800mm

The dynamic feeling of a non-living kite meeting a living bird is worth pondering.

p. 139
领地
Territory, 2023–24
600 × 800mm

pp. 140–41
行路
On the Way, 2020
1000 × 800mm

p. 143
围城之内
Within the Siege, 2020–24
600 × 800mm

pp. 144–45
最后的倔强
The Last Stubbornness, 2020
1000 × 800mm

p. 146
喊你的名字
Calling You, 2022
600 × 800mm

p. 147
逃避
Evade, 2020
600 × 800mm

p. 146
介入
Intervention, 2020
600 × 800mm

pp. 150–51
搁浅
Stranding, 2018–24
1000 × 800mm

pp. 152–53
看海
See the Sea, 2020
600 × 800mm

p. 155
影君子
A Shadowed Gentleman, 2020
600 × 800mm